THE LITERARY CRITICISM
OF FRANK NORRIS

THE
LITERARY CRITICISM
OF
FRANK NORRIS

EDITED BY DONALD PIZER

UNIVERSITY OF TEXAS PRESS, AUSTIN

Published with the assistance of a grant from the Ford Foundation
under its program for the support of publications in the humanities
and social sciences.

Printed in the United States of America
by the Printing Division of the University of Texas;
bound by Universal Bookbindery, Inc.
San Antonio, Texas

FOR MARY

PREFACE

Few contemporary literary movements have been so variously described and evaluated as has American naturalism. One of the reasons for this diversity has been the lack of clear understanding of the late nineteenth-century origins of the movement. In particular, there has been much confusion concerning the critical beliefs of Frank Norris, our earliest theorist of naturalism. Norris' criticism should (and indeed does) isolate tendencies in the naturalistic attitude which illumine later American fiction. But despite the importance of Norris for the history of modern American literature, and despite the intrinsic worth of both his best novels and (as I hope to show) his best criticism, the only collection of his criticism available has been the posthumous *The Responsibilities of the Novelist*, first published in 1903 and thereafter republished unchanged in the various editions of Norris' works.[1]

The Responsibilities of the Novelist has several key deficiencies as a representation of Norris' critical beliefs. Its essays were neither selected nor arranged by Norris, but rather were haphazardly thrown together by his publisher.[2] The only organizing principle operative in the book is a tendency to place the more important essays first. Moreover, the volume contains no selections from two important sources—Norris' extensive critical writing for the San Francisco *Wave* during 1896–1897, and his "Weekly Letter" to the *Chicago American Literary and Art Review* during the summer of 1901. The first omission is particularly serious, since *The Responsibilities of the Novelist* was thus limited entirely to essays written during 1901–1902. The essays from these two sources, as well

---

[1] *The Responsibilities of the Novelist and Other Literary Essays* (New York: Doubleday, Page & Company, 1903). A London edition was published by Grant Richards that same year. The work appeared as *Essays on Authorship* in Volume IV of *The Complete Works of Frank Norris* (New York: P. F. Collier & Son, 1903); as Volume VII of *The Complete Works of Frank Norris*, Golden Gate Edition (New York: Doubleday, Page & Company, 1903); as Volume VII in *The Argonaut Manuscript Limited Edition of Frank Norris's Works* (Garden City, New York: Doubleday, Doran & Company, 1928); and as Volume VII in the trade edition (*The Complete Edition of Frank Norris*) of the Argonaut Edition, also published in 1928. In 1949 the Alicat Bookshop Press of New York republished six of the essays under the title *Six Essays on the Responsibilities of the Novelist*. In 1962 Walter-de Berry, Inc., of Cambridge, Massachusetts, reissued the *Responsibilities* in a volume containing also W. D. Howells' *Criticism and Fiction*.

[2] Norris died in late 1902 without leaving any indication that he had ever planned a collection of his criticism. The Doubleday records for this period have been destroyed. The most likely supposition is that the work was based on scrapbook clippings owned by Norris' widow, Mrs. Jeannette Norris, which were then selected and arranged by his brother Charles, Jeannette, and someone in the Doubleday office. Since both Jeannette and Charles were then in their early twenties, the major portion of the selecting and editing was probably done at Doubleday's.

as additional material omitted from the *Responsibilities*, shed much light on Norris' general critical position, on the development of his critical ideas, and on certain hitherto obscure areas of his thought and opinion. In all, this new material constitutes approximately 40 percent of the present volume.

This collection of Norris' criticism therefore has a twofold purpose: to make available the full range of his critical writing, and to explicate his critical beliefs by means of a thematic organization and interpretative introductions. In order to supersede the original *Responsibilities*, I have included all of that work. I have omitted chiefly the two-minute reviews which Norris describes in his essay on "Newspaper Criticisms" and a number of literary gossip columns written for the *Chicago American*. For a complete bibliography of Norris' critical writing, see the checklist at the end of this volume.

Finally, a few words about the plan of this book. The first two parts contain Norris' basic theory; the last three show his application of theory to specific literary problems, events, and works. The general Introduction summarizes Norris' critical position and some of its background. The ideas discussed there are examined more fully in later introductions.

I wish to thank the following libraries for their aid and courtesy: the Bancroft Library of the University of California, Berkeley, the Howard-Tilton Memorial Library of Tulane University, and the California State Library at Sacramento. Anyone interested in Frank Norris owes a special debt of gratitude to James D. Hart for his efforts in gathering together the material which now forms the Frank Norris and the Franklin D. Walker collections at the Bancroft Library, University of California. Franklin D. Walker, James D. Hart, Kenneth A. Lohf, and Robert D. Lundy have graciously replied to my questions. I have profited greatly from the careful reading of my manuscript by R. H. Fogle, G. W. Meyer, and E. P. Bollier. A portion of my Introduction to the section entitled "Definitions" has appeared in *Modern Fiction Studies*. I am grateful to the editor of that journal for permission to republish it. The Book Club of California has kindly granted me permission to quote from Professor Walker's edition of *The Letters of Frank Norris*.

I am indebted to the Tulane University Council on Research for grants in aid of research and publication.

CONTENTS

Definitions

PART TWO: THE WRITER AND SOCIETY

The Responsibilities of the Novelist

The Novelist as American

Popular Fiction

PART THREE: THE WRITER AS BUSINESSMAN

INTRODUCTION

1

Most discussions of Norris' ideas, or lack of them, owe much to Franklin Walker's biography of Norris. In that work Walker stressed Norris' "boyish enthusiasm" and his code of "feeling" raised above "thought." Walker implied by this emphasis that Norris was not a systematic thinker and that it would be futile to search for a coherent intellectual position in his fiction or criticism. But Walker's characterization of Norris is misleading for two reasons. A writer under thirty does not have to appear solemn to think seriously. And the rejection of "thought" for "feeling" is itself capable of expansion into an elaborate intellectual position. Because Norris advised others to feel does not mean that his advice was not reasoned. Indeed, in the history of man much thought has been devoted to the creation of anti-intellectual philosophies.

At the heart of the unified and coherent system of ideas underlying Norris' criticism is a primitivistic anti-intellectualism.[1] One method of describing this system is to adopt as convenient counterwords the key terms in Norris' cry that life is better than literature. Superficially, he affirmed by this statement that firsthand experience ("life") is better than secondhand experience ("literature"). But when the terms are placed in the context of Norris' critical essays, one realizes that they are Norris' inadequate symbols for two rich and opposing clusters of ideas and values. I therefore use "life" and "literature" both with a recognition of their deficiencies as generally viable critical terminology and with an appreciation of their usefulness and appropriateness when analyzing Norris' critical ideas.

To Norris, "life" included the emotions and the instincts. It incorporated both the world of nature (the outdoors and the country) and the kind of life which Norris believed "natural" (the life of passion and violence, and the life of the low and fallen) because such life was closest to the primitive in man and furthest from the cultivated. "Literature," on the other hand, included thought, culture, overeducation, refinement, and excessive spirituality. "Life" was dominated by connotations of masculinity, naturalness, and strength; "literature" by suggestions of effeminacy, artificiality, and weakness. "Life" was the source of good art—from it sprang art which moved and led men—whereas from "literature" came imitative and affected art, written entirely for money or for the approval

---

[1] It should be clear that I use "primitivism" in its cultural rather than chronological sense. Norris' primitivism establishes certain key values in nature; he does not claim that these values flourished more in the past than in the present.

of a cult, or because the artist was unfortunate and unknowing enough to overrefine his temperament and to neglect the crude, raw, often violent world of action and affairs—the world of men and of nature.

From this primitivistic center Norris' critical system branches out in several important directions. Norris believed that the greatest attribute of the writer is sincerity, because the sincere writer rejects the artificialities of literary schools, vogues, and style, and turns rather to the true sources of power and worth—his own "heart" and his immersion in the rough and tumble of active life. By being faithful to his own vision of life, and by dealing with the full compass of life, including the sordid, the sincere writer avoids the two great interdependent flaws of "literature"—rejection of "life" and imitation of others. The correct formula for sincerity is individual knowledge of "life" and then individual use of one's vision of "life" as the material of fiction. Norris' faith in the intuitive or instinctive is thus the common foundation both for his mystique of sincerity and his call for "life, not literature."

Norris' primitivism and anti-intellectualism also contain the seeds for two other aspects of his critical system—his belief in the critical judgment of the "People" and his demand for the practical and useful, in both life and fiction.[2] Norris' minimizing of thought implied his confidence in the instinctive judgment shared by all men, regardless of position or education. He insisted that though the sincere writer who failed to conform to popular imitative vogues might not be immediately successful, the People in the long run would confirm his worth. Moreover, since Norris made action rather than the mind the center of experience, he valued the demonstrably useful in men's affairs above the independent cultivation or stimulation of the mind. He believed that the best fiction does not merely describe or amuse. Rather, it serves the practical moral purpose of revealing both the primary truths of human experience and the full extent of human injustice and deprivation, so that man might learn and mend his ways. The predominantly middle-class direction which Norris gave to his primitivistic values is revealed both by his faith in the majority and by his moral pragmatism.

Norris' ideas on the relationship of the American writer to the American scene also derive from his basic core of values. The American writer, confronted by a huge new reading public easily influenced by fiction, should above all recognize his responsibility to be sincere, to deal with

---

[2] My understanding of the social implications of Norris' anti-intellectualism has been aided by two excellent articles: Merle Curti, "Intellectuals and Other People" (*American Historical Review,* LX [January, 1955], 259–282), and Walter E. Houghton, "Victorian Anti-Intellectualism" (*Journal of the History of Ideas,* XIII [June, 1952], 291–313).

life as it is, and to reveal the underlying realities of life as he finds it. But because American life is still heterogeneous, the American novelist must be a regionalist—not the describer of surface eccentricities, however, but the perceiver of fundamental regional characteristics.

Finally, naturalism—as defined by Norris—is the literary mode capable of encompassing the entire complex of ideas contained in the rejection of "literature" for "life." To Norris, naturalism was the only modern literature concerned with "life"—with the attempt to deal honestly with the richness and diversity of contemporary life, including the violent and low, and to describe the great forces underlying all experience. It was the method which penetrated beneath the commonplace outer surfaces of "civilization" and got at the heart of "life"—man at his most instinctive, emotional, and fundamental. It was the method to be used by the sincere American writer attempting to "prove something" both about man and about his region. In short, Norris defined naturalism primarily as a mode capable of expressing the values clustered around his idea of "life."

But now one comes to a vital paradox in Norris' critical thought. For Norris combined with his primitivistic ideas an equally confirmed faith in what he called "the mechanics of fiction"—that is, a belief that the form and technique of fiction have certain rules, "tricks," and procedures which can not only be described and codified, but which can also be taught, and which must be acquired through arduous discipline and application. In other words, as far as the form of the novel is concerned, Norris attacked the instinctive, the emotional, the natural. He believed that fictional form is an intellectual problem in selection and organization for the achievement of plausibility, effect, and theme, and that there are few substitutes for a considered and painstaking intellectual solution. It is upon this fundamental duality, then, that Norris' critical system rests—"life, not literature" as far as theme and content are concerned, but "literature, not life" as far as form is concerned. Of the two, he gave the first priority, as can be seen in his story "Dying Fires" and in his essays on New York as a literary center. Without "life" as a foundation, no amount of technical training would benefit a writer. The best novelist, however, was primitivistic in content and theme, sophisticated in form.

This duality in Norris' critical system anticipates and clarifies a major development in the American novel. A strong current of primitivistic anti-intellectualism had always existed in nineteenth-century American fiction, from Leatherstocking baiting Obed Bat in *The Prairie* to Huck Finn deciding to obey his heart rather than his conscience. This faith in the life of action, instinct, and emotion continues as a central force in the modern American novel, as in the work of Faulkner, Hemingway, and

Steinbeck. There is little doubt that it is one of our distinctive national faiths.[3] The importance of Norris' criticism is that he is our earliest critic to found a complete aesthetic of the novel upon this faith. Moreover, Norris wrote at a time when there was an increasing sense of the artistic qualities and capacities of the novel. He thus combines with his primitivism a demand that the novel be cultivated as an art form, and thereby represents a major bridge between the ungainly novels of a Cooper or Twain and the virtuoso techniques of a Hemingway or Faulkner. Much of our best modern fiction therefore answers Norris' key demands, since it often combines an intense thematic primitivism with a striking facility in the manipulation of point of view, time, scene, and symbol. In short, the sophisticated primitivism which Norris required is a primary characteristic of twentieth-century American fiction. One finds this quality both among the established novelists and among the more promising postwar writers, such as Mailer, Bellow, and Styron. Whatever the crudities, the lapses, the journalistic short cuts of Norris' criticism, then, that criticism is important not only for the obvious reasons that it tells us much about Norris' own practice of fiction and that it clarifies the literary issues and temper of his age. His criticism is also significant because it increases our understanding of some of the most basic and seemingly most enduring characteristics of American fiction.

2

Norris' critical ideas were influenced by his reading and by his university experience. While at the University of California during 1890–1894, he accepted the image of "life" present in the fiction of Kipling, Davis, Stevenson, and Zola. He found, however, that his formal literary studies at the university—his theme writing and his literature courses—were antithetical to the fiction his temperament was seeking out. Norris always sought sharp and absolute dualisms, and even at this early date he no doubt began to distinguish between the "literature" of his English courses (with their formal, derivative themes and their study of style) and the "life" of his reading. He may also have recognized this duality in the two prescribed texts of his freshman English course—William Minto's *Manual of English Prose Literature . . . Designed Mainly To Show Characteristics of Style* and George H. Lewes' *The Principles of Success in Literature.* The first, an anthology much hated by Berkeley students,[4] was

---

[3] For discussions of the literary expression of this faith see Philip Rahv, "The Cult of Experience in American Writing," *Image and Idea* (Norfolk, Connecticut: New Directions, 1949), pp. 6–21, and Lionel Trilling, "Reality in America," *The Liberal Imagination* (New York: The Viking Press, 1950), pp. 3–21.

[4] It, along with the freshman mathematics text, was publicly burned each year in a traditional freshman ceremony—the Bourdon.

used for exercises similar to the categorizing of metaphors which Norris described in his "The 'English Courses' of the University of California." Lewes' work, on the other hand, forcefully preached many of the doctrines which Norris ultimately incorporated into his own criticism—calls for sincerity and originality rather than imitation, for trust in the public, for art based upon personal experience, and for disregard of "fine writing."[5]

When Norris went to Harvard in 1894 for an additional year of training as a writer, he responded favorably to the teaching methods of Lewis Gates. Rather than prose analysis or formal themes, the students in Gates' composition class wrote whatever they pleased, so long as it was their own work. And Gates himself praised not the cultivation of style, but concrete and direct expression, based preferably on "the facts of daily life."[6] It was at Harvard that Norris began writing *Vandover and the Brute* and *McTeague.*

By the time Norris became a reporter for the San Francisco *Wave* in early 1896, he had established a roughhewn but coherent aesthetic. Fiction, he believed, should boldly and vigorously capture the actual. The writer's first duty, therefore, was to abjure the safe, imitative work of schools and the popular, and to attack with honesty the raw, often violent and extraordinary, life about him. Norris' critical writing in the *Wave* is thus less the theoretical counterpart of his conventional and derivative short stories of this period than of his already written naturalistic novels. And these novels, despite their indebtedness to Zola, are above all products of Norris' own personal response to his San Francisco world and to the problems of experience which absorbed him.[7]

Norris' literary criticism of 1901–1902 continues to rest on the foundation of the "life, not literature" theme of his *Wave* editorials. This later criticism, however, shifts the emphasis within that doctrine from the excitement of "life" to the social usefulness and duties of the sincere writer. The novelist must now not only delineate "life," but in so doing must

[5] Robert D. Lundy, in his "The Making of *McTeague* and *The Octopus*" (unpublished Ph.D. dissertation, University of California, 1956), is the first to point out the possible influence of Lewes on Norris.

[6] Lewis Gates, "The Return to Conventional Life," *Studies and Appreciations* (New York: The Macmillan Company, 1900), p. 39. Characteristic of Gates is his praise of Mrs. Browning's *Aurora Leigh*: "And everywhere the reader is kept within sound of the busy rumour of daily life; he breathes the actual air of the smoky London streets; he explores squalid tenements; he watches the pageantry of church weddings . . .; he is never for long allowed to lose sight of the expressive visage of the great world of fact" (p. 41). See also John S. Coolidge, "Lewis E. Gates: The Permutations of Romanticism in America," *New England Quarterly*, XXX (March, 1957), 23–38.

[7] See my "Evolutionary Ethical Dualism in Frank Norris' *Vandover and the Brute* and *McTeague*," *PMLA*, LXXVI (December, 1961), 552–560.

picture vast social and racial truths and particular social injustices. He must now be a committed writer vitally concerned with his role as leader of men's thoughts and actions.

This increased social emphasis in Norris' thought is the result primarily of his own natural development along lines determined by his maturing experience as a creative writer and by his full exploration of his values and their implications. His primitivistic anti-intellectualism had implied from the first both a faith in mass man and a belief that truth must be functional in the world of affairs, and these ideals lead literature outward into social involvement. His position is antithetical to that of an art-for-art's-sake writer, whose ideal of elite intellectualism causes him to reject any broad social or moral role for art. Some basis for this development in Norris' critical thinking is also present in his early admiration for the epic breadth of Hugo and Zola. Perhaps, too, it owes something to Tolstoy's widely discussed beliefs on the moral duties of the writer in *What is Art?* (1898).

Just as much of Norris' criticism in the *Wave* derives from his own practice in *Vandover* and *McTeague*, so much of his critical writing of 1901–1902 is closely related to *The Octopus*, which he completed in late 1900. *The Octopus*, for example, is intensely regional, yet it also reflects Norris' desire to present both universal social and natural forces and a prevailing social wrong. It is, in short, the work of a sincere American author attempting to "prove something" in a highly complex fictional form. And though *The Octopus* has little of the "low" material of *Vandover* and *McTeague*, its central theme is still that of "life, not literature." The novel depicts the transformation of three young men from intellectualism to an imaginative and emotional reliance upon the natural world and its processes.[8]

In a sense, then, Norris' failure to codify his critical beliefs is partially compensated for by the existence of *The Octopus*. For that work constitutes an almost complete exemplum, in organic form, of Norris' expanded critical system—of his primary convictions concerning both the craft and the social role of fiction.

3

Norris' criticism divides neatly into two periods: his contributions to the San Francisco *Wave* during 1896–1897,[9] and his free-lance writing

---

[8] See my "The Concept of Nature in Frank Norris' *The Octopus*," *American Quarterly,* XIV (Spring, 1962), 73–80.

[9] Norris actually published several short stories in the *Wave* while he was a student at the University of California during 1890–1894. In addition, he contributed a number of

for various newspapers and magazines during 1901–1902. The *Wave* had been founded in the late 1880's to publicize the Southern Pacific's resort hotel at Del Monte. At first it had been almost exclusively a society journal, directed toward "those in the swim." By the time Norris joined the weekly, it had broadened its coverage to include the general affairs and activities of the San Francisco area. The staff of the *Wave* consisted of John O'Hara Cosgrave as editor, Norris as reporter and subeditor, and several local writers who contributed either occasional stories, reviews, and articles, or weekly columns on social gossip, bicycle-club news, and like matters.

Norris' duties for the week usually combined any number of the following: a feature article on some aspect of San Francisco or its vicinity, an interview with a visiting theatrical personality, a short story, and one or more reviewing tasks—books, stage, sports, art. Occasionally, too, he would contribute an unsigned comment on literature or education to the editorial section. Sometimes he would write a full review of a book by an author who interested him, such as Howells, Zola, and Crane, but for the most part his reviewing was confined to grinding out brief paragraphs on books ranging from studies of insects to collections of Christmas calendars. His editorials were another matter. They were perhaps written as last-minute space fillers, but their contents and quality suggest otherwise. For example, on June 6, 1896, Norris reviewed Zola's *Rome* and mentioned that the novel was intensely romantic. On June 27 he contributed an editorial on Zola as a romantic, a sequence which suggests the natural birth of an idea rather than a forced delivery. Moreover, his editorials —those on Zola, on the English courses at Berkeley, on the short story, on the need for a San Francisco Kipling, on selection in fiction—were written with verve and spirit. Their freshness differs from the sense of labored effort in many of his essays of 1901–1902.

Norris left the *Wave* in early 1898 to work in the New York editorial offices of Doubleday and McClure. For several years he devoted himself almost entirely to his editorial duties (moving to Doubleday, Page in January, 1900) and to the writing of novels. It was not until mid-1901 that he returned to critical writing, prompted both by his desire to give up his editorial job and by his need to support his growing family.

In the early spring of 1901 Norris visited Chicago to gather information for *The Pit*. While in Chicago he sold the idea of a weekly literary column to the Sunday supplement of Hearst's newly founded *Chicago*

articles to the magazine in the fall of 1895, after he returned from Harvard and before he left for South Africa. Among these was his first published critical article, "Our Unpopular Novelists" (*Wave*, XIV [October 5, 1895], 7). However, he did not become a member of the staff of the *Wave* until April, 1896.

American. His column, "Frank Norris' Weekly Letter," ran for thirteen weeks, from May to August, 1901. Datelined "New York," it was, as Norris described it to a friend, "rather general in character and included, on different occasions, book reviews, and beastly 'personal gossip' of the doings of the literary celebrities of the Metropolis."[10] Many of the columns consist entirely of such "personal gossip." In others, however, Norris developed the technique of expanding a minor literary problem or news item into a full essay by placing it in the context of a more basic literary issue.

By late summer Norris was having financial difficulties with the *American*, and he began to cast around for another home for his column.[11] He found one in November in the *Boston Evening Transcript,* which published twelve of his pieces during the winter of 1901–1902. Rather than the potpourri of most of his *American* columns, each of Norris' *Transcript* essays dealt with a single topic and in general was a more elaborate exercise in critical analysis. Meanwhile, in addition to his *Transcript* articles, he had begun late in 1901 to contribute intermittent essays to *World's Work.* A forerunner of the modern news magazine, this monthly usually carried very little criticism. However, it was published by Doubleday, Page, and Norris had several friends among its editors, one of whom, Arthur Goodrich, urged him to contribute critical essays.[12] Of all his criticism written in 1901–1902, Norris' essays in *World's Work* deal most fully and effectively with his ideas on the responsibilities of the novelist. As with his editorials in the *Wave,* he apparently wrote these essays not to meet deadlines but to speak his mind on what were to him vital issues.

Norris' last *Transcript* article appeared on February 5, 1902. Sometime soon after, Jeannette Gilder, editor of the influential *Critic,* invited him to contribute a regular monthly column.[13] For the first time Norris' criticism was to be published in a literary journal rather than in general circulation newspapers or magazines. His column, "Salt and Sincerity," ran for six months, from May till the month of his death, October, 1902. His form was an elaboration of his *Chicago American* device, the use of contemporary literary news as a basis for the introduction of larger critical or intellectual problems. Yet despite the opportunities they offered, Norris' "Salt and Sincerity" columns are among the least important of his critical

[10] Norris to Isaac Marcosson, September 10, 1901, *The Letters of Frank Norris,* ed. Franklin D. Walker (San Francisco: Book Club of California, 1956), p. 78. This volume is referred to hereafter as *Letters.*

[11] Norris to Marcosson, September 10, 1901, *Letters,* p. 78.

[12] *Letters,* p. 95.

[13] So Jeannette Norris recalled in an interview with Franklin Walker on May 16, 1930. Walker's notes for his biography of Norris are in the Franklin Walker Collection, Bancroft Library, University of California. They are referred to hereafter as FWC.

essays of 1901–1902. A full year of extensive critical writing had exhausted Norris' store of ideas. There is scarcely a new thought in all of "Salt and Sincerity," though there is much useful amplification of almost all his basic themes.

Norris died in San Francisco on October 25, 1902, while preparing for a trip to the South Seas. After the posthumous publication of two critical articles—including his most famous essay, "The Responsibilities of the Novelist"—there appeared his last critical series, a group of eight essays syndicated during January-March, 1903. (At least they are reputed to have appeared. No newspaper publication of them has been found. See "A Note on Authorship and the Text" below.) This last series, which contains some of the weakest essays in *The Responsibilities of the Novelist*, was apparently prepared by Norris to be syndicated while he and his wife were on their South Sea journey. The essays are almost all popular reworkings of his principal themes of 1901–1902.

The critical writings of Norris differ in quality, but in general they suffer the defects of hurried composition. His newspaper contributions in particular are slow-paced and repetitious and overrely on such worn devices as the expansion of a minor news item or the discrediting of a popular misconception. Many of his essays also contain weak counterparts of prominent features of his fictional style, such as overextended analogies (similar to his frequently excessive fictional symbolism) and a heavy-breathing rhetoric. But despite these and other evidences of the harried professional (the novelist with "royalties," as Norris described him in "Fiction Writing as a Business"), Norris' essays of 1901–1902 do not misrepresent his critical position or ideals. They are "sincere" in his sense of the term, in that they express his ingrained interests and beliefs, though they often falsify that impression by their reliance on the superficial techniques and rhetoric of popular journalism.

Norris' rhetoric in his essays, however, suggests one of their important characteristics—their tone and style of his gradually assumed role of popular moralist. He had always partially played that role, but in his writings of 1901–1902, as he reached a continually widening audience, he became more and more the instructor of the public conscience. This tendency perhaps reached a peak in his "Salt and Sincerity" columns, as, for example, in his long articles on education and newspapers, in which he acts as public censor. Norris' increasing consciousness of this role thus combines with certain permanent qualities of his prose to give his critical writing a distinctly "public" style. This style contains exaggeration, over-sharp distinctions, internal repetition, rhetorical emphasis, and extended concrete analogies.

But when Norris was most deeply engaged—as in his early articles on

Zola as a romantic or on the need for a San Francisco Kipling, or in his later essays on the responsibilities and true rewards of the novelist—his criticism has the dash, the excitement, and the convincingness of popular exhortation at its best.

A NOTE ON AUTHORSHIP AND THE TEXT

Since the *Wave* had a small staff, a substantial portion of Norris' work appeared anonymously or pseudonymously to disguise the fact that much of each issue was prepared by two or three writers. Of Norris' twenty-two contributions of literary criticism to the *Wave*, eight were neither signed nor initialed by him. Two of these eight are signed "Justin Sturgis," a pseudonym which Norris adopted early in 1897 for light material or for items in issues containing several of his contributions.[1] Four of the anonymous contributions appeared in the editorial section, where articles were seldom signed, and two were reviews. These six anonymous items are immediately and undoubtedly attributable to Norris on the basis of content, style, allusion, and theme. Franklin Walker identified several of them in his 1932 biography, and recently Kenneth A. Lohf and Eugene P. Sheehy (Norris' bibliographers) and Robert D. Lundy have noted others.[2] (The checklist at the end of this volume indicates the signature for each of Norris' contributions to the *Wave*.) Finally, two of Norris' early contributions to *World's Work* are anonymous, but have also long been attributed to him.

The text of the present volume, with one major group of exceptions, is that of the original publication of each item. Norris had no hand in the text of *The Responsibilities of the Novelist*, which was apparently prepared in the Doubleday, Page offices from clippings. Although the *Responsibilities* text is in general accurate, it varies considerably from original publication in spelling (Doubleday followed English convention) and punctuation. In addition, the *Responsibilities* text contains occasional changes in wording. Since the original publication of each item is that closest to Norris, I have used it, even though this has resulted in some inconsistency in spelling and punctuation. The one exception to this pro-

---

[1] Walker questioned Cosgrave in 1930 about the use of Justin Sturgis, but Cosgrave could not remember whether Norris shared the pseudonym or used it exclusively (FWC). Joseph M. Backus, in "Gelett Burgess: A Biography of the Man Who Wrote 'The Purple Cow' " (Ph.D. dissertation, University of California, 1961), states that from mid-March to mid-May, 1897, Burgess replaced Norris as subeditor of the *Wave* and that the pieces in the *Wave* during this period which are signed Justin Sturgis are by Burgess. (Burgess himself left for New York in May, 1897.) Since the only signed contribution by Norris to the magazine during this period was the article "A 'Lag's' Release," XVI (March 27, 1897), 4, which could have been written earlier, Backus is probably right. However, all other pieces in the *Wave* signed Justin Sturgis seem definitely to be by Norris (including the two republished in this book), and it is significant that the pseudonym was not used after Norris left the journal in early 1898.

[2] Walker noted "Zola as a Romantic Writer" and "The 'English Courses' of the University of California." Lohf and Sheehy accept these as well as "Stephen Crane's Stories of Life in the Slums" and "The Decline of the Magazine Short Story." Lundy adds "Zola's *Rome*" and "The Modern Short Story."

cedure is the group of nine essays syndicated in 1902–1903 (one early in 1902, eight early in 1903). The only reference to their syndication is in the bibliography appended to the 1903 *Responsibilities*, a bibliography prepared, according to Charles G. Norris, by Jeannette Norris and Isobel Strong.[3] Since I and several other researchers have failed to locate these essays, the seven which were published in *Responsibilities* are here reprinted from that text. I have, however, Americanized their spelling.

I have silently corrected obvious typographical errors. I have also standardized throughout the punctuation of titles and numbers, and the spelling and punctuation of foreign names, words, and expressions, since in these matters there is little to be gained by reproducing the vagaries of journalistic usage.

[3] Recalled by Charles in an interview with Franklin Walker, July 8, 1931 (FWC). Isobel Strong was Robert Louis Stevenson's daughter-in-law. The Norrises had met the Stevenson clan in New York and had later negotiated with Mrs. Stevenson for the purchase of a cabin near San Francisco. Jeannette spent considerable time with Mrs. Strong after Norris' death.

PART ONE
THE WRITER AND HIS CRAFT

The Training of the Novelist

INTRODUCTION

Norris believed that the writer should be educated and trained in the techniques of fiction and in the practice of an originality based upon "life." But he saw, both in his own education and in contemporary conceptions of the artist, that there were major forces which opposed the proper training of the novelist. His articles on the preparation of the novelist, therefore, often consider that preparation primarily in terms of the handicaps facing it.

He particularly relied upon two of his own experiences as examples of the obstacles placed in the way of the correct training of the writer. One such obstacle was American business civilization, which—though Norris applauded it for other reasons—had no place in its values for the selection and encouragement of youthful artistic talent. Norris himself had felt this lack, for his father, a wealthy self-made businessman, had assumed that his son would pursue a similar career. It was only the intervention of Norris' artistically minded mother which permitted him to attend art schools and then to undertake the "literary course" at the University of California.

But once in college, Norris found yet another obstacle—the prescribed themes and prose analysis of the conventional composition course. Later, he used his experiences at California and Harvard as examples of the false and the correct ways to encourage literary ability. The considerable basis for this contrast is apparent from a series of articles in the *Dial* during 1894, in which various university English departments described their programs. Whereas Charles Mills Gayley pointed out that at California "academic scholarship does not look with favor upon the attempt to stimulate or foster creative production," Barrett Wendell gave much attention to the elective writing courses at Harvard, and noted that in them "little importance is attached to theoretical knowledge of rhetoric as distinguished from constant practice in writing under the most minute practical criticism."[1] At one university, in short, Norris was required to write themes on such topics as "What Characteristics of *The Vicar of Wakefield* Make It a Classic";[2] at the other he could write *McTeague*.

---

[1] Charles Mills Gayley, "English at the University of California," *Dial*, XVII (July 16, 1894), 31, and Barrett Wendell, "English at Harvard," *Dial*, XVI (March 1, 1894), 132. Norris' attitude toward the English courses at California was no doubt influenced by his personal dislike of William Dallam Armes, his freshman English teacher. (Charles and Jeannette Norris recalled this dislike in interviews with Walker, FWC.)

[2] The University of California *Occident* (XIX [October 24, 1890], 60) listed four possible topics for freshman themes, of which the one I cite is characteristic.

Besides reacting against those handicaps which had affected him personally, Norris attacked several popular misconceptions which he felt
were interfering with the training of the novelist. Two such beliefs were
those concerning the writer as gentleman-scholar and the writer as genius.
The first prevented that contact with the world of men and action which
Norris believed should serve as the basis for fiction. He assumed that the
youthful writer who prepared himself for a literary career by cultivating
the New England tradition of scholarly inquiry and gentlemanly aloofness was bound to neglect "life" for "literature"—was bound to be what
we today would call a writer in the genteel tradition. The correct method
of preparation was rather that of Strelitz, a writer in Norris' story "His
Sister," who wanders the streets looking for "dramas of the curbstone."
Or perhaps the best method was to immerse oneself in the raw, primitive
life of some remote area, where there would be no opportunity to play
the gentleman-scholar. This had been the method of both Kipling and
Richard Harding Davis, and Norris himself may have attempted to dupli-
cate it by his trip to South Africa.

The second popular belief which Norris rebelled against undermined
his emphasis on the trained fictional craftsman. Although Norris often
called for the writer to practice self-reliance, he distinguished between the
correctness of a writer's faith in the inherent truth of his vision of life
and the falsity of a writer's dependence upon an inherent capacity to mold
that vision into successful artistic form. He attacked, in other words, the
convention of the artist as genius, as possessed of a God-given instinctive
ability independent of external forces.[3] Norris believed that the transla-
tion of creative insight into a novel required a trained understanding of
the tools and methods of fiction. Schools and books which attempted to
codify and teach fictional techniques were therefore not to be scorned.
These techniques had to be learned, and explicit instruction might aid
and shorten the process. Look into your heart, Norris seems to be saying,
but before you write, know something about "life" and about the craft of
fiction.

The central paradox in Norris' aesthetic, which I have described in my
general Introduction, is thus reflected in his conception of the preparation
of the writer. On the one hand, the novelist is to be trained to cultivate
originality and to avoid bookishness. On the other, he is encouraged to
concern himself with established, successful literary forms and techniques,

---

[3] During the 1880's and 1890's there was much controversy between those critics who
continued to stress the innate capacity of the artist and those, influenced by Taine and by
evolutionary ideas, who emphasized the role of external social and literary forces in determining literary production. See my "Evolutionary Ideas in Late Nineteenth-Century
English and American Literary Criticism," *Journal of Aesthetics and Art Criticism*, XIX
(Spring, 1961), 305–310.

which can be learned from books and schools. The paradox in this instance is partially the result of Norris' distinction between the content and the form of fiction, a distinction so sharp it permitted him to outline a different training for success in each. This distinction, however, was more logical than absolute. For, like most novelists, Norris strove for organic unity in his fiction, though, like most critics, he distinguished between form and content in his critical analysis.

THE "ENGLISH COURSES" OF THE UNIVERSITY OF CALIFORNIA[4]

In the "announcement of courses" published annually by the faculty of the University of California the reader cannot fail to be impressed with the number and scope of the hours devoted by the students to recitations and lectures upon the subject of "literature." At the head of this department is Professor Gayley (the same gentleman who is to edit the volumes of Shakespeare for Macmillan at the expense of the State of California).[5] Be pleased for a moment to consider these "literary" courses. They comprise "themes" written by the student, the subject chosen by the instructor and the matter found in text books and encyclopedias. They further include lectures, delivered by associate professors, who, in their turn have taken their information from text books and "manuals" written by other professors in other colleges. The student is taught to "classify." "Classification" is the one thing desirable in the eyes of the professors of "literature" of the University of California. The young Sophomore, with his new, fresh mind, his active brain and vivid imagination, with ideas of his own, crude, perhaps, but first hand, not cribbed from text books. This type of young fellow, I say, is taught to "classify," is set to work counting the "metaphors" in a given passage. This is actually true—tabulating them, separating them from the "similes," comparing the results. He is told to study sentence structure. He classifies certain types of sentences in De Quincey and compares them with certain other types of sentences in Carlyle. He makes the wonderful discovery—on suggestion from the instructor—that De Quincey excelled in those metaphors and similes relating to rapidity of movement. Sensation!

In his Junior and Senior years he takes up the study of Milton, of Browning, of the drama of the seventeenth and eighteenth centuries, English comedy, of advanced rhetoric, and of aesthetics.[6] "Aesthetics," think of that! Here, the "classification" goes on as before. He classifies "lyrics" and "ballads." He learns to read Chaucer as it was read in the

---

[4] *Wave*, XV (November 28, 1896), 2–3.

[5] An involved allusion. California state law required that textbooks used in state-supported institutions be written preferably by residents of the state. Charles Mills Gayley, chairman of the University of California English department, was also active in the university extension movement, where he prepared several courses in Shakespeare. Norris is apparently alluding to an edition of Shakespeare that Gayley would edit for these courses, which would be paid for by the state, though Gayley would also be able to sell the copyright to Macmillan for publication elsewhere. However, no such edition of Shakespeare by Gayley was ever published.

[6] Norris is more or less describing his own career at Berkeley. Besides the required freshman composition and sophomore literature courses, he took courses entitled Poets of the Fourteenth and Fifteenth Centuries, the English Drama, Milton, Literary Criticism, English Comedy, Browning, and Poets of the Nineteenth Century.

fourteenth century, sounding the final *e*; he paraphrases Milton's sonnets, he makes out "skeletons" and "schemes" of certain prose passages. His enthusiasm is about dead now; he is ashamed of his original thoughts and of those ideas of his own that he entertained as a Freshman and Sophomore. He has learned to write "themes" and "papers" in the true academic style, which is to read some dozen text books and encyclopedia articles on the subject, and to make over the results in his own language. He has reduced the writing of "themes" to a system. He knows what the instructor wants, he writes accordingly, and is rewarded by first and second sections. The "co-eds" take to the "classification" method even better than the young men. They thrive and fatten intellectually on the regime. They consider themselves literary. They write articles on the "Philosophy of Dante" for the college weekly, and after graduation they "read papers" to literary "circles" composed of post-graduate "co-eds," the professors' wives and daughters and a very few pale young men in spectacles and black cutaway coats. After the reading of the "paper" follows the "discussion," aided and abetted by cake and lemonade. This is literature! Isn't it admirable!

The young man, the whilom Sophomore, affected with original ideas, does rather different. As said, by the time he is a Junior or Senior, he has lost all interest in the "literary" courses. The "themes" must be written, however, and the best way is the easiest. This is how he ofttimes goes about it: He knows just where he can lay his hands upon some fifty to a hundred "themes" written by the members of past classes, that have been carefully collected and preserved by enterprising students. It will go hard if he cannot in the pile find one upon the subject in hand. He does not necessarily copy it. He rewrites it in his own language. Do you blame him very much? Is his method so very different from that in which he is encouraged by his professor; viz., the cribbing—for it is cribbing—from text books? The "theme" which he rewrites has been cribbed in the first place.

The method of English instruction of the University of California often develops capital ingenuity in the student upon whom it is practiced. We know of one young man—a Senior—who found himself called upon to wrote four "themes," yet managed to make one—re-written four times —do for the four. This was the manner of it. The four "themes" called for were in the English, chemical, German and military courses respectively. The young fellow found a German treatise on the manufacture of gunpowder, translated it, made four copies, and by a little ingenuity passed it off in the four above named departments. Of course the thing is deplorable, yet how much of the blame is to be laid at the door of the English faculty?

The conclusion of the whole matter is that the literary courses of the

University of California do not develop literary instincts among the students who attend them. The best way to study literature is to try to produce literature. It is original work that counts, not the everlasting compiling of facts, not the tabulating of metaphors, nor the rehashing of text books and encyclopedia articles.

They order this matter better at Harvard. The literary student at Cambridge has but little to do with lectures, almost nothing at all with text books. He is sent away from the lecture room and told to look about him and think a little. Each day he writes a theme, a page if necessary, a single line of a dozen words if he likes; anything, so it is original, something he has seen or thought, not read of, not picked up at second hand. He may choose any subject under the blue heavens from a pun to a philosophical reflection, only let it be his own. Once every two weeks he writes a longer theme, and during the last six weeks of the year, a still longer one, in six weekly installments. Not a single suggestion is offered as to subject.[7] The result of this system is a keenness of interest that draws three hundred men to the course and that fills the benches at every session of the class. The class room work consists merely in the reading by the instructor of the best work done, together with his few critical comments upon it by the instructor in charge. The character of the themes produced under this system is of such high order that it is not rare to come across one of them in the pages of the first-class magazines of the day. There is no sufficient reason to suppose that the California collegians are intellectually inferior to those of the Eastern States. It is only a question of the means adopted to develop the material.

FRANK NORRIS' WEEKLY LETTER[8]

Kim, Kipling's newest—and some say his best—begins to loom over the horizon of forthcoming publications. The author spent more time, effort and pains upon this than upon any other of his books. He rewrote it entire three separate times, and the final manuscript is so emended, edited, corrected and changed about that the typewriting of it was twice as long as it would have been under ordinary circumstances. The plot—slow in movement at first—warms up after the first third of the story is done, and develops swiftly into a thrilling and intensely interesting drama.

Apropos of this book, an interesting bet has been made between the business managers of his rival publishing houses of New York. The wager

---

[7] That Norris is here describing the method used in Gates' course can be seen by his Harvard themes in the Frank Norris Collection, Bancroft Library, University of California. See also the description of English 22 in *Harvard University: Announcement of the Department of English, 1894–1895* (in the Harvard archives).

[8] *Chicago American*, June 8, 1901, p. 5.

is $1000 that 200,000 copies of *Kim* are sold within six months after publication.[9]

Another book to be published this month, and which is bound to attract universal attention, is *A Modern Antaeus,* by the unknown author of *An Englishwoman's Love Letters.*[10] It is a novel, modern in point of time, and written in the form of the life history of the hero, Tristram Gaveny. In the preface of the book its author thus indicates its aims and scope:

This that follows is the story of one to whom her [the earth's] breast was still sweet and her strength piercing. In him she had back in her arms a contented suckling of huge appetite—a blithe piece of clay shaped to take in the oil and wine of gladness which still flow from her veins. In the beginning you shall still see him at suck, and in the end you shall not find him properly weaned. In the meanwhile her milk is sound to his taste. Others, not I, must judge where the fault has lain.

The style of the writing is the extreme of florid, so overladen with metaphor and simile as to be at times quite unintelligible. The book—of course—will sell, and be widely read. But it is fair to doubt whether it will please many besides the retailers, who see it only in the false shine of one silver dollar and one twenty-five cent piece.

Lately there has come to notice the report of the almost simultaneous opening of two novel institutions, one in New York and one upon the Pacific Coast—this latter, I believe, conducted by W. C. Morrow. These institutions are conducted for the purpose of instruction in the art of novel writing. Absurd? One is not so sure about that. I do not know what the curriculum or courses are in either of these schools. They may very well be absurd—in fact, could easily become so—but I do know and am of the firm belief that there is not only place for but actual need of instruction in the art—or, rather, let us say the mechanics—of fiction.

Some certain people—foolish people—often say: "Teach how to write novels! It must be born in you. There is no other way." I do not believe this. Nobody is born with the ability to write fiction. The greatest writers have to learn it all for themselves. If they taught themselves they could to a very large extent teach others. It is not at all impossible of belief that the fundamentals of construction in fiction could be in a manner codified, formulized and studied with as much good results as the fundamentals of any other of the professions.

[9] *Kim* was appearing serially in *McClure's* at this time, and was to be published in book form by Doubleday, Page in October, 1901. Norris would know of the condition of the manuscript and of the bet through his editorial position with Doubleday. The two publishing houses are presumably McClure and Doubleday, Page.

[10] Laurence Housman (brother of A. E. Housman) was the author of these two novels, both published by Doubleday, Page. Norris, but for the uncomplimentary remarks which follow, would appear to be publicizing the books of his own firm.

All other of the fine arts demand preparatory courses of training—sculpture, painting, music, acting, architecture, and the like. Why should fiction be the one—the only one—to be ignored? Be well assured of this: The construction of a novel is as much of an exact science as the construction of a temple or a sonnet. The laws and rules of this construction have never been adequately formulated, but they exist. Such men as Mr. Kipling, M. Zola, Mr. Lew Wallace and Mr. Dickens knew them and built their novels upon them, and because they knew them so well their novels are interesting and powerful.

The mechanics of fiction—much, very much, can be said under this head. Judged from this point of view, how many of the wretched, sprawling, loose-jointed novels of the day, overbalanced, unsymmetrical, out of proportion, would stand inspection? A false note in music, a false tone in a painting, bad modeling in a statue, clumsy lines in a public building are at once condemned, and recognized as faults and blemishes, even by the uncritical. But a work of fiction may be as slovenly in workmanship as its author chooses—it may even be as badly constructed as *The Heavenly Twins*[11]—and pass muster for all that.

As a matter of course it is not to be assumed that the bent toward the composing of fictitious scenes, people, etc., can be developed, or even aroused, but many a young writer could be taught that the axiom, "The whole is greater than the part," is as true for a novel as it is for a proposition of geometry. He could be shown that the divisions of the drama—i.e., (1) the start, (2) the rise, (3) the height, (4) the close—are equally essential to the novel and conducive to the readers' interest—which is always the same as artistic finish. Possibly it might be hammered into his understanding that it is better, nine times out of ten, to treat but of one thing in one chapter, to keep to one time and one place as much as is possible, and to hold to but one theme from cover to cover.

In the meanwhile the Eastern and Western "schools of instruction" have started work.

If only they teach the aspirants of the colossal difficulty of producing even a fairly well constructed piece of fiction they will do good. It is difficult to see how they could do very much harm.

NOVELISTS OF THE FUTURE: THE TRAINING THEY NEED[12]

It seems to me that a great deal could be said on this subject—a great deal that has not been said before. There are so many novelists these latter days. So many whose works show that they have had no training and it

---

[11] A long, sentimental, wandering novel (published in 1893) by Sarah Grand (pseudonym of Mrs. David C. McFall).

[12] *Boston Evening Transcript*, November 27, 1901, p. 14.

does seem that so long as the fiction writers of the United States go fumbling and stumbling along in this undisciplined fashion, governed by no rule, observing no formula, setting for themselves no equation to solve, that just so long shall we be far from the desirable thing—an American school of fiction. Just now (let us say that it is a pity) we have no school at all. We acknowledge no master, and we are playing at truant, incorrigible, unmanageable, sailing paper boats in the creek behind the schoolhouse, or fishing with bent pins in the pools and shallows of popular favor. That some catch goldfish there, is no great matter, and is no excuse for the truancy. We are not there for the goldfish, if you please, but to remain in the school at work till we have been summoned to stand up in our places and tell the master what we have learned.

There's where we should be, and if we do not observe the rules and conform to some degree of order, we should be rapped on the knuckles or soundly clumped on the head, and by vigorous discipline taught to know that formulas $(a-b)$ $(a+b)$ are important things for us to observe, and that each and all of us should address ourselves with all diligence to finding the value of x in our problems.

It is the class in the Production of Original Fiction which of all the school contains the most truants. Indeed, its members believe that schooling for them is unnecessary. Not so with the other classes. Not one single member of any single one of them who does not believe that he must study first if he would produce afterwards. Observe, there on the lower benches, the assiduous little would-be carpenters and stonemasons; how carefully they con their tables of measurement, their squares and compasses. "Ah, the toilers," you say, "the grubby manual fellows—of course they must learn their trade!"

Very well, then. Consider—higher up the class, on the very front row of benches—the Fine Arts row, the little painters and architects and musicians and actors of the future. See how painfully they study, and study and study. The little stomemason will graduate in a few months; but for these others of the Fine Arts classes, there is no such thing as graduation. For them there shall never be a diploma, signed and sealed, giving them the right to call themselves perfected at their work. All their lives they shall be students. In the vacations—maybe—they write, or build, or sing or act, but soon again they are back to the benches studying, studying always; working as never carpenter or stonemason worked. Now and then they get a little medal, a bit of gold and enamel, a bow of ribbon, that is all; the stonemason would disdain it, would seek it for the value of the metal in it. The Fine Arts people treasure it as the veteran treasures his cross.

And these little medals you—the truants, the bad boys of the paper boats and the goldfish—you want them, too; you claim them and clamor for them. You who declare that no study is necessary for you; you who are not content with your catch of goldfish, you must have the bits of ribbon and enamel, too. Have you deserved them? Have you worked for them? Have you found the value of x in your equation? Have you solved the parenthesis of your problem? Have you even done the problem at all? Have you even glanced or guessed at the equation? The shame of it be upon you! Come in from the goldfish and go to work, or stay altogether at the fishing and admit that you are not deserving of the medal which the master gives as a reward of merit.

"But there are no books that we can study," you contest. "The architect and the musician, the painter and the actor—all of these have books ready to hand; they can learn from codified, systematized knowledge. For the novelist, where is there of cut-and-dried science that he can learn that will help him?"

And that is a good contention. No, there are no such books. Of all the arts, the art of fiction has no handbook. By no man's teaching can we learn the knack of putting a novel together in the best way. No one has ever risen to say, "Here is how the plan should be; thus and so should run the outline."

We admit the fact, but neither does that excuse the goldfishing and the paper boat business. Some day the handbook may be compiled—it is quite possible—but meanwhile, and *faute de mieux,* there is that which you may study better than all handbooks.

Observe, now. Observe, for instance, the little painter scholars. On the fly leaves of their school books they are making pictures—of what? Remember it, remember it and remember it—of the people around them. So is the actor, so the musician—all of the occupants of the Fine Arts bench. They are studying one another, quite as much as their books— even more, and they will tell you that it is the most important course in the curriculum.

You—the truant little would-be novelist—you can do this, quite as easily as they, and for you it is all the more important, for you must make up by the intimate knowledge of your fellows what you are forced to lack in the ignorance of forms. But you cannot get this knowledge out there behind the schoolhouse—hooking goldfish. Come in at the tap of the bell and, though you have no books, make pictures on your slate, pictures of the Fine Arts bench struggling all their lives for the foolish little medals, pictures of the grubby little boys in the stonemason's corner, jeering the art classes for their empty toiling. The more you make these pictures, the better you shall do them. That is the kind of studying you can do, and from the study of your fellows you shall learn more than from the study of all the textbooks that ever will be written.

But to do this you must learn to sit very quiet, and be very watchful, and so train your eyes and ears that every sound and every sight shall be significant to you and shall supply all the deficiency made by the absence of textbooks.

This, then, to drop a very protracted allegory, seems to be the proper training of the novelist: The achieving less of an aggressive faculty of research, than of an attitude of mind—a receptivity, an acute sensitiveness. And this can be acquired.

But it cannot be acquired by shutting one's self in one's closet, by a withdrawal from the world, and that, so it would appear, is just the mistake so many would-be fiction writers allow themselves. They would make the art of the novelist an aristocracy, a thing exclusive, to be guarded from contact with the vulgar, humdrum, bread-and-butter business of life, to be kept unspotted from the world, considering it the result of inspirations, of exaltations, of subtleties and—above all things—of refinement, a sort of velvet-jacket affair, a studio hocus-pocus, a thing loved of women and of aesthetes.

What a folly! Of all the arts it is the most virile; of all the arts it will not, will not, will not flourish indoors. Dependent solely upon fidelity to life for existence, it must be practised in the very heart's heart of life, on the street corner, in the market place, not in the studios. God enlighten us! It is not an affair of women and aesthetes, and the muse of American fiction is no chaste, delicate, super-refined mademoiselle of delicate roses and "elegant" attitudinizings, but a robust, red-armed *bonne femme,* who rough-shoulders her way among men and among affairs, who finds a healthy pleasure in the jostlings of the mob and a hearty delight in the honest, rough-and-tumble, Anglo-Saxon give-and-take knockabout that for us means life. Choose her, instead of the sallow, pale-faced statue-creature, with the foolish tablets and foolish, upturned eyes, and she will lead you as brave a march as ever drum tapped to. Stay at her elbow and obey her as she tells you to open your eyes and ears and heart, and as you go she will show things wonderful beyond wonder in this great, new, blessed country of ours, will show you a life untouched, untried, full of new blood and promise and vigor.

She is a Child of the People, this muse of our fiction of the future, and the wind of a new country, a new heaven and a new earth is in her face and has blown her hair from out the fillets that the old world muse has bound across her brow, so that it is all in disarray. The tan of the sun is on her cheeks, and the dust of the highway is thick upon her buskin, and the elbowing of many men has torn the robe off her, and her hands are hard with the grip of many things. She is hail-fellow-well-met with every one she meets, unashamed to know the clown and unashamed to face the king, a hardy, vigorous girl, with an arm as strong as a man's and a heart as sensitive as a child's.

Believe me, she will lead you far from the studios and the aesthetes, the velvet jackets and the uncut hair, far from the sexless creatures who cultivate their little art of writing as the fancier cultivates his orchid. Tramping along, then, with a stride that shall tax your best paces, she will lead you—if you are humble with her and honest with her—straight into a World of Working Men, crude of speech, swift of action, strong of passion, straight to the heart of a new life, on the borders of a new time, and there and only there, will you learn to know the stuff of which must come the American fiction of the future.

NOVELISTS TO ORDER—WHILE YOU WAIT[13]

Not at all absurd, "Novelists to order—while you wait," provided you order the right sort, and are willing to wait long enough. In other words, it is quite possible to make a novelist, and a good one, too, if the thing is undertaken in the right spirit, just as it is possible to make a painter, or an actor, or a business man.

I am prepared to hear the old objections raised to this: "Ah, it must be born in you"; "no amount of training can 'make' an artist"; "poets are born and not made," etc., etc. But I am also willing to contend that a very large percentage of this talk is sheer nonsense, and that what the world calls "genius" is, as often as not, the results of average ability specialized and developed. The original "spark" in the child-mind, that later on "kindles the world into flame with its light,"[14] I do believe could be proved to be the same for the artist, the actor, the novelist, the inventor, even the financier and "magnate." It is only made to burn in different lamps. Nor does any one believe that this "spark" is any mysterious, supernatural gift, some marvelous, angelic "genius," God-given, Heaven-given, etc., etc., etc., but just plain, forthright, rectangular, everyday common sense, nothing more extraordinary or God-given than sanity. If it were true that Genius were the gift of the gods, it would also be true that hard work in cultivating it would be superfluous. As well be without genius if some plodder, some dullard, can by such work equal the best you can do—you with your God-given faculties.

Is it not much more reasonable—more noble, for the matter of that—to admit at once that all faculties, all intellects are God-given, the only difference being that some are specialized to one end, some to another, some not specialized at all. We call Rostand and Mr. Carnegie geniuses, but most of us would be unwilling to admit that the genius of the Ameri-

---

[13] Syndicated, February 23, 1903.
[14] Unidentified, though perhaps proverbial rather than literary.

can financier differed in kind from the genius of the French dramatist. However, one believes that this is open to debate. As for my part, I suspect that, given a difference in environment and training, Rostand would have consolidated the American steel companies and Carnegie have written *L'Aiglon*. But one dares to go a little further—a great deal further—and claims that the young Carnegie and the young Rostand were no more than intelligent, matter-of-fact boys, in no wise different from the common house variety, grammar school product. They have been trained differently, that is all.

Given the ordinarily intelligent ten-year-old, and, all things being equal, you can make anything you like out of him—a minister of the gospel or a green-goods man, an electrical engineer or a romantic poet, or—return to our muttons—a novelist. If a failure is the result, blame the method of training, not the quantity or quality of the ten-year-old's intellect. Don't say, if he is a failure as a fine novelist, that he lacks genius for writing, and would have been a fine business man. Make no mistake, if he did not have enough "genius" for novel-writing he would certainly have not had enough for business.

"Why, then," you will ask, "is it so impossible for some men, the majority of them, to write fine novels, or fine poems, or paint fine pictures? Why is it that this faculty seems to be reserved for the chosen few, the more refined, cultured, etc.? Why is it, in a word, that, for every artist (using the word to include writers, painters, actors, etc.) that appears there are thousands of business men, commercial "geniuses"?

The reason seems to lie in this: and it is again a question of training. From the very first the average intelligent American boy is trained, not with a view toward an artistic career, but with a view to entering a business life. If the specialization of his faculties along artistic lines ever occurs at all it begins only when the boy is past the formative period. In other words, most people who eventually become artists are educated for the first eighteen or twenty years of their life along entirely unartistic lines. Biographies of artists are notoriously full of just such instances. The boy who is to become a business man finds, the moment he goes to school, a whole vast machinery of training made ready for his use, and not only is it a matter of education for him, but the whole scheme of modern civilization works in his behalf. No one ever heard of obstacles thrown in the way of the boy who announces for himself a money-making career; while for the artist, as is said, education, environment, the trend of civilization are not merely indifferent, but openly hostile and inimical. One hears only of those men who surmount—and at what cost to their artistic powers—those obstacles. How many thousands are there who succumb unrecorded!

So that it has not often been tried—the experiment of making a novelist while you wait—i.e., taking a ten-year-old of average intelligence and training him to be a novelist. Suppose all this modern, this gigantic perfected machinery—all this resistless trend of a commercial civilization were set in motion in favor of the little aspirant for honors in artistic fields, who is to say with such a training he would not in the end be a successful artist, painter, poet, musician or novelist. Training, not "genius," would make him.

Then, too, another point. The artistic training should begin much, much earlier than the commercial training—instead of, as at present, so much later.

Nowadays, as a rule, the artist's training begins, as was said, after a fourth of his life, the very best, the most important has been lived. You can take a boy of eighteen and make a business man of him in ten years. But at eighteen the faculties that make a good artist are very apt to be atrophied, hardened, unworkable. Even the ten-year-old is almost too old to begin on. The first ten years of childhood are the imaginative years, the creative years, the observant years, the years of a fresh interest in life. The child "imagines" terrors or delights, ghosts or fairies, creates a world out of his toys, and observes to an extent that adults have no idea of. ("Give me," a detective once told me, "a child's description of a man that is wanted. It beats an adult's every single time.") And imagination, creation, observation and an unblunted interest in life are exactly the faculties most needed by novelists.

At eighteen there comes sophistication—or a pretended sophistication, which is deadlier. Other men's books take the place of imagination for the young man; creation in him is satisfied by dramas, horse-races and amusements. The newspapers are his observation, and oh, how he assumes to be above any pleasure in simple, vigorous life!

So that at eighteen it is, as a rule, too late to make a fine novelist out of him. He may start out in that career, but he will not go far—so far as he would in business. But if he was taken in hand as soon as he could write in words of three syllables, and instead of being crammed with commercial arithmetic (How many marbles did A have? If a man buys a piece of goods at $12\frac{1}{2}$ cents and sells it for 15 cents, etc., etc.) —

If he had been taken in hand when his imagination was alive, his creative power vigorous, his observation lynxlike, and his interest keen, and trained with a view toward the production of original fiction, who is to say how far he would have gone?

One does not claim that the artist is above the business man. Far from it. Only, when you have choked the powers of imagination and observation, and killed off the creative ability, and deadened the interest in life, don't call it lack of genius.

Nor when some man of a different race than ours, living in a more congenial civilization, whose training from his youth up has been adapted to a future artistic profession, succeeds in painting the great picture, composing the great prelude, writing the great novel, don't say he was born a "genius," but rather admit that he was made "to order" by a system whose promoters knew how to wait.

"Life, Not Literature"

INTRODUCTION

I have already introduced the idea that a primitivistic anti-intellectualism underlies Norris' demand for "life, not literature." What remains to be discussed is the important relationship between Norris' particular mode of expressing that demand and the literary and cultural movements of his time.

That Norris' inner core of values assumes an outer shape determined in part by his age is revealed by a major difference between his beliefs and those of earlier and later romantic writers with generally similar values. The central dichotomy in such writers as Hawthorne and Thoreau or Steinbeck and Faulkner is not only between the emotional-instinctive life and the intellectual life, but also, and more far-reaching, between the organicism of nature and the mechanization of science or industrialism. Norris differs from these figures in that he praises the advances of modern industrialism. He views scientific mechanization as no threat to man, but rather as a means toward universal betterment. He fulfills, in short, Lois Whitney's description of the capacity of the popular mind to hold at the same time beliefs in cultural primitivism and in mechanical progress.[1] Norris, however, not only displays this perennial capacity, but is also very much of his time. For unlike the romantics of the early nineteenth or of the twentieth centuries, most writers of the late nineteenth century accepted that age's faith in industrial progress, though they often criticized abuses arising from uncontrolled industrialism.[2] Norris, for example, quarrelled with the railroad in *The Octopus* primarily because it was a monopoly. Elsewhere in the novel he displayed a faith in the benevolent powers of industrialism and commerce. And it is significant that on several occasions in his essays he used the Baldwin locomotive as a symbol of America's mechanical acuteness, its industrial strength, its world leadership, and its ability to aid other nations.

Norris, then, does not participate in the nature-machine conflict of earlier and later romantics.[3] Rather, he substitutes for the machine the

---

[1] Lois Whitney, *Primitivism and the Idea of Progress in English Popular Literature of the Eighteenth Century* (Baltimore: Johns Hopkins Press, 1934), p. 137.

[2] See Walter F. Taylor, *The Economic Novel in America*, (Chapel Hill, North Carolina: The University of North Carolina Press, 1942), p. 325.

[3] Critics seeking to document such a conflict in Norris have overrelied on the scene in *The Octopus* in which a railroad engine massacres a flock of sheep. See, for example, Leo Marx, "Two Kingdoms of Force," *Massachusetts Review*, I (Fall, 1959), 62–95. This scene, however, serves principally to characterize a particular railroad company, and must be compared with Norris' general statements elsewhere concerning industrialism and mechanization.

contemporary aesthetic movement, and—with some justice—views that movement as the major threat to the primitivistic values present in his conception of "life." He is caught up, not so much in the realism-romanticism controversy of the nineties as in that decade's conflict between a decadent aestheticism and an emerging school of manliness, adventure, and the outdoors.

This latter, more pertinent conflict is more clearly defined in England than in America, since our own aesthetic movement was primarily a weak imitation of English and French currents. (Our full-fledged rebellion against middle-class values occurred in the twenties.) In England, however, a genuine, vicious, and much-publicized battle was fought between the school of Wilde, Beardsley, and the *Yellow Book* and that of Henley, Kipling, and Stevenson.[4] This struggle reached a climax in the trial of Wilde in 1895 and in the apparent victory of the forces of "decency," virility, and moral art. But its ramifications continued into the early years of the new century, kept alive in part by the vogue of bohemianism and by the discussion of Nordau's thesis in *Degeneration* (1895) that almost all modern art was degenerate.[5]

To Norris, therefore, as late as 1902 "literature" was characterized by the stylistics of Pater, by the "spirituality" of Ruskin, and most of all by Wilde's doctrines of art's moral neutrality and of the superiority of art to nature. "I was a man who stood in symbolic relations to the art and culture of my age," Wilde wrote, and one can see a rather twisted application of that statement in Norris' tendency to characterize "literature" in sexual terms as effeminate, with some suggestions of homosexuality. Indeed, much of the emotional force present in Norris' attack on literary style can be understood only in relation to his revulsion from the eroticism and homosexuality associated with Wilde, Beardsley, and Huysmans.

In opposition to these figures was the group of writers, led by Henley, whom Jerome Buckley has called the "counter-decadents."[6] This counter-movement reached its fulfillment in the work of Kipling. And just as Norris' description of "literature" often seems an epitome of the popular conception of Wilde, so his idea of "life" is intimately related both to the fiction and to the aesthetic theory of Kipling. Like Norris, Kipling

[4] The most useful discussions of the aesthetic movement in England are by Jerome Buckley, *The Victorian Temper* (Cambridge, Massachusetts: Harvard University Press, 1951) and William Gaunt, *The Aesthetic Adventure* (New York: Harcourt, Brace and Company, 1945).

[5] See Grant C. Knight, *The Critical Period in American Literature* (Chapel Hill, North Carolina: The University of North Carolina Press, 1951), pp. 70–75.

[6] Jerome Buckley, *William Ernest Henley: A Study in the "Counter-Decadence" of the 'Nineties* (Princeton: Princeton University Press, 1945).

asserted the intrinsic value of both nature and machine. (The two faiths are strikingly combined in the two halves of *Captains Courageous*—the boy's "education" off the Grand Banks, the father's brilliant railroad journey. Kipling and Norris differ in this respect from Zola, who—for all his scientific pretensions—usually distrusted the machine.) Like Norris, Kipling posited aestheticism as the chief obstacle to the portrayal of "life," and like Norris he located aestheticism in literary centers and in universities.[7] Almost all of Kipling's basic aesthetic theory appears in *The Light That Failed*, a novel which Norris read early in the 1890's. In that work Dick, the artist-correspondent, takes part in battles and then paints them in all their violence, brutality, and dirt. He finds, however, that London art dealers and editors want neat, tidy battle scenes. (Norris' idea of sincerity also owes something to Dick's struggle between his sense of truth and the demands of public taste.) Maisie, on the other hand, is a sheltered, imitative, innocuous painter concerned almost entirely with gaining popular success. This contrast, and Dick's frequently expressed contempt for "Art" (always capitalized), supplied Norris with much of the rhetoric for his "life"-"literature" dualism.

In all, then, a Wilde-Kipling antithesis runs through Norris' description of "literature" and "life." But he also incorporated into that description certain distinctly American characteristics. For example, he tended in such articles as that on the "nature revival" to give a particularly Rooseveltian, outdoors, strenuous-life quality to his description of "life."[8] And in his attack on magazines for rejecting all stories not suitable for young girls, he joined in the American writer's bitterness toward the restrictions of the Iron Madonna and of the "daughter test,"[9] the point

---

[7] See particularly Kipling's poems "In Partibus" and "The 'Mary Gloster'." The first deals with London literary life as follows:

> But I consort with long-haired things
> In velvet collar-rolls,
> Who talk about the Aims of Art
> And "themes" and "goals,"
> And moo and coo with women-folk
> About their blessed souls.

The second characterizes a Cambridge man:

> "For you muddled with books and pictures, an' china an' etchings an' fans,
> "And your rooms at college was beastly—more like a whore's than a man's."

James Lane Allen, in his "Two Principles in Recent American Fiction" (*Atlantic Monthly*, LXXX [October, 1897], 433–441), named Kipling as the leader of the "masculine principle" which had been replacing the "feminine principle" in recent fiction.

[8] See Grant C. Knight, *The Strenuous Age in American Literature* (Chapel Hill, North Carolina: The University of North Carolina Press, 1954).

[9] See Leonard Lutwack, "The Iron Madonna and American Criticism in the Genteel Era," *Modern Language Quarterly*, XV (December, 1954), 343–348. The term "Iron

being, in Norris' case, that such restrictions stifled the publication of a literature derived from "life."

Moreover, though America lacked a figure comparable to Wilde, Norris discovered useful native butts for his attack on "literature" in Les Jeunes and in the New York literati. Les Jeunes were a group of San Francisco artists and writers, led by Gelett Burgess and Bruce Porter, who founded a little magazine called the *Lark* in 1895.[10] Vaguely imitative of the *Yellow Book* and the Chicago *Chap-Book*, the *Lark*, however, was more whimsical and eccentric than morbidly decadent. In addition, Norris knew and liked several of Les Jeunes.[11] Nevertheless, he reacted against the mannered and precious quality of the *Lark* (it was, for example, printed on bamboo paper with unjustified type) and against its appeal to the "specialized interest of the few."[12] When in 1897 he discussed the possibility of Kiplingesque exploitation of San Francisco, he pointedly contrasted literary virility with the work of Les Jeunes. And later in his career, when he needed a prototype of the over-aesthetic artist (most notably for Corthell in *The Pit*), he was always to use Bruce Porter.

More complex, however, is Norris' relationship to his primary symbol of aestheticism in America, the New York literary scene. For Norris himself had participated in the general migration of San Francisco writers to New York during the nineties, a journey which was viewed in San Francisco as a necessary step in the progress of a literary career.[13] When Norris was called to New York in 1898, he heralded his move as a victory.[14] Yet within a few years he pictured New York as representing all that was false in "literature."

Madonna" was popularized by Hjalmar Boyesen in his article "Why We Have No Great Novelists" (*Forum*, II [February, 1887], 615–622).

[10] See James D. Hart's Introduction to Gelett Burgess, *Bayside Bohemia: Fin de Siècle San Francisco and Its Little Magazines* (San Francisco: Book Club of California, 1954), and Oscar Lewis, *Bay Window Bohemia: An Account of the Brilliant Artistic World of Gaslit San Francisco* (Garden City, New York: Doubleday & Company, 1956). Besides Burgess and Porter, Les Jeunes included Willis Polk, Porter Garnett, Ernest Peixotto, and Yone Noguchi. The *Lark* published its last number (an *Epi-Lark*) in May, 1897.

[11] He had met Burgess at Berkeley, where Burgess taught topographical drawing, and later knew him in connection with the *Wave*, which Burgess contributed to frequently. Ernest Peixotto was a close friend from his Paris art student days. But Norris knew almost all Les Jeunes, and Jeannette Norris and others (FWC) recalled his friendships with them.

[12] Bruce Porter, *Epi-Lark*, May, 1897, n.p.

[13] While Norris was working on the *Wave* that magazine often noted the New York accomplishments of such former San Francisco writers and artists as Juliet Wilbor Tompkins, Geraldine Bonner, Ernest Peixotto, and Gelett Burgess. Eventually Cosgrave himself made the "jump."

[14] He greeted his call by McClure as "good news" in a letter to Eleanor Davenport (February 12, 1898, *Letters*, p. 5).

Norris' rejection of New York was foreshadowed by his early absorption of Kipling's attitude toward London and by his own experiences in the minor literary center of San Francisco. One suspects that he transferred characteristics of both Les Jeunes and his mother's Browning club to his descriptions of New York literary life. But Norris also no doubt encountered in New York that fringe of sophisticated dilettantism often found in literary capitals—the "New Bohemia" and the literary salons of his day, the publishers' cocktail circuit of ours.

What compels interest in Norris' depiction of this group (in his articles on New York and in his story "Dying Fires") is the power he attributes to it—the power to wreck completely a promising career. His heavy emphasis on New York's ability to corrupt suggests a similarity between these accounts and other works by him—such as *Vandover* and *Blix*—in which he dramatizes (and exaggerates) his personal fears. For Norris, like his imaginary provincial novelist, thought of himself as a writer of crude, raw, but honest fiction (*McTeague*) which had been praised for its strength. Like his provincial writer, he had them come to New York, had gone to work for a publisher, and had been prompted—in Norris' case by reviewers, including Howells[15]—to refine his art, to get more "beauty," "spirituality," and "intellect" into his work. And there is some reason to believe that the second half of *A Man's Woman*, with all its high-minded quibbling, is a slight yielding to that prompting. But unlike his provincial writer, Norris felt that he had not capitulated completely. He had rather caught himself up in time, had recognized his true talent, and now, in late 1899, as he wrote Isaac Marcosson, was

going back *definitely* . . . to the style of MacT. and stay with it right along. I've been sort of feeling my way since the "Moran" days and getting a twist of myself. Now I think I know where I am at and what game I play the best. The Wheat series will be straight naturalism with all the guts I can get into it.[16]

And this "going back," it seems clear, included a repudiation of his earlier goal of New York.

The significance of this autobiographical element in Norris' attack on New York is that it clarifies the personal quality of the masculine-feminine rhetoric in his entire "life"-"literature" antithesis. It was personally important for Norris to assert the masculinity of true art—whether it was the art of Kipling, or that of his imaginary provincial writer before coming to New York, or that of his own visceral naturalism. There were several reasons for this need. An an artist, Norris wished to stress the masculinity of art in order to insure the masculinity of the artist, par-

---

[15] Howells, *Literature*, N.S. I. (March 24, 1899), 241–242.
[16] Norris to Marcosson, November, 1899, *Letters*, p. 48.

ticularly in an age when *Punch* and Gilbert and Sullivan summed up the popular association of the artist with effeminacy and even homosexuality. Moreover, his emphasis on the masculinity of a literature of "life" allied that literature with the honorific masculinity of the world of affairs, where men "got things done" and aided the world's work. In other words, underlying such particulars as Norris' rejection of New York was his need to find contemporary applicable formulas—perhaps somewhat like Hemingway's use of hunting and bullfighting—for the expression of the masculinity of his talent and his career.

As with his other major critical ideas, Norris' association of masculinity with "life" and effeminacy with "literature" is also prominent in his fiction. It is a primary theme, for example, in two of his popular novels, *Moran* and *Blix*. In these works women possessing a masculine strength of body and mind reject feminine superficialities for a full participation in some aspect of life, whereas young men must make a like decision if they are to progress from effeminacy to masculinity. And here, as in Norris' criticism, masculinity includes moral force, effeminacy moral indecision or weakness.

OUR UNPOPULAR NOVELISTS: DISAPPEARANCE OF AMERICAN FICTION FROM THE BOOK STORES[17]

For those who have faith in American authors of fiction there is nothing more discouraging than a walk through the book stores of an afternoon and a talk with the booksellers. Where are our American story tellers? One has heard, of course, of Howells, and Crawford, and Harold Frederic, and Nelson Page, and Wallace, and our own dear Harding Davis. But look at the shelves of the popular books; here and there, at wide intervals, one sees a *Ben Hur,* a *Ralstons,* and perhaps a *Gallegher* or two, or a *Van Bibber and Others,* but they are *rari* in a *gurgite vasto.*[18] Look at the stream, look at the flood, look at the very tidal wave of English fiction that overflows the shelves, that pours itself out upon the long tables, that is diked up in the show windows, that overwhelms the city, the whole country, in fact.

It is like an invasion, a reconquest, a literary revanche; it is an army with banners flying. Look at them as they come; Trilby is still at the head, and close upon her bare, list-slippered heels comes the Minister of France, with his sword and robes; Sherlock Holmes, very stealthy and smelling of cocaine—if cocaine smells—and the Manxman in his beret and worsted Jersey (one is sure that *he* smells of drying fish and of the ocean).[19]

These are the "steadies," the sure ones, the veterans. The sale of these books is to be counted on—they are staple. But besides them are the books of the hour, "the latest things out," the fads, and these, too, are English every one—*Beside the Bonnie Briar Bush, The Prisoner of Zenda, The Stark-Munro Letters,* and others. Go to, say, four of the principal retail book stores in the city and ask the salesman to name to you five of the most popular books of the month in their order of popularity. This is the answer you receive: at Doxey's—*Beside the Bonnie Briar Bush, The Prisoner of Zenda, The Manxman, The Gentleman of France, Memoirs of a Minister of France.* At The Popular Book Store—*Beside the Bonnie Briar Bush, The Stark-Munro Letters, The Master* (by Zangwill), *The Manxman, The Memoirs of a Minister of France.* At Beach's—*Beside the Bonnie Briar Bush, The Prisoner of Zenda, The Gentleman of France, The Stark-Munro Letters, The Moss Hags,* (this last a guess, as it is not yet out). At Cooper's only *The Gentleman of*

[17] *Wave,* XIV (October 5, 1895), 7.
[18] The works mentioned are Lew Wallace's *Ben Hur* (1880), F. M. Crawford's *The Ralstons* (1895), and Richard Harding Davis' *Gallegher and Other Stories* (1891) and *Van Bibber and Others* (1892).
[19] Referred to are *Trilby* (1894) by George du Maurier, *From the Memoirs of a Minister of France* (1895) by Stanley J. Weyman, *Adventures of Sherlock Holmes* (1892) by Arthur Conan Doyle, and *The Manxman* (1894) by Hall Caine. All were best sellers of 1894 or 1895.

France is selling; at Cooper's nothing else goes; the stock of fiction is dead. What a fearful gloom upon this establishment Cooper! At Robertson's it is *Beside the Bonnie Briar Bush* again, *The Prisoner of Zenda*, *The Stark-Munro Letters*, Zangwill's *Master*, and *The Honorable Peter Sterling*, by John Ford, *American*. Print it in large caps, print it in red ink; tell it at the four corners of the city. Here for once, at least, the American has beaten them all. Robertson has sold more *John Sterlings* than of any three other English novels of the year (*Trilby* scratched).[20]

Now, why should this thing be? Why do the American public buy three English novels to one written by an American? It is almost impossible to say. The booksellers themselves cannot agree upon any one explanatory theory. Here are three of the theories put forward by most of them. The first is, that American authors have written themselves out; the old authors are dead either in a literal or a literary sense, and no new ones have risen to take their places. The second is, that it is the publisher who makes the book. The English novelists have publishers who know how to make a demand for a novel, know how to make it popular, know how to give it a "boom." The third accounts for the mystery by "tendencies" and "reactions." There has been a "reaction" against the realistic school of the American authors of ten years ago, and a "marked tendency" toward the romantic fiction now in process of production by English story-writers. This last may be the true reason; but you should remember that there is nothing, nothing on God's green earth, that cannot be plausibly accounted for by "tendencies" and "reactions." If a novel, a realistic novel say, is successful, it is due to a "reaction" against the tame and insipid productions of the romanticists. If it is a failure, one accounts for it by saying that the "tendencies" of modern fiction are to the clean, the wholesome, or adventurous and imaginative. Now, all this is a great pity. One is even led to regret the very invention of the terms of "romanticism," "realism," "naturalism." Human nature is the same no matter whether one regards it with the eyes of a romanticist, a realist, or a naturalist; art in composition is the same. Don't higgle with your terms; don't belong to any "school." If you read books instead of writing them, read with a view to the *general effect produced*. If the book is good, it is good whether it is *Ivanhoe, The Rise of Silas Lapham*, or *La Bête Humaine* of M. Zola. Why cannot the writers of new novels work independently of schools or theories? Why not do their best work without half an eye upon the style and tenets of their favorite author?

[20] Works not already identified are: Ian Maclaren *Beside the Bonnie Briar Bush* (1894), Anthony Hope, *The Prisoner of Zenda* (1894), Arthur Conan Doyle, *The Stark Munro Letters* (1895), Stanley J. Weyman, *A Gentleman of France* (1894), and S. R. Crockett, *The Men of the Moss-Hags* (1895). The novel by Ford is *The Honorable Peter* (not *John*) *Stirling* (not *Sterling*), by Paul (not *John*) L. Ford.

THE DECLINE OF THE MAGAZINE SHORT STORY[21]

Is it possible that the short story—the American short story—is on the decline? And if so is it because the authors have ceased to produce work of a high standard, or because the public—that particular circle of the public for whom the magazines cater—have ceased to demand it?

Four years ago the name of Richard Harding Davis was in everybody's mouth. Now he is writing syndicate articles for the daily press on "special topics," and Gallegher Travers and Cortlandt Van Bibber are fast fading from the public's memory.[22] Is Mr. Davis a type? Has he reached the limit of his productive capacity, or have the magazine editors—who feel the tastes of their public as a skillful rider feels his horse's mouth—dropped him as an author who has lost popular favor? In either event the result remains the same; Mr. Davis' stories have ceased to appear in the magazines. But on the other hand, one would expect to see his place filled by a new popular favorite. According to immemorial custom this should be the case, yet somehow a successor has failed to appear. Owen Wister claimed attention for some dozen or so issues, but now he too is dropped, is out of the race, is a back number. Kipling is never seen in the three big magazines, and but rarely in *McClure's*. Now why should this thing be? Why is it that the best magazines should fail to publish the best class of stories? Why are not the names of Kipling and of Arthur Morrison and Stephen Crane seen in *Harper's* and in the *Century* and in *Scribner's* as often as those old, old familiar standbys, the veterans, the "steadies," Brander Matthews, Octave Thanet, Charles Dudley Warner, Thomas Janvier, Ruth McEnery Stuart and so many other "magazinists"? Do you remember how Caliban spoke of Setebos, how that some day he might "doze, doze, doze, as good as die"?[23] That expresses it exactly. These good people, these professional magazinists write, and write, and write; to all ends and purposes they died long ago. Can there be anything staler than Brander Matthews' stories of New York life? anything flatter than Min Stuart's dialect stories? anything more unprofitable than the foolish maunderings of Thomas Janvier, with his "out of the way hotels," his foreigner, his new-married couple? The three more important magazines have shoveled this tasteless, vapid sort of thing at one so long and so persistently that one has at last come to accept it without a great deal of comment; one takes it as a whole, much the same as one would shrimps.

To put it tersely, the stuff is absolutely stupid. We have met the same characters, witnessed the same scenes, gone through the same worn,

---

[21] *Wave*, XVI (January 30, 1897), 3.

[22] Davis' two most famous characters, the first a clever boy from the slums, the second a New York society "thoroughbred." Norris imitated them in his early stories.

[23] Robert Browning, "Caliban upon Setebos" (1. 283). Norris adds an extra "doze."

hackneyed, hashed-up situations again and again and yet again. The short stories of *Harper's, Scribner's* and the *Century* have become deadly dull. There is in them no freshness, no originality, no vitality, no close, keen grip on life or nature. They are mere empty forms, out of which the substance has long since vanished, and one accepts them only because of the reputation of the magazines in which they are published. We ourselves have read stories in recent issues of the *Century Magazine* which, had they been sent anonymously to this paper, would have been decisively and promptly rejected with a distinct understanding that their "unavailability" did most certainly "imply a lack of literary merit."

The great merit of the stories of these "magazinists"—the one quality which endears them to the editors, is that they are what in editorial slang is called "safe." They are safe, it is true, safe as a grave yard, decorous as a church, as devoid of immorality as an epitaph. They have not the vigor or decisiveness to offend the most invertebrate taste. They adorn the center table. They do not "call a blush to the cheek of the young." They can be placed—Oh crowning virtue, Oh supreme encomium—they can be "safely" placed in the hands of any young girl the country over.

It is the "young girl" and the family center table that determine the standard of the American short story.

AN OPENING FOR NOVELISTS: GREAT OPPORTUNITIES FOR FICTION WRITERS IN SAN FRANCISCO[24]

There are certain cities in the world which are adaptable to the uses of the writer of fiction, and there are others which are not. Things can happen in some cities and the tale of them will be interesting; the same story laid in another city would be ridiculous. It is hard to say, why this is so, but a moment's review of the world's centers with this thought in mind will prove the truth of the statement beyond any shadow of doubt. Paris, London and Rome are "good material." Berlin, Vienna and Hamburg are not. Stories of New Orleans or of Constantinople could easily be made interesting, but no romancer has yet had the hardihood to attempt to write of Chicago or Buffalo. Imagine a novel of Chicago.[25] The fact is very curious and the choice very arbitrary. There seems to be no rule applicable. A city need not necessarily be old, nor a seaport, nor "cosmopolitan," nor picturesque, nor beautifully built, nor large nor small. Any one who has the instinct for fiction can tell on the instant

[24] *Wave*, XVI (May 22, 1897), 7.

[25] Norris was apparently unaware of H. B. Fuller's *The Cliff-Dwellers* (1893) and *With the Procession* (1895), both set in Chicago, and of Hamlin Garland's *Rose of Dutcher's Coolly* (1895), partially set in Chicago. Nor, of course, did he anticipate his own *The Pit* (1903).

whether or not it is suitable as a background for a novel, a short story or a drama.

But consider San Francisco. It is not necessary to hesitate a moment. "Things can happen" in San Francisco. Kearny street, Montgomery street, Nob Hill, Telegraph Hill, of course Chinatown, Lone Mountain, the Poodle Dog, the Palace Hotel and the What Cheer House, the Barbary Coast, the Crow's Nest, the Mission, the Bay, the Bohemian Club, the Presidio, Spanish town, Fisherman's wharf.

There is an indefinable air about all these places that is suggestive of stories at once. You fancy the names would look well on a book's page. The people who frequent them could walk right into a novel or short story and be at home.

It occurs to me that there is perhaps one feature of the city that conduces to this effect, that is its isolation. Perhaps no great city of the world is so isolated as we are. Did you ever think of that? There is no great city to the north of us, to the south none nearer than Mexico, to the west is the waste of the Pacific, to the east the waste of the deserts. Here we are set down as a pin point in a vast circle of solitude. Isolation produces individuality, originality. The place has grown up independently. Other cities grow by accretion from without. San Francisco must grow by expansion from within; and so we have time and opportunity to develop certain unhampered types and characters and habits unbiased by outside influence, types that are admirably adapted to fictitious treatment.

It is a significant fact that the little that has been done in the way of gripping hold upon and impressing this life of ours between the covers of works of fiction has been done in the way of short stories. London had her Dickens, New Orleans her Cable, New York her Davis, Boston her Howells, Paris her Zola, but San Francisco still waits for her novelist. She will wait long, we believe. The conditions of our life are suited finely to the short story, but not as yet to the novel. We are growing and living, as it were, in spots, here a little and there a little, scattered bits of life and movement, quite independent of each other—short stories that are happening every day. But we are not settled enough yet for the novelist, who demands large, co-ordinated, broad and simple lines upon which to work, something far more unified than we can yet give him.[26] But the short stories. There's the chance. Who shall be our Kipling? Where is the man

---

[26] A somewhat anomalous remark considering that Norris had completed *Vandover and the Brute* and had almost finished *McTeague*. Indeed, he had subtitled *Vandover*, "A Study of Life and Manners in an American City at the End of the Nineteenth Century," and that city was San Francisco. There is also a discrepancy in the title of this article, since it should rightly be "An Opening for Short-Story Writers." Norris answered his own plea, for in the months following this article he published a San Francisco story in almost every issue of the *Wave*.

that shall get at the heart of us, the blood and bones and fiber of us, that shall go a-gunning for stories up and down our streets and into our houses and parlors and lodging houses and saloons and dives and along our wharves and into our theaters; yes, and into the secretest chambers of our homes as well as our hearts?

Les Jeunes. Yes, there are Les Jeunes, and the *Lark* was delightful— delightful fooling, but there's a graver note and a more virile to be sounded. Les Jeunes can do better than the *Lark*. Give us stories now, give us men, strong, brutal men, with red-hot blood in 'em, with un- leashed passions rampant in 'em, blood and bones and viscera in 'em, and women, too, that move and have their being, people that love and hate something better now than Vivettes and Perilles and Goups.[27] They are here, these living men and women. Think of the short stories that are happening every hour of the time. Get hold of them, some of you younger writers, grip fast upon the life of them. It's the Life that we want, the vig- orous, real thing, not the curious weaving of words and the polish of literary finish. Damn the "style" of a story, so long as we get the swing and rush and trample of the things that live. While you are rounding a phrase a sailor has been shanghaied down there along the water front; while you are sustaining a metaphor, another See Yup has been hatcheted yonder in Gambler's Alley; a man has time to be stabbed while you are composing a villanelle; the crisis of a life has come and gone while you have been niggling with your couplet. "Murder and sudden death," say you? Yes, but it's the life that lives; it's reality, it's the thing that counts. We don't want literature, we want life. We don't want fine writing, we want short stories. Kipling saw it here and Stevenson as they passed through—read the unwritten tales of us as they ran.[28]

The tales are here. The public is here. A hundred clashing presses are hungry for you, future young story-writer of San Francisco, whoever you may be. Strike but the right note, and strike it with all your might, strike it with iron instead of velvet, and the clang of it shall go the round of the nations.

A qui le tour, who shall be our Kipling?

FRANK NORRIS' WEEKLY LETTER[29]

Only two or three days ago I heard a story about a young man of letters that not only impressed me at the time, but has ever since been, as it were,

---

[27] Vivette and Perilla (not *Perille*) were imaginary characters of refinement and sensi- tivity to whom many of the essays in the *Lark* were either dedicated or addressed. Goops (not *goups*) were boneless figures drawn by Burgess for cartoons in the *Lark*.

[28] Norris refers to passages on San Francisco in Kipling's *American Notes* (1891) and Stevenson's *The Wrecker* (1892). Loudon Dodd in *The Wrecker* (always one of Norris' favorite novels) thought San Francisco the most interesting city in America.

[29] *Chicago American,* August 24, 1901, p. 8.

a sort of obsession. The thing depressed me. I have not been able to get it out of my mind. It was not only because the story was sad in itself, but because there is every reason to believe—oh, let us say it is positively true—that there are hundreds of stories like this one of my young fellow working themselves out in every city in the union; more especially so in New York.

The story distinctly has a moral and for the sake of those beginners in letters who have yet to arrive—even for those whose "first book" is already published—the story shall be set down in this place.

The name of the young man does not matter, though he has been before the public. I doubt if there are one hundred people who would recall his name. He came of good people in Pennsylvania. His father was a lawyer in a small city, had been editor of the "city paper," and thence no doubt came the literary twist in our young man.

When he was twenty-two he wrote a novel. The novel was not great, but it was distinctly promising in that it was all his own. By some miraculous good fortune he had got started straight with his very first effort; had not been influenced by some favorite author, had not been Kiplingized or Davised or Anthony Hoped. This sort of thing happens oftener than you would suppose in little out of the way communities, where a boy will begin to write before he has, one may almost say, begun to read, and where there are no "literary" people to bother him and sidetrack him.

The stuff, then, was all his own. There was a fresh note in it that no one had ever heard before. Nothing astonishing about it, a book you would maybe yawn over, but it was his own. You can imagine, or I will ask you to understand, how carefully and with what meticulous nicety such a career, thus begun, should have been nurtured. Some writers work twenty years before attaining to their own style, before becoming original. But this young fellow was one of those country boys who grow up unnoticed and are close enough to the soil to get a good, vigorous growth early in life.

Well, his book was published by a New York firm and one of the editors of this firm (who saw the promise in the work and the prospects of a good investment in a potential genius of the near future) sent for the young man to come to New York and gave him a minor place on the editorial staff.

In New York the boy fell foul of a literary set first off. He was invited to an "evening." There he met a few of the vast army of "third-raters." Short-haired women and long-haired men, minor poets whose opportunity in life is the blank space left in the magazine between the end of an article and the bottom of the page; authors who because of a story or two printed in the *Century* or *Harper's* or *Scribner's* were considered to have "arrived"; book reviewers who hacked for the literary weeklies and spoke of themselves as critics; and—worst of all—a number of women who neither wrote nor reviewed, but who "took an interest in young writers." They took an interest in this boy of mine—some of them had read his little book—and they fluttered and buzzed about him.

He never knew the difference. He had never been in a large city before and he thought this was the real thing. He thought these people were the real literary force of New York, and naturally enough he was flattered, dazed, confused. He began to foregather with this set continually. He was made a lion of when his book reached its little pinnacle of popularity—perhaps it sold 2500 copies. The set kow-towed to him and spoke of his book as a masterpiece. It was like Stevenson, they said, only with more polish. They said this for an actual fact—Stevenson with more polish!—POLISH.

Then some of the women who "influenced" and some of the half-baked "magazinists" took him in hand. Ah, they understood his temperament. They could see where his forte lay. Thus and thus he should write; the spiritual element (there was a healthy, sane animalism in the young man's book, a thing that hurt nobody and that he would modify in time)—the spiritual element was the great thing, the higher plane, the upward trend, and they quoted Walter Pater and Ruskin and Matthew Arnold, and by and by the boy began to think he saw his future in a different light. Began to think he really was Stevenson with more polish and that he must "strive for the spiritual" and "trend upward."

He learned the lingo of the "third-raters." He began to speak of certain books as "convincing" or "not convincing." He knew all about "catholicity of taste." He knew the difference between a metaphor and a simile and a "split infinitive" made him shudder.

In this spirit and with these surroundings to influence him he retired to himself for a few months and wrote his second book; wrote as those certain women of the set would have him write. The originality and unconventionality of his first book he looked upon as crudity—I suppose he said it "failed to convince."

His second book, of course, was a failure. His publisher would have none of it. Said it was "not the thing." The boy had the greatest difficulty in securing a publisher for it at all, and when it finally appeared it sold a few hundred copies, then stopped, and the real critics—the kind that do not appear in sets—hardly so much as noticed it.

The young fellow came back to the set to talk it over. Then, too, in his disappointment he wanted to be told again that he was "Stevenson with more polish."

But the set—the same women and magazinists and fakers who had ruined his one chance in life—could hardly find time to notice him now.

When they did it was to tell him that he must strive to be more worthy of his better self, to find the "true note," his "individual medium of expression."

They hardly had time to say even this, however. A new little lion was among them—a Filipino poet with wild eyes and who looked like a fencing master.

The young man shouldered off, went by himself into a corner to think it over. His eyes were opened and he saw what these people had done to him. Saw the Great Mistake and that he had wasted his substance. He was eating husks with swine. He had sinned before heaven and the great good thing that had once been his he had allowed to be stripped from him, in return receiving a farrago of empty phrases.

He tried to pull out. He "arose and went to his father," but in his case it was too late. It was gone—the faint little spark that might, with care, have burst into a blaze. He could not now get back that fresh, untrammeled view of things that he had at first. His chance was gone and the light was dead within him.

He has gone back to Pennsylvania by now and is a law clerk in his father's office. He spends most of his time in serving papers and ruling forms and thinking how he will manage when his next chance comes.

It won't come again, however. But if he had kept away from literary sets and from the women who influence he would not have furnished a warning to the many others of his kind who are this very day going exactly the same gait.

WHY WOMEN SHOULD WRITE THE BEST NOVELS: AND WHY THEY DON'T[30]

It is rather curious upon reflection and upon looking over the rank and file of achievement during the period of recorded history, to observe that of all the occupations at first exclusively followed by men, that of writing has been—in all civilizations and among all people—one of the very first to be successfully—mark the qualification of the adverb—to be successfully invaded by women. We hear of women who write poetry long before we hear of women who paint pictures or perform upon musical instruments, or achieve distinction upon the stage.

It would seem as if of all the arts, that of writing is the one to which women turn the quickest. Great success in the sciences or in mercantile pursuits is of course out of the question, so that—as at the first—it may be said, speaking largely, that of all the masculine occupations that of writing is the first to be adopted by women.

[30] *Boston Evening Transcript,* November 13, 1901, p. 20.

If it is the first it must be because it is the easiest. Now to go very far back to the earliest beginnings, all occupations, whether artistic or otherwise, were the prerogative of the male; considering this fact I say does it not follow, or would not the inference be strong, that—given an equal start—women would write more readily than men, would do so because they could do so; that writing is a feminine—not accomplishment merely—but gift.

So that the whole matter leads up to the point one wishes to make, namely, that here, in our present day and time, it should be easier for women to write well than for men. And as writing today means the writing of fiction, we arrive, somewhat deviously and perhaps—after jumping many gaps and weak spots en route—a little lamely at the very last result of all, which is this: Women should be able to write better novels than men.

But under modern conditions there are many more reasons for this success of women in fiction than merely a natural inherent gift of expression.

One great reason is leisure. The average man, who must work for a living, has not time to write novels, much less to get into that frame of mind, or to assume that mental attitude by means of which he is able to see possibilities for fictitious narrative in the life around him. But as yet, few women (compared with the armies of male workers) have to work for a living and it is an unusual state of affairs in which the average woman of moderate circumstances could not, if she would, take from three to four hours a day from her household duties to devote to any occupation she deemed desirable.

Another reason is found, one believes, in the nature of women's education. From almost the very first the young man studies with an eye to business, or to a profession. In many State colleges now-a-days all literary courses, except the most elementary—which indeed have no place in collegiate curriculums—are optional. But what girls' seminary does not prescribe the study of literature through all its three or four years, making of this study a matter of all importance? And while the courses of literature do not, by any manner of means, make a novelist, they familiarize the student with style and the means by which words are put together. The more one reads, the easier one writes.

Then, too (though this reason lies not so much in modern conditions as in basic principles), there is the matter of temperament. The average man is a rectangular, square-cut, matter-of-fact, sober-minded animal who does not receive impressions easily, who is not troubled with emotions and has no overmastering desire to communicate his sensations to anybody. But the average woman is just the reverse of all these. She is impressionable, emotional and communicative. And impressionableness, emotionality and communicativeness are three very important qualities of mind that make for novel writing.

The modern woman, then, in a greater degree than her contemporaneous male, has the leisure for novel writing, has the education, and has the temperament. She should be able to write better novels, and as a matter of fact she does not. It is, of course, a conceded fact that there have been more great men novelists than women novelists, and that today the producers of the best fiction are men and not women. There are probably more women trying to write novels than there are men, but for all this it must be admitted that the ranks of the "arrived" are recruited from the razor-using contingent.

Why, then, with such a long start and with so many advantages of temperament, opportunity and training should it be that women do not write better novels than men?

One believes that the answer is found in the fact that life is more important than literature, and in the wise, wise, old, old adage that experience is the best teacher. Of all the difficult things that enter into the learning of a most difficult profession, the most difficult of all for the intended novelist to acquire is the fact that life is better than literature. The amateur will say this with conviction, will preach it in public and practise the exact reverse in private. But it still remains true that all the temperament, all the sensitiveness to impressions, all the education in the world will not help one little, little bit in the writing of the novel if life itself, the crude, the raw, the vulgar, if you will, is not studied. An hour's experience is worth ten years of study—of reading other people's books. But this fact is ignored, and the future writer of what it is hoped will be the great novel of his day and age studies the thoughts and products of some other writer, of some other great novel, of some other day and age, in the hope that thereby much may be learned. And much will be learned—very much, indeed—of the methods of construction; and if the tyro only has wits enough to study the great man's formula, well and good. But the fascination of a great story writer—especially upon the young, untried little story writer—is strong, and before the latter is well aware he is taking from the big man that which he has no right to take. He is taking his code of ethics, his view of life, his personality, even to the very incidents and episodes of his story. He is studying literature and not life.

If he had gone direct to life itself, all would have been different. He would have developed in his own code, his own personality, and he would have found incidents and episodes that were new—yes, and strikingly forceful, better than any he could have imagined or stolen, and which were all his own. In the end, if the gods gave him long life and a faculty of application, he would have evolved into something of a writer of fiction.

All this digression is to try to state the importance of actual life and actual experience, and it bears upon the subject in hand in this, that women who have all the other qualifications of good novelists are, because of the nature and character that invariably goes with these qualifications, shut away from the study of, and the association with, the most important thing of all for them—real life. Even making allowances for the emancipation of the New Woman, the majority of women still lead, in comparison with men, secluded lives. The woman who is impressionable is by reason of this very thing sensitive (indeed, sensitiveness and impressionableness mean almost the same thing), and it is inconceivably hard for the sensitive woman to force herself into the midst of that great, grim complication of men's doings that we call life. And even admitting that she finds in herself the courage to do this, she lacks the knowledge to use knowledge thus gained. The faculty of selection comes even to men only after many years of experience.

So much for causes exterior to herself, and it is well to admit at once that the exterior causes are by far the most potent and most important; but there are perhaps causes to be found in the make-up of the woman herself which keep her from success in fiction. Is it not a fact that protracted labor of the mind tells upon a woman quicker than upon a man? Be it understood that no disparagement, no invidious comparison is intended. Indeed it is quite possible that her speedier mental fatigue is due to the fact that the woman possesses the more highly specialized organ.

A man may grind on steadily for an almost indefinite period, when a woman at the same task would begin, after a certain point, to "feel her nerves," to chafe, to fret, to try to do too much, to polish too highly, to develop more perfectly. Then come fatigue, harassing doubts, more nerves, a touch of hysteria occasionally, exhaustion, and in the end complete discouragement and a final abandonment of the enterprise: and who shall say how many good, even great, novels have remained half written, to be burned in the end, because their women authors mistook lack of physical strength for lack of genuine ability?

NEW YORK AS A LITERARY CENTER[31]

It has been given to the present writer to know a great many of what one may call The Unarrived in literary work, and of course to be one himself of that "innumerable caravan," and speaking authoritatively and

[31] Syndicated, January 19, 1902.

of certain knowledge, the statement may be made, that of all the ambitions of the Great Unpublished, the one that is strongest, the most abiding, is the ambition to get to New York. For these, New York is the *point de départ*, the pedestal, the niche, the indispensable vantage ground; as one of the unpublished used to put it: "It is a place that I can stand on and holler."

This man lived in a second-class town west of the Mississippi, and one never could persuade him that he might holler from his own, native heath, and yet be heard. He said it would be "the voice of one crying in the wilderness." New York was the place for him. Once land him in New York and all would be gas and gaiters.

There are so many thousands like this young man of mine that a word in this connection seems appropriate; and the object of this present writing is to protest against this blind and unreasoned hegira, and to urge the point that tradition, precedent to the contrary notwithstanding, New York is not a literary center.

I am perfectly well aware that this statement savors of heresy, but at the same time I think it can be defended. As for instance:

Time was when Boston claimed the distinction that one now denies to New York. But one asserts that Boston made her claims good. In those days the reactionary movement of populations from the cities toward the country had not set in. A constant residence winter and summer in the country was not dreamed of by those who had the leisure and the money to afford it. As much as possible the New England writers crowded to Boston, or to Cambridge, which is practically the same thing, and took root in the place. There was their local habitation; there they lived, and thence they spread their influence. Remember that at the height of the development of the New England school there were practically no other writers of so great importance the length and breadth of the land. This huddling about a common point made it possible to visit all the homes of nearly all of the most eminent American literati in a single day. The younger men, the aspirants, the Unpublished, however, thrown into such society, could not fail to be tremendously impressed, and, banded together as these great ones were, their influence counted enormously. It was no unusual sight to see half a dozen of these at the same dinner table. They all knew each other intimately, these Bostonians, and their word was *Lex,* and the neophytes came from all corners of the compass to hear them speak, and Boston did in good earnest become the Hub, the center of literary thought and work in the United States.

But no such conditions obtain in New York to-day. During the last ten years two very important things have happened that bear upon this question. First has come the impulse toward a country life—a continued winter and summer residence in the country. Authors more than any other class of workers can afford this since their profession can be carried anywhere. They need no city offices. They are not forced to be in touch with the actual business life of Broadway.[32] Secondly, since the day of the Bostonian supremacy a tremendous wave of literary production has swept over the United States. New England has ceased to be the only place where books are written. Poems are now indited in Dakota, novels composed in Wyoming, essays written in Utah, and criticisms flourish in Kansas. A thousand and one Little Centers have sprung up. Literary groups are formed everywhere, in Buffalo, in San Francisco, in Indianapolis and Chicago.

All this detracts from the preponderance of any one city, such as New York, as literary dictator. You shall find but a very small and meager minority of the Greater Men of Letters who have their homes in Manhattan. Most of them preferred to live in the places whereof they treat in their books, in New Orleans, in Indiana, in Kentucky, or Virginia, or California, or Kansas, or Illinois. If they come to New York at all it is only temporarily, to place their newest book or to arrange with publishers for future work.

The result of this is as is claimed. New York is not a literary center. The publishing houses are there, the magazines, all the distributing machinery, but not the writers. They do not live there. They do not care to come there. They regard the place simply as a distributing point for their wares.

Literary centers produce literary men. Paris, London and Boston all have their long lists of native-born writers—men who were born in these cities and whose work was identified with them. But New York can claim but ridiculously few of the men of larger caliber as her own. James Whitcomb Riley is from Indiana, Joel Chandler Harris is a Southerner. Howells came from Boston, Cable from New Orleans, Hamlin Garland from the West. Bret Harte from California, Mark Twain from the Middle West, Harold Frederic and Henry James found England more congenial than the greatest city of their native land. Even among the younger generation there are but few who can be considered as New Yorkers. Although Richard Harding Davis wrote accurately and delightfully of New York people, he was not born in New York, did not receive his first impetus from New York influences, and does not now live in New York. Nor is his best work upon themes or subjects in any way related to New York.

[32] Norris himself had spent the winter of 1900–1901 at Roselle, New Jersey, and had returned to New Jersey for the summer of 1901.

In view of all these facts it is difficult to see what the Great Unpublished have to gain by a New York residence. Indeed, it is much easier to see how very much they have to lose.

The writing of fiction has many drawbacks, but one of its blessed compensations is the fact that of all the arts it is the most independent. Independent of time, of manner and of place. Wherever there is a table and quiet, there the novel may be written. "Ah, but the publishing houses are in New York." What has that to do with it? Do not for a moment suppose that your novel will be considered more carefully because you submit it in person. It is not as though you were on the lookout for odd jobs which, because of a personal acquaintance with editors and publishers, might be put in your way. The article, the story, the essay, poem or novel is just as good, just as available, just as salable whether it comes from Washington Territory or Washington Square.

Not only this, but one believes that actual residence in New York is hostile and inimical to good work. The place, admittedly, teems with literary clubs, circles, associations, organizations of pseudo-literati, who foregather at specified times to "read papers" and "discuss questions." It is almost impossible for the young writer who comes for a first time to the city to avoid entangling himself with them; and of the influences that tend to stultify ambition, warp original talent and definitely and irretrievably stamp out the last spark of productive ability one knows of none more effective than the literary clubs.

You will never find the best men at these gatherings. You will never hear the best work read in this company, you will never evolve any original, personal, definite ideas or ideals under such influence. The discussions of the literary clubs are made up of puerile arguments that have done duty for years in the college text-books. Their work—the papers quoted and stories read aloud—is commonplace and conventional to the deadliest degree, while their "originality"—the ideas that they claim are their very own—is nothing but a distortion and dislocation of preconceived notions, mere bizarre effects of the grotesque and the improbable. "Ah, but the spur of competition." Competition is admirable in trade—it is even desirable in certain arts. It has no place in a literary career. It is not as though two or more writers were working on the same story, each striving to better the others. That would, indeed, be true competition. But in New York, where the young writer—any writer—may see a dozen instances in a week of what he knows is inferior work succeeding where he fails, competition is robbed of all stimulating effect and, if one is not very careful, leaves only the taste of ashes in the mouth and rancor and discontent in the heart.

With other men's novels the novelist has little to do. What this writer is doing, what that one is saying, what books this publishing house is handling, how many copies so-and-so's book is selling—all this fuss and feathers of "New York as a literary center" should be for him so many distractions. It is all very well to say "let us keep in touch with the best thought in our line of work." "Let us be in the movement." The best thought is not in New York; and even if it were, the best thought of other men is not so good for you as your own thought, dug out of your own vitals by your own unaided efforts, be it never so inadequate.

You do not have to go to New York for that. Your own ideas, your own work will flourish best if left alone untrammeled and uninfluenced. And believe this to be true, that wherever there is a table, a sheet of paper and a pot of ink, there is a Literary Center if you will. You will find none better the world over.

THE "NATURE" REVIVAL IN LITERATURE[33]

It has been a decade of fads, and "the people have imagined a vain thing," as they have done from the time of Solomon and as no doubt they will till the day of the New Jerusalem. And in no other line of activity has the instability and changeableness of the taste of the public been so marked as in that of literature. Such an overturning of old gods and such a setting up of new ones, such an image-breaking, shrine-smashing, relic-ripping carnival I doubt has ever been witnessed in all the history of writing. It has been a sort of literary Declaration of Independence. For half a century certain great names, from Irving down to Holmes, were veritable Abracadabras—impeccable, sanctified. Then all at once the *fin de siècle* irreverence seemed to invade all sorts and conditions simultaneously, and the somber, sober idols were shouldered off into the dark niches, and not a man of us that did not trundle forth his own little tin-god-on-wheels, kowtowing and making obeisance, and going before with cymbals and a great noise, proclaiming a New Great One; now it was the great Colonial Image, now the Great Romantic Image, now the Great Minor-German Kingdom Image.

There are a great many very eminent and very wise critics who frown upon and deplore the reaction. But it is a question if, after all, the movement will not prove—ultimately—beneficial. Convention, blind adherence to established forms, inertia, is the dry rot of a national literature. Better the American public should read bad books than no books, and that same public is reading now as never before. It is a veritable unheaval, a breaking-up of all the old grounds. Better this than supineness;

[33] Syndicated, February 16, 1903.

better this than immobility. Once the ground turned over a bit, harrowed and loosened, and the place is made ready for the good seed.[34]

Some of this, one chooses to believe, has already been implanted. In all the parade of the new little tin-gods some may be discovered that are not tin, but sterling. Of all the fads, the most legitimate, the most abiding, the most inherent—so it would appear—is the "Nature" revival. Indeed, it is not fair to call it a fad at all. For it is a return to the primitive, sane life of the country, and the natural thing by its very character cannot be artificial, cannot be a "fad." The writers who have followed where Mr. Thompson Seton blazed the way are so numerous and so well known that it is almost superfluous in this place to catalogue or criticize them. But it is significant of the strength of this movement that such an outdoor book as *Bob, Son of Battle,* was unsuccessful in England, and only attained its merited popularity when published here in America. We claimed the "good gray dog" as our own from the very first, recognizing that the dog has no nationality, being indeed a citizen of the whole world. The flowers in *Elizabeth's German Garden*—also world citizens—we promptly transplanted to our own soil. Mr. Mowbray, with his mingling of fact and fiction, made his country home for the benefit—I have no doubt—of hundreds who have actually worked out the idea suggested in his pages. The butterfly books, the garden books, the flower books, expensive as they are, have been in as much demand as some very popular novels. Mr. Dugmore astonished and delighted a surprisingly large public with his marvelous life-photographs of birds, while even President Roosevelt himself deemed Mr. Wallihan's *Photographs of Big Game* of so much importance and value that he wrote the introductory notice to that excellent volume.[35]

It is hardly possible to pick up a magazine now that does not contain the story of some animal hero. Time was when we relegated this sort to the juvenile periodicals. But now we cannot get too much of it. Wolves, rabbits, hounds, foxes, the birds, even the reptilia, all are dramatized, all figure in their little roles. Tobo and the Sand-hill Stag parade upon the same pages as Mr. Christie's debutantes and Mr. Smedley's business men, and, if you please, have their love affairs and business in precisely the same spirit.[36] All this cannot but be significant, and, let us be assured, sig-

---

[34] One of Norris' frequently expressed ideas of 1901–1902. See my Introduction to "Popular Fiction" below.

[35] Norris refers to Alfred Ollivant, *Bob, Son of Battle* (1893); Mary Russell, *Elizabeth and her German Garden* (1898); J. P. Mowbray (pseudonym of Andrew C. Wheeler), *The Making of a Country Home* (1901); Arthur R. Dugmore, *Bird Homes* (1900); and Allen G. Wallhan (not *Wallihan*), *Camera Shots at Big Game* (1901). The last three books were published by Doubleday, Page. Ernest Thompson Seton was a leading writer of nature books.

[36] Lobo (not *Tobo*) the Wolf and Sandhill Stag were animal characters created by

nificant of good. The New England school for too long dominated the entire range of American fiction—limiting it, specializing it, polishing, refining and embellishing it, narrowing it down to a veritable cult, a thing to be safeguarded by the elect, the few, the aristocracy. It is small wonder that the reaction came when and as it did; small wonder that the wearied public, roused at length, smashed its idols with such vehemence; small wonder that, declaring its independence and finding itself suddenly untrammeled and unguided, it flew off "mobishly" toward false gods, good only because they were new.

All this is small wonder. The great wonder is this return to nature, this unerring groping backward toward the fundamentals, in order to take a renewed grip upon life. If you care to see a proof of how vital it is, how valuable, look into some of the magazines of the seventies and eighties. It is astonishing to consider that we ever found an interest in them. The effect is like entering a darkened room. And not only the magazines, but the entire literature of the years before the nineties is shadowed and oppressed with the bugbear of "literature." Outdoor life was a thing apart from our reading. Even the tales and serials whose *mise en scène* was in the country had no breath of the country in them. The "literature" in them suffocated the life, and the humans with their everlasting consciences, their heated and artificial activities, filled all the horizon, admitting the larks and the robins only as accessories; considering the foxes, the deer and the rabbits only as creatures to be killed, to be pursued, to be exterminated. But Mr. Seton and his school, and the Mowbrays, and the Ollivants, the Dugmores and the Wallihans opened a door, opened a window, and mere literature has had to give place to life. The sun has come in and the great winds, and the smell of the baking alkali on the Arizona deserts and the reek of the tar-weed on the Colorado slopes; and nature has ceased to exist as a classification of science, has ceased to be *mis*-understood as an aggregate of botany, zoology, geology and the like, and has become a thing intimate and familiar and rejuvenating.

There is no doubt that the estate of American letters is experiencing a renaissance. Formality, the old idols, the demigorgons and autocrats no longer hold an absolute authority. A multitude of false gods are clamoring for recognition, shouldering one another about to make room for their altars, soliciting incense as if it were patronage. No doubt these "draw many after them," but the "nature revival" has brought the galvanizing, vital element into this tumult of little inkling sham divinities and has

---

Ernest Thompson Seton. Howard Chandler Christy (not *Christie*) and William T. Smedley were illustrators for such magazines as *Harper's* and the *Century*.

shown that life is better than "literature," even if the "literature" be of human beings and the life be that of a faithful dog.

Vitality is the thing, after all. Dress the human puppet never so gaily, bedeck it never so brilliantly, pipe before it never so cunningly, and, fashioned in the image of God though it be, just so long as it is a puppet and not a person, just so long the great heart of the people will turn from it, in weariness and disgust, to find its interest in the fidelity of the sheep-dog of the North o' England, the intelligence of a prairie wolf of Colorado, or the death-fight of a bull moose in the timberlands of Ontario.

The Mechanics of Fiction

INTRODUCTION

Norris' idea of the form of the novel begins with two negatives—that fiction is not the product of "pure imagination," and that it is not, conversely, a literal transcription of life. Rather, Norris accepted a basically Lockean conception of the creative faculty. This acceptance was probably influenced by his reading of Lewes' *The Principles of Success in Literature* during his freshman year and by a course in literary criticism which he took from Charles Mills Gayley during his senior year. Both Lewes and Gayley believed that the artist was dependent upon experience for the raw material of his art, though the finished work of art was a recombined and reshaped version of experience. Lewes argued this belief from his philosophical empiricism, whereas Gayley assumed it within his conception of the evolution of literature, in which art and the literary and social environment were intrinsically linked.[1] Moreover, Norris probably soon inferred a connection between this theory of artistic creation and the fictional technique of detailed documentation which he had found in Kipling and Zola, and which he himself had quickly made a primary technique in his own fictional method.

Norris' concept of form, therefore, is best approached through his essay "Fiction is Selection," with its image of the artist as mosaicist carefully selecting and arranging the blocks of experience into fresh and meaningful patterns. He had opened this essay with one of his favorite ideas—that literal accuracy is not art, an idea derived from his belief that fiction must be plausible, and that events in life are often improbable or unconvincing. In later essays he therefore usually contrasted accuracy with truth, in order to stress that art was fundamentally the selection and arrangement of the blocks of experience into a pattern which persuasively revealed a truth of human experience. For Norris, successful fiction revealed the Aristotelian paradox of falsity to the specific in order to achieve a general validity.

Norris thus believed that since the communication of an impression of truth was the artist's primary task, almost all problems of form resolved to the need to express that truth with the greatest possible emotional and

---

[1] Norris was a student in several of Gayley's courses, including English XV, Problems of Literary Criticism, which he took the first semester of his senior year. There is no description of this course in the *University of California Register* for 1893–1894, but the previous year it was described as consisting of two subjects, "the theory of literature as an expression of aesthetic values" and "the evolution of literature, and the differentiation of literary species." For Gayley's views on the evolution of literature, see his "A Society of Comparative Literature," *Dial*, XVII (August 1, 1894), 57.

thematic effect. Each novel will have its own best way of realizing this end. Yet there were certain "rules" for the achievement of effect common to all fiction, and only the untrained or the hurried, careless writer ignored these rules.

One such requirement was that a novel must be constructed around a "pivotal event." It must, in other words, have a carefully foreshadowed climactic scene which made its impact by elaborate preparation and by a gradually accelerating anticipation rather than by overwriting of the scene itself. Norris himself, as his career progressed, tended increasingly to build his novels around such scenes, usually locating them about three-quarters through the novel, as in *The Octopus* and *The Pit*. In a letter to Isaac Marcosson he explained his use of this principle of construction in *The Octopus*. "The movement of the whole business is very slow at first," he wrote—

don't really get under way till after the first 15,000 words (it's about 200,000 words long), then, with the first pivotal incident it quickens a bit, and from then on, I've tried to accelerate it steadily till at last you are—I hope—just whirling and galloping and tearing along till you come *bang!* all of a sudden to a great big crushing *END*, something that will slam you right between your eyes and knock you off your feet—all this I *hope* for.[2]

Indeed, Norris was so conscious of the role of planned effect in fiction that he criticized Doubleday and McClure for printing a chapter of *A Man's Woman* with its close at the bottom of the right-hand page. "If the reader thinks there is more of the chapter to follow," he wrote his English publisher, "it spoils its climactic effect and by the time he has turned the page and found out his mistake the right psychological moment is gone."[3]

Norris' emphasis on effect also underlies his other major ideas about form. His call, for example, for the removal of the author as personality and for the communication of theme through scene and action is founded on the belief that authorial presence dulls the reader's response to the inherent power of scene, action, and character. His panegyric on simplicity is also related to the belief that clarity and directness are the primary means of attaining a moving effect. And both of these demands— for an objective, dramatic method and for simplicity in style—increase the author's task, rather than diminish it. It is the slovenly, undisciplined author, Norris argued, who sacrifices intensity for ease of authorial intervention and for superficially emotional rhetoric.

In Norris' own fiction, however, these last two requirements are fre-

---

[2] Norris to Isaac Marcosson, September 13, 1900, *Letters,* pp. 67–68.
[3] Norris to Grant Richards, May 25, 1900, *Letters,* p. 56.

quently neglected. His own style is too often burdened with purple passages, and he has great difficulty removing himself from his novels, though he is present less as an overt personality than as a disconcertingly moral point of view in supposedly objective descriptions and analyses. But despite his own lack of success in completely fulfilling these requirements, his statement of them foreshadows their widespread adoption both as critical commonplaces and as accepted practice. They are central to one of the major traditions of the modern novel—the Hemingway convention of dramatic method, of clipped, bare prose, and of establishment of theme largely through the symbolic potentialities of the concrete rather than authorial analysis. Indeed, the typical Hemingway novel, with its gradual rise to a climactic scene (a fiesta, a bridge dynamiting), seems to fulfill many of Norris' basic demands.

Norris' ideas of form are thus a critical reflection of a major transition occurring in the art of fiction, as the novel moved from its typically loose, author-dominated, overwritten nineteenth-century character toward a contemporary convention of tight construction and objective method. His attitude toward form reflects the belief of many late nineteenth-century writers, epitomized by James, that the novel, though a popular art, was not thereby less capable of controlled craftsmanship. Indeed, Norris' ideas are similar to James' in yet another important respect. Both writers have the practicing artist's awareness that form is primarily the achievement of the illusion of truth rather than the expression of experience itself.[4]

In all, there is a practical hardheadedness in Norris' discussion of form, despite such a characteristic lapse toward sentimentality as his remarks on the arrested childhood of "story-teller" novelists. His theory of fictional form does not explore the novel as an abstraction, but rather deals with the permanent and immediate requirements of the novelist—the need to tell a concrete story that embodies an acceptable general truth, and the need to tell that story in a way which communicates it with the most force. Art is no miraculous gift, Norris states. It is rather the painstaking shaping of experience into the plausible and the convincing. The best artists are therefore those who know something about the techniques of fiction and who practice those techniques, whether they involve the careful search for a significant short-story incident or the logistic preparations for the climactic scene in a 200,000-word novel.

4 See René Wellek, "Henry James's Literary Theory and Criticism," *American Literature*, XXX (November, 1958), 293–321.

THE MODERN SHORT STORY[5]

There is one type of the modern short story that is a sort of great-grandchild of the novel of fifty years ago, but that, finding no abiding place between the broad covers of a printed book, has been adapted and nurtured by the monthly magazine. Originally the short story was but a miniature novel, having all the features of a novel—introduction, plot, complication, development of character and the like—every characteristic in fact but that of length. Balzac introduced this type—the type of the long short story, and it still survives in the present day in the form of the serial of two numbers that appears from time to time in *Harper's* or *Century*, or more especially in the "Novelette" of *Lippincott's*. Among the best examples of this type are Stevenson's "Dr. Jekyll and Mr. Hyde," Amélie Rives' "Quick or the Dead," and Mr. Hope's "Indiscretion of the Duchess." These stories may be read at a single sitting. They are hardly more than condensed novels. The introduction is entirely dispensed with, the action is generally simple, the movement rapid, the range very limited. But the writer, however, still retains the succession of incidents and episodes of the larger forms of fiction, and by means of these evolves a considerable amount of complication. But ever since the introduction of the short story as a form of fiction the tendency has been towards brevity. The short story has been getting shorter and shorter, not so much, I am confident, because of limited time on the part of the reading public as because of limited space on the part of the magazines. The popular magazine must cover in a given and fixed amount of space a great variety of subjects—art, literature, science, travel, biography, history and fiction, to say nothing of the space consumed by illustrations. All matter, fiction or otherwise, must consequently be reduced to the shortest possible length. Editors all over the country are constantly returning "available" matter to the authors with suggestions to condense. The short story is no exception. It has become shorter and shorter from year to year, until from being a shorter form of novel of incidents and episodes, it has been reduced in some cases to the relation of a single incident by itself, concise, pungent, direct as a blow. There have been successful stories written upon an incident so brief that the whole matter can be summed up in a single sentence. For instance, "An English officer's return to his regiment after years of imprisonment in Siberia." There does not seem to be material enough for even a very short story in this statement. Yet Mr. Kipling saw possibilities in it when he conceived the idea of "The Man Who Was." Or again, the impulse of a good-hearted young New Yorker to remove a little girl from the bad influences of stage life and return her to her father, is all

[5] *Wave*, XV (December 26, 1896), 3.

that Mr. Davis permits himself to relate in "Her First Appearance," perhaps the best story he ever wrote.

Short stories of this latter description are entirely different from that first type which we have chosen to call the long short story. The first type were merely condensed novels; but stories such as "The Man Who Was" and "Her First Appearance" are, as it were, chapters—the most significant ones—taken from the heart of unwritten novels; all the preceding chapters, the introduction, etc., are suggested; all those that follow are left to the reader's imagination. It is the custom for critics at this point to expatiate upon the difficulty of writing short stories such as these. It does not necessarily follow that the "very" short story requires any greater amount of cleverness of handling than the longer one. Popular belief to the contrary, I hold that the writing of a novel is by far the most arduous and exacting task within the province of literature. It is true, however, that a really good short story is one of the rarest things an editor meets with. But the difficulty lies not so much in the actual writing, in the condensing and suggesting, etc., as it does in the invention or selection— call it what you like—of the original idea, the motive. Consider the nature of the thing required. The author must devise or discover a single scene, a bit, an episode so full of meaning, so dramatic, so tremendously significant that it suggests to the mind of the reader an entire volume of explanatory matter. The reader must not only read between the lines, but between the very words. And all this must be accomplished within the compass of, at the very most, thirty-five hundred words. I say at the very most. Some of Mr. Kipling's strongest effects have been attained by means of two thousand.

The writing of the short story, whether it be the "long" short story or the "short" short story, has developed in many authors a certain amount of trick work that it is very amusing to note. The word "trickery" as applied to an artistic production may appear to be an ill-chosen term, though this literary "trickery," this legerdemain as used by Kipling, and especially by Davis and Anthony Hope, is no more blameworthy than that of the clever sketch artist who makes a couple of dots do for a line and a couple of lines suggest a mass of shadow.

One of the most fetching "tricks" of the short story writer is his handling of the very last paragraph or sentence of his story. By its very position the last sentence of a tale gathers the enormous emphasis it may possess. The reader will invariably consider the last sentence with great seriousness, weighing every word with the greatest attention and earnestness. Many short story writers who are clever enough to realize this weakness—if it be a weakness—on the part of their public, are also clever enough to take advantage of it, by withholding the real point and meaning of their story until the last sentence or paragraph is reached, then suddenly unfolding it in a few brief words, as one might suddenly unravel an apparently hopeless tangle of skeins with a few deft turns of the wrist. This is trickery of course, but it is very clever trickery, since it discloses the whole purport of the story in a single instant, and the reader receives the accumulated effect of the preceding pages with the suddenness and force of a mild electric shock.[6]

Richard Harding Davis terminates "The Princess Aline" in this fashion, having scrupulously withheld from the reader until that last instant all suspicion of the fact that Aline is in love with Carlton. Mr. Davis is very fond of these little *coups de théâtre*. His "Unfinished Story" and "The Other Woman" both end in this manner, while Anthony Hope uses the same machinery in almost every one of the *Dolly Dialogues.*

What is to be the future of the short story it would be difficult to say. It cannot continue indefinitely to shorten in length. There must inevitably come a time when it will reach its limit, a limit of brevity which if overpassed would bring it into the province of the anecdote. It is probably as short now as it ever will be, and as movements in art go by extremes, it would not be surprising if the short story of the twentieth century goes back to its original type, so that instead of the short long story of to-day, we should again be reading the long short story of Balzac and of Bulwer.

FICTION IS SELECTION[7]

To the man who has ever so modestly assumed the pose of a writer of fiction is given a certain experience which is usually trying, sometimes amusing, but that on rare occasions is profitable and entertaining to the last degree. People who wish him well give him "ideas" for stories, come to him with the remark "here's something you ought to make into a story," or "there's a character you ought to put in a book." More often than otherwise they clinch their recital with the remark: "This really happened, you know," as though it were any better for actually having happened. Take, for instance, a case like this: A very good friend of the writer's, a capital chap, but without the sense for fiction, tells him a yarn of a romantic elopement. As usual, he says, "this is something that actually happened, you know." Here is what actually happened: A young fellow is in love with a girl—parents on both sides opposed to the match—relentless. Young couple decide to elope—secret appointment at the gate at the bottom of the garden—carriage and horses there—start for the flight—pur-

---

[6] Norris used this technique in a number of his *Wave* stories. See, for example, "The Third Circle" and "His Dead Mother's Portrait."

[7] *Wave*, XVI (September 11, 1897), 3.

suit—girl's brother on a horse (black for preference)—pistol shots ex-
changed—black horse of pursuing brother killed—down he goes with a
hideous sliding clatter—next town is reached and marriage performed—
subsequent reconciliation, etc., etc., etc. "Now isn't that a story for you?"
he exclaims. "That actually happened at ———" and he names the town
and backs up his story with all manner of detail. "There's a story you
ought to write," says he, in conclusion. No, indeed, not if the copy were
paid for at the rate of twenty-five dollars per hundred words. The thing
may have happened. There can be no doubt that such stories have happened. But the truth of a story in this sense of the word has nothing to do
with its availability, from the point of view of good fiction. In a written
tale it would not seem real. It would seem like a rehash of some tawdry
yellow-covered romance of fifty or a hundred years ago. Fiction is what
seems real, not what is real.

But for all this, the story writer must go to real life for his story. You
can never think out, or invent or imagine a tale that will be half so good
as the things that have "really happened." The complications of real life
are infinitely better, stronger and more original than anything you can
make up. The only difference is in the matter of selection of details. The
story writer's position in regards to the life of the world is like that of a
maker of mosaics in front of a vast pile of tiny many-colored blocks. He
doesn't make the blocks nor color them—the story writer does not invent
nor imagine the parts of his story. Writer and mosaicist alike select and
combine. The maker of a mosaic has a design in his brain, or, better still,
infinitely better, sees in the pile of little colored blocks in front of him a
certain little group or tiny heap that, by merest accident, has tumbled into
a design of its own. The design is rough, very crude, the blocks do not
fit together, and here and there a green or blue or red block jars in the
color scheme. But, for all that, there is a suggestion of design there, much
more original than any design he could work out. Well, he takes this
group of blocks in hand, picks out and throws away the red and blue and
the green that jar and fight, trims off the edges of the blocks and makes
them fit compactly together; perhaps a gap or two is left. The whole vast
heap is at his command. Deftly he goes over it, picking out here and there
the blocks that he needs, a circular one here, a triangular one there, now
one of a bright vermillion, now one of a sombre grey. Little by little he
pieces together that crude and rough design, gets everything to fit, everything to harmonize; possibly he combines the first design with another;
possibly these two designs suggest a third still better; so he proceeds. At
last the final design is complete. A little polishing, a very little, for in
roughness there is strength and in sharp contrast, vividness; and there
you are, a rounded whole, a definite, compact and complete thing, taken

out of and isolated from a formless heap and jumble of shape and colors.

There may be—in fact, there is—in the heap a hundred and one other combinations of forms and shapes already arranged, "actually existing," made to hand, as it were, but the designer over-passes them because these combinations have been used by other designers before him, used so often that there is no longer any originality or freshness in them.

Some one objects at this point: "What about imagination? What about fancy? What about invention?" There is no such thing as imagination. What we elect to call imagination is mere combination of things not heretofore combined. The designer, before his heap of mosaic blocks, can only pick and choose. If he is daring enough, thoughtful enough, careful enough to combine two colors that have never before been combined, or two shapes never before fitted together, we call it "imagination." It is only observation, after all. The designer does not make his little blocks, does not color them. They are already made and colored for him. The fiction writer of the wildest and most untrammelled fancy cannot get away from real life. Imagination! There is no such thing; you can't imagine anything that you have not already seen and observed.

Like the skilled mosaic maker, any one with an eye accustomed to looking for short stories can run his glance over the heap of things we have elected to call life and here and there see combinations of form and color that are original, telling and worth working up. Such a one would not have given the elopement combination half a thought. The design may be in the heap, almost perfect as it lies; the story may have really happened; both are worthless for all that. Sometimes, however, the design does not exist at all except in your brain; you must go to your heap nevertheless. Here, for instance, is an "idea" for another kind of story. It has never happened, but it was told me by a man who has the fiction-sense rather keenly developed. Observe the difference between it and the other one of the elopement, but bear in mind that this last story is yet in its crude original state—needs, in fact, no end of handling and piecing and re-arranging. It's a mere handful of blocks, so far. A Jew—sweats old clothes in a sordid basement—a wretched benighted man, squatting all day cross-legged in that sordid basement—has a wife no less sordid than himself. The Jew has no emotions, no fancies, no illusions. There is no poetry in the man. He sweats old clothes. Has not seen the country in fifteen or twenty years. However, in front of his shop stands a poplar tree—tall, very beautiful. Jew has a sort of blind, unreasoned attachment for the tree—looks at it in the evening after he is done with sweating old clothes—has watched its leaves come and go with the seasons—loves the tree, but doesn't know why—hardly knows that he does love the tree. All the starved poetry of the sordid man's life is centered about the tree. One day the tree is suddenly cut down—consternation—something gone out of the Jew's life—don't know exactly what—becomes morose and gloomy—goes from bad to worse—develops latent melancholia—insanity perhaps—quarrels with the sordid wife. All his peace of mind and little happiness gone—goes from worse to worst of all—one day kills the sordid wife without knowing why—is adjudged insane and strait-jacketed in a sanitarium—would it all have happened if the tree had been left standing?

FRANK NORRIS' WEEKLY LETTER[8]

The news in literary New York just now is that there is no news. It is the quiet season. Almost every author of note—some of the publishers, too—are out of town and the seeker after a sign must look for them in the mountains, in the country, even—even at the seaside. With the average writer the season for work is the Winter. During Summer he watches the reception of his latest book, published in the previous March or April, and only toward Fall gathers himself together, overlooks his notes and begins to think of his next effort.

Early Spring and early Fall are the two great publishing seasons, but of late several noteworthy books have been launched so late as June. Of these the most promising, to my notion, is Mr. Lusk's *Autocrats*. It is a serious attempt to make an American story out of modern American issues. It is not "historical." The "click of rapiers" does not "ring on every page." It is neither a "what-ho-without-there" story, nor a "why-how-now-Mistress-Nancy" tale; and, because of this, let us take off our hats to its author, who looks for interest and drama in the things that he sees, instead of in the things he has read about. He has tried to make a picture of modern complication—the struggle over and around a franchise for a street railway. He has attempted to know at first hand what he is talking about, and seeing all abuse, has struck at it with such strength as was his own.

And apropos of this a story is told. The publishers of the book, appreciating its good points, had decided to drive it hard, to "boom" it—in a word to advertise in the daily press. No town, it was argued, would respond better to such efforts than the one in which the story was supposed to have happened. So the most important newspaper in that town was selected in which to place the largest "ad" issued. It was a half page affair, voluminous, striking, a real effort—and most expensive. Great results were expected.

Imagine the surprise in the office when the copy of the "ad" was re-

[8] *Chicago American,* July 13, 1901, p. 8.

turned from the paper in question with an abrupt note to the effect that the manager declined to print it. Followed much telegraphing, letters and finally explanations, with this result:

Mr. Lusk in his novel had introduced the character of an editor, who, bought up by the Autocrats, had sold out his editorial columns to further the launching of their corrupt deal. The paper—if not the editor—had its counterpart in real life and it was in this very paper of all others that the publishers of the *Autocrats* had determined to make their great attempt to start the sale of the story.[9]

Frank T. Bullen, "first mate," the author of *The Cruise of the Cachalot,* which I hold to be one of the best books of the last ten years, is at work upon a novel which this Fall will be published simultaneously in England, Canada and the United States. Of all the forthcoming publications it is to this one I shall look forward with the greatest degree of curiosity. If it is as good as *The Cruise*—but of course that is out of the question. No man could turn out two books like that one. Even if it was as good, it must be different. Such a book as Mr. Bullen's first effort is possible only once in the life time of even the greatest man.

A sailor before the mast—if he is a good able seaman—cannot record his impressions in readable form. And a writer cannot be an able seaman. That is, not more than once in a thousand times. But in this book—by direct intervention of kind providence—we have both. I hold and maintain that *The Cruise* is valuable in precisely the same way as are Amiel's *Journal* and *The Diary of Miss Bashkirtseff.* I am well aware of the strangeness of the assertion. What! The impressions of an over-refined, supersensitive, delicately poised gentleman; and the half hysterical outpourings of a "woman-artist," also over-refined, also supersensitive, also delicately poised. What! These two to be classed with the narrative of the killing of whales; a greasy record—decks awash with oil, scuppers spouting with it; a hecatomb of leviathans, smells, blood, men fighting, murders and all the rest of it. I say *The Cruise, The Diary* and the *Journal* are alike in kind; and if there is any difference in degree I claim it for the sailor and not for the artist.

The common ground whereon these three writers meet is that of their individuality and the power to record it. It is this, I believe, that hits the hardest in Mr. Bullen's book. He has recorded himself in *The Cruise.* The mere informative side of this book is not of the first importance. Most readers know a great deal about the manner of killing whales, and those that don't know don't care much about it. Only in the details of the business has the mate told us anything new. It is the mate himself, his ideas, his notions, his reflections, and the scant, scrimped, half-hinted-at auto-

[9] Norris probably knew this anecdote because *The Autocrats,* by Charles K. Lush (not *Lusk*), was published by Doubleday, Page.

biography that he occasionally permits to slip into his pages that holds one. The book is a human document. I know a new man now, have made a new acquaintance, have got a glimpse into a new corner. That's the thing to be thankful for.

Which suggests a question—how far is the author justified in putting himself into his work? Is it good art or bad? Is it his duty to present only his story and his characters, suppressing himself, keeping in the background, or, like Thackeray, occupying the center of the stage himself, talking in his own person, explaining and commenting?

Is it better to be like M. Zola, who never under any pretense or pretext shows his hand, the story moving forward of itself automatically, as it were, seemingly of its own vitality?

In fiction I hold with the theory of the suppression of the author's personality—so far as possible. In books other than novels, records of impressions, of travels, of adventures, I think the writer himself—provided his personality is interesting—is the important thing. Take Stevenson (our own Robert Louis) from the essays and there is not much left. But drop him out from *The Wrecker* (autobiographical though it is in form), *The Ebb Tide, Ballantrae,* or *Kidnapped,* and the books still stand, just about as interesting as before.

After all in fiction the main thing is fiction. In a novel I look for and want a picture of certain things that have happened, certain characters that have been studied, certain scenes that have occurred. The man behind the pen—what has the public to do with him? The more he differentiates himself from his story, the more remote his isolation, the more real will appear the things and people of which he treats, the more will his story seem to have a life of its own. I am free to confess—heresy though it seems to be—that Mr. Thackeray's disquisitions, where he himself takes the stage, are, for me, dull to a degree. They strike one as out of place. If the artist stood by his painting with a pointer and "explained" his work, or if the dramatist commented upon his play in the midst of the action, one would be inclined to resent the intrusion. Why is the intrusion of the novelist any less forgiveable? If his story is not self-explanatory, it is a bad story, and if in spite of all willful self-suppression the point of view of the writer—his ideals, his ideas, his personality, in a word—does not appear in his work indirectly—mind I say indirectly—he had best give over the attempt to produce readable fiction; as well have the cinematograph and the phonograph.

A PROBLEM IN FICTION: TRUTH VERSUS ACCURACY[10]

So many people—writers more especially—claim stridently and with a deal of gesturing, that because a thing has happened it is therefore

[10] *Boston Evening Transcript,* November 6, 1901, p. 20.

true. They have written a story, let us say, and they bring it to you to criticise. You lay your finger upon a certain passage and say, "Not true to life." The author turns on you then and annihilates you—in his own mind—with the words, "But it actually happened." Of course, then, it must be true. On the contrary, it is accurate only.

For the assumption is that truth is a higher power of accuracy, that the true thing includes the accurate; and assuming this, the authors of novels—that are not successful—suppose that if they are accurate, if they tell the thing just as they saw it, that they are truthful. It is not difficult to show that a man may be as accurate as the spectroscope and yet lie like a Chinese diplomat. As for instance: Let us suppose you have never seen a sheep, never heard of sheep, don't know sheep from shavings. It devolves upon me to enlighten your ignorance. I go out into the field and select from the flock a black sheep, bring it before you, and, with the animal there under our eyes, describe it in detail, faithfully, omitting nothing, falsifying nothing, exaggerating nothing. I am painfully accurate. But you go away with the untrue conviction that all sheep are black! I have been accurate, but I have not been true.

So it is with very, very many novels, written with all earnestness and seriousness. Every incident has happened in real life, and because it is picturesque, because it is romantic, because, in a word, it is like some other novel, it is seized upon at once, and serves as the nucleus of a tale. Then, because this tale fails of success, because it fails to impress, the author blames the public, not himself. He thinks he has gone to life for his material, and so must be original, new and true. It is not so. Life itself is not always true; strange as it may seem, you may be able to say that life is not always true to life—from the point of view of the artist. It happened once that it was my unfortunate duty to tell a certain man of the violent death of his only brother, whom he had left well and happy but an hour before. This is how he took it: He threw up both hands and staggered back, precisely as they do in melodrama, exclaiming all in a breath, "O my God! This is terrible! What will mother say?" You may say what you please, this man was not true to life. From the point of view of the teller of tales, he was theatrical, false, untrue, and though the incident was an actual fact and though the emotion was real, it had no value as "material," and no fiction writer in his senses would have thought of using it in a story.

Naturally enough it will be asked what then is the standard. How shall the writer guide himself in the treatment of a pivotal, critical scene, or how shall the reader judge whether or not he is true? It is a crux, one admits. But the incident must be handled so as to seem true. Perhaps after all the word "seem," and not the word "true" is the most important. Of course no good novelist, no good artist, can represent life as it actually is. Nobody can, for nobody knows. Who is to say what life actually is? It seems easy, easy for us who have it, and live in it and see it and hear it and feel it every millionth part of every second of the time. I say that life is actually this or that, and you say it is something else, and number three says "Lo here," and number four says "Lo there." Not even science is going to help you; no two photographs, even, will convey just the same impression of the same actuality; and here we are dealing not with science, but with art, that instantly involves the personality of the artist and all that that means. Even the same artist will not see the same thing twice exactly alike. His personality is one thing today and another thing tomorrow; is one thing before dinner and another thing after it. How then to determine what life actually is?

The point is just this. In the fine arts we do not care one little bit about what life actually is, but what it looks like to an interesting, impressionable man, and if he tells his story, or paints his picture, so that the majority of intelligent people will say, "Yes, that must have been just about what would have happened under those circumstances," he is true. His accuracy cuts no figure at all. He need not be accurate if he does not choose to be. If he sees fit to be inaccurate in order to make his point—so only his point be the conveying of a truthful impression—that is his affair. We have nothing to do with that. Consider the study of a French cuirassier by Detaille; where the sunlight strikes the brown coat of the horse, you will see, if you look close, a mere smear of blue, light blue. This is inaccurate. The horse is not blue, nor has he any blue spots. Stand at the proper distance and the blue smear resolves itself into the glossy reflection of the sun, and the effect is true.

And in fiction—take the fine scene in *Ivanhoe,* where Rebecca, looking from the window, describes the assault upon the outer walls of the castle to the wounded knight, lying on the floor in the room behind her. If you stop and think, you will see that Rebecca never could have found such elaborate language under the stress of so great excitement—those cleverly managed little climaxes in each phrase, building up to the great climax of the paragraph, all the play of rhetoric, all the nice chain and adjustment of adjectives; she could not possibly have done it. Neither you nor I, nor any of us, with all the thought and time and labor at our command, could have ever written the passage. But is it not admirably true, true as the truth itself? It is not accurate, it is grossly, ludicrously inaccurate; but the fire and leap and vigor of it; there is where the truth is. Scott wanted you to get an impression of that assault on the barbican, and you do get it. You can hear those axes on the outer gate as plainly as Rebecca could; you can see the ladders go up, can hear them splinter, can see and feel and know all the rush and trample and smashing of that fine fight, with the Fetterlock Knight always to the fore, as no merely accurate description—accurate to five points of decimals—could ever present it.

So that one must remember the distinction, and claim no more for accuracy than it deserves—and that's but little. Anybody can be accurate, the man with the footrule is that. Accuracy is the attainment of small minds, the achievement of the commonplace, a mere machine-made thing that comes with niggardly research and ciphering and mensuration and the multiplication table, good in its place, so only the place is very small. In fiction it can under certain circumstances be dispensed with altogether. It is not a thing to be striven for. To be true is the all-important business, and once attaining that, "all other things shall be added unto you." Paint the horse pea-green, if it suits your purpose; fill the mouth of Rebecca with gasconades and rodomontades interminable: these things do not matter. It is truth that matters, and the point is whether the daubs of pea-green will look like horseflesh and the mouth-filling words create the impression of actual battle.[11]

THE MECHANICS OF FICTION[12]

We approach a delicate subject. And if the manner of approach is too serious it will be very like the 40,000 men of the King of France who marched terribly and with banners to the top of the hill with the meagre achievement of simply getting there. Of all the arts, as one has previously observed, that of novel writing is the least mechanical. Perhaps after all rightly so; still it is hard to escape some formality, some forms. There must always be chapter divisions, also a beginning and an end, which implies a middle, continuity, which implies movement, which in turn implies a greater speed or less, an accelerated, retarded or broken action; and before the scoffer is well aware he is admitting a multitude of set forms. No one who sets a thing in motion but keeps an eye and a hand upon its speed. No one who constructs but keeps watch upon the building, strengthening here, lightening there, here at the foundations cautious and conservative, there at the cornice fantastic and daring. In all human occupations, trades, arts or business, science, morals or religion, there exists way at the bottom a homogeneity and a certain family likeness, so that, quite possibly after all the discussion of the importance of

---

[11] Norris also used this distinction between accuracy and truth in his definitions of realism, romanticism, and naturalism. See his "Weekly Letter" of August 3, 1901, pp. 73–75 below.

[12] *Boston Evening Transcript,* December 4, 1901, p. 22.

the mechanics of fiction may be something more than mere speculative sophistry.

A novel addresses itself primarily to a reader, and it has been so indisputably established that the reader's time and effort of attention must be economized that the fact need not be mentioned in this place—it would not economize the reader's time nor effort of attention.

Remains then the means to be considered, or in other words: How best to tell your story.

It depends naturally upon the nature of the story. The formula which would apply to one would not be appropriate for another. That is very true, but at the same time it is hard to get away from that thing in any novel which, let us call, the pivotal event. All good novels have one. It is the peg upon which the fabric of the thing hangs, the nucleus around which the shifting drifts and currents must—suddenly—coagulate, the sudden releasing of the brake to permit for one instant the entire machinery to labor, full steam, ahead. Up to that point the action must lead; from it, it must decline.

But—and here one holds at least one mechanical problem—the approach, the leading up to this pivotal event must be infinitely slower than the decline. For the reader's interest in the story centres around it and once it is disposed of attention is apt to dwindle very rapidly—and thus back we go again to the economy proposition.

It is the slow approach, however, that tells. The unskilled, impatient of the tedium of meticulous elaboration, will rush at it in a furious gallop of short chapters and hurried episodes, so that he may come the sooner to the purple prose declamation and drama that he is sure he can handle with such tremendous effect.

Not so the masters. Watch them during the first third—say—of their novels. Nothing happens, or at least so you fancy. People come and go, plans are described, localities, neighborhoods; an incident crops up just for a second, for which you can see no reason, a note sounded that is puzzlingly inappropriate. The novel continues. There seems to be no progress; again that perplexing note, but a little less perplexing. By now we are well into the story. There are no more new people but the old ones come back again and again, and yet again; you remember them now after they are off the stage, you are more intimate with the two main characters. Then come a series of petty incidents in which these two are prominent. The action still lags, but little by little you are getting more and more acquainted with these principal actors. Then perhaps comes the first acceleration of movement. The approach begins—ever so little—to rise, and that same note which seemed at first so out of tune sounds again and this time drops into place in the progression, beautifully harmonious, correlating the whole gamut. By now all the people are "on," by now all the groundwork is prepared. You know the localities so well that you could find your way about among them in the dark; hero and heroine are intimate acquaintances.

Now the action begins to increase in speed. The complication suddenly tightens, all along the line there runs a sudden alert. An episode far back there in the first chapter, an episode with its appropriate group of characters, is brought forward and coming suddenly to the front collides with the main line of development and sends it off upon an entirely unlooked for tangent. Another episode of the second chapter—let us suppose—all at once makes common cause with a more recent incident and the two produce a wholly unlooked for counter influence which swerves the main theme in still another direction and all this time the action is speeding faster and faster, the complication tightening and straining to the breaking point and then at last a "motif" that has been in preparation ever since the first paragraph of the first chapter of the novel suddenly comes to a head, and in a twinkling the complication is solved with all the violence of an explosion and the catastrophe, the climax, the pivotal event fairly leaps from the pages with a rush of action that leaves you stunned, breathless and overwhelmed with the sheer power of its presentation. And there is a master-work of fiction.

Reading as the uninitiated do without an eye to the mechanics, without a consciousness of the wires and wheels and cogs and springs of the affair, it seems inexplicable that these great scenes of fiction—short as they are—some of them less than a thousand words in length—should produce so tremendous an effect by such few words, such simple language; and that sorely overtaxed word, "genius," is made to do duty as the explanation. But the genius is rare that in one thousand simple words, taken by themselves, could achieve the effect—for instance—of the fight aboard *The Flying Scud* in Stevenson's *Wrecker*. Taken by itself, the scene is hardly important except from the point of view of style and felicity of expression. It is the context of the story that makes it so tremendous, and because Osbourne and Stevenson prepared for that very scene from the novel's initial chapter.

And it seems as if here in a phrase one could resume the whole system of fiction-mechanics—preparation of effect.

The unskilled will invariably attempt to atone for lack of such painstaking preparation for their "Grande Scenes" by hysteria, and by exclamation in presenting the catastrophe. They declaim, they shout, stamp, shake their fists and flood the page with sonorous adjectives, call upon heaven and upon God. They summon to their aid every broken down device to rouse the flaccid interest of the reader and conclusively, irretrievably and ignominiously fail. It is too late for heroic effort then, and the reader, uninterested in the character, unfamiliar with the locale, unattracted by any charm of "atmosphere," lays down the book unperturbed and forgets it before dinner.

Where is the fault? Is it not in defective machinery? The analogies are multitudinous. The liner with hastily constructed boilers will flounder when she comes to essay the storm, and no stoking, however vigorous, no oiling, however eager, if delayed till then, will avail to aid her to ride through successfully. It is not the time to strengthen a wall when the hurricane threatens, prop and stay will not brace it then. Then the thing that tells is the plodding, slow, patient, brick-by-brick work, that only half shows down there at the foot half-hidden in the grass, obscure, unnoted. No genius is necessary for this sort of work, only great patience and a willingness to plod, for the time being.

No one is expected to strike off the whole novel in one continued fine frenzy of inspiration. As well expect the stone mason to plant his wall in a single day. Nor is it possible to lay down any rule of thumb, any hard and fast schedule in the matter of novel writing. But no work is so ephemeral, so delicate, so—in a word—artistic that it cannot be improved by systematizing.

There is at least one indisputably good manner in which the unskilled may order his work—besides the one of preparation already mentioned. He may consider each chapter a unit, distinct, separate, having a definite beginning, rise, height and end, the action continuous, containing no break in time, the locality unchanged throughout—no shifting of the scene to another environment. Each chapter thus treated is a little work in itself, and the great story of the whole novel is told thus as it were in a series of pictures, the author supplying information as to what has intervened between the end of one chapter and the beginning of the next by suggestion or by actual résumé. As often as not the reader himself can fill up the gap by context.

This may be over-artificial, and it is conceivable that there are times when it is necessary to throw artificiality to the winds. But it is the method that many of the greatest fiction writers have employed, and even a defective system is—at any rate in fiction—better than none.

SIMPLICITY IN ART[13]

Once upon a time I had occasion to buy so uninteresting a thing as a silver soup ladle. The salesman at the silversmith's was obliging and for my inspection brought forth quite an array of ladles. But my purse was flaccid, anemic, and I must pick and choose with all the discrimination in the world. I wanted to make a brave showing with my gift, to get a great deal for my money. I went through a world of soup ladles, ladles with gilded bowls, with embossed handles, with chased arabesques, but there were none to my taste. "Or perhaps," says the salesman, "you would care to look at something like this," and he brought out a ladle that was as plain and as unadorned as the unclouded sky—and about as beautiful. Of all the others this was the most to my liking. But the price! ah, that anemic purse; and I must put it from me! It was nearly double the cost of any of the rest. And when I asked why the salesman said:

"You see, in this highly ornamental ware the flaws of the material don't show, and you can cover up a blow hole or the like by wreaths and beading. But this plain ware has got to be the very best. Every defect is apparent."

And there, if you please, is a conclusive comment upon the whole business—a final basis of comparison of all things, whether commercial or artistic, the bare dignity of the unadorned that may stand before the world all unashamed, panoplied rather than clothed in the consciousness of perfection. We of this latter day, we painters and poets and writers— artists—must labor with all the wits of us, all the strength of us, and with all that we have of ingenuity and perseverance to attain simplicity. But it has not always been so. At the very earliest, men—forgotten, ordinary men—were born with an easy, unblurred vision that today we would hail as marvelous genius. Suppose, for instance, the New Testament was all unwritten and one of us were called upon to tell the world that Christ was born, to tell of how we had seen Him, that this was the Messiah. How the adjectives would marshal upon the page, how the exclamatory phrases would cry out, how we would elaborate and elaborate, and how our rhetoric would flare and blazen till—so we should imagine—the ear would ring and the very eye would be dazzled; and even then we would believe that our words were all so few and feeble. It is beyond words, we should vociferate. So it would be. That is very true—words of ours. Can you not see how we should dramatize it? We would make a point of the transcendent stillness of the hour, of the deep blue of the Judean midnight, of the lip-lapping of Galilee, the murmur of Jordan, the peacefulness of sleeping Jerusalem. Then the stars, the descent of the angel, the shepherds—all the accessories. And our narrative would be as commensurate with the subject as the flippant smartness of a "bright" reporter in the Sistine chapel. We would be striving to cover up our innate incompetence, our impotence to do justice to the mighty theme by elaborateness of design and arabesque intricacy of rhetoric.

But on the other hand—listen:

"The days were accomplished that she should be delivered, and she brought forth her first born son and wrapped him in swaddling clothes and laid him in a manger, because there was no room for them in the inn."

Simplicity could go no further. Absolutely not one word unessential, not a single adjective that is not merely descriptive. The whole matter stated with the terseness of a military report, and yet—there is the epic, the world epic, beautiful, majestic, incomparably dignified, and no ready writer, no Milton nor Shakespeare, with all the wealth of their vocabularies, with all the resources of their genius, with all their power of simile or metaphor, their pomp of eloquence or their royal pageantry of hexameters, could produce the effect contained in these two simple declarative sentences.

The mistake that we little people are so prone to make is this: that the more intense the emotional quality of the scene described, the more "vivid," the more exalted, the more richly colored we suppose should be the language.

When the crisis of the tale is reached there is where we like the author to spread himself, to show the effectiveness of his treatment. But if we would only pause to take a moment's thought we must surely see that the simplest, even the barest statement of fact, is not only all-sufficient but all-appropriate.

Elaborate phrase, rhetoric, the intimacy of metaphor and allegory and simile is forgivable for the unimportant episodes where the interest of the narrative is languid; where we are willing to watch the author's ingenuity in the matter of scrolls and fretwork and mosaics—rococo work. But when the catastrophe comes, when the narrative swings clear upon its pivot and we are lifted with it from out the world of our surroundings, we want to forget the author. We want no adjectives to blur our substantives. The substantives may now speak for themselves. We want no metaphor, no simile to make clear the matter. If at this moment of drama and intensity the matter is not of itself preëminently clear no verbiage, however ingenious, will clarify it. Heighten the effect. Does exclamation and heroics on the part of the bystanders ever make the curbstone drama more poignant? Who would care to see Niagara through colored fire and calcium lights?

The simple treatment, whether of a piece of silversmith work or of a momentous religious epic, is always the most difficult of all. It demands more of the artist. The unskilful story-teller as often as not tells the story to himself as well as to his hearers as he goes along. Not sure of exactly how he is to reach the end, not sure even of the end itself, he must feel his way from incident to incident, from page to page, fumbling, using

many words, repeating himself. To hide the confusion there is one resource—elaboration, exaggerated outline, violent color, till at last the
unstable outline disappears under the accumulation and the reader is to
be so dazzled with the wit of the dialogue, the smartness of the repartee,
the felicity of the diction, that he will not see the gaps and lapses in the
structure itself. Just as the "nobby" drummer wears a wide and showy
scarf to conceal a soiled shirt bosom.

But in the master works of narrative there is none of this shamming,
no shoddyism, no humbug. There is little more than bare outline, but in
the care with which it is drawn, how much thought, what infinite pains
go to the making of each stroke, so that when it is made it falls just at the
right place and exactly in its right sequence. This attained what need is
there for more? Comment is superfluous. If the author make the scene
appear terrible to the reader he needs not say in himself or in the mouth
of some protagonist "It is terrible!" If the picture is pathetic so that he
who reads must weep, how superfluous, how intrusive should the author
exclaim, "It was pitiful to the point of tears." If beautiful we do not want
him to tell us so. We want him to make it beautiful and our own appreciation will supply the adjectives.

Beauty, the ultimate philosophical beauty, is not a thing of elaboration,
but on the contrary of an almost barren nudity; a jewel may be an exquisite gem, a woman may have a beautiful arm, but the bracelet does not
make the arm more beautiful, nor the arm the bracelet. One must admire
them separately, and the moment that the jewel ceases to have a value or
a reason upon the arm it is better in the case where it may enjoy an un-
divided attention.

But after so many hundreds of years of art and artists, of civilization
and progress, we have got so far away from the sane old homely un-
complex way of looking out at the world that the simple things no longer
charm, and the simple declarative sentence, straightforward, plain, seems
flat to our intellectual palate—flat and tasteless and crude.

What we would now call simple, our forbears would look upon as a
farrago of gimcrackery, and all our art—the art of the better-minded of
us—is only a striving to get back to the unblurred, direct simplicity of
those writers who could see that the Wonderful, the Counsellor, the
mighty God, the Prince of Peace, could be laid in a manger and yet be
the Saviour of the world.

It is this same spirit, this disdaining of simplicity that has so warped
and inflated The First Story, making of it a pomp, an affair of gold-
embroidered vestments and costly choirs, of marbles, of jeweled windows
and of incense, unable to find the thrill as formerly in the plain and
humble stable, and the brown-haired, grave-eyed peasant girl, with her

little baby; unable to see the beauty in the crumbling mud walls, the low ceiled interior, where the only incense was the sweet smell of the cow's breath. The only vestments the swaddling clothes, rough, coarse fibered, from the hand looms of Nazareth. The only pomp the scanty gifts of three old men, and the only chanting the crooning of a young mother holding her firstborn babe upon her breast.

STORY-TELLERS VS. NOVELISTS[14]

It is a thing accepted and indisputable that a story-teller is a novelist, but it has often occurred to one that the reverse is not always true and that the novelist is not of necessity a story-teller. The distinction is perhaps a delicate one, but for all that it seems to be decisive, and it is quite possible that with the distinction in mind a different judgment might be passed upon a very large part of present-day fiction. It would even be entertaining to apply the classification to the products of the standard authors.

The story-telling instinct seems to be a gift, whereas—we trend to the heretical—the art of composing novels—using the word in apposition to stories, long or short—may be an acquirement. The one is an endowment, the other an accomplishment. Accordingly throughout the following paragraphs the expression: novelists of composition, for the time being will be used technically, and will be applied to those fiction-writers who have not the story-telling faculty.

It would not be fair to attempt a proof that the one is better or worse than the other. The difference is surely of kind and not of degree. One will only seek to establish the fact that certain eminent and brilliant novel-writers are quite bereft of a sense of fiction, that some of them have succeeded in spite of this deficiency, and that other novel-writers possessing this sense of fiction have succeeded *because* of it, and in spite of many drawbacks such as lack of training and of education.

It is a proposition which one believes to be capable of demonstration that every child contains in himself the elements of every known profession, every occupation, every art, every industry. In the five-year-old you may see glimpses of the soldier, trader, farmer, painter, musician, builder and so on to the end of the roster. Later, circumstances produce the atrophy of all these instincts but one, and from that one specialized comes the career. Thus every healthy-minded child—no matter if he develops in later years to be financier or boot-maker—is a story-teller. As soon as he begins to talk he tells stories. Witness the holocausts and carnage of the leaden platoons of the nursery table, the cataclysms of

14 *World's Work*, III (March, 1902), 1894–96.

the Grand Trans-Continental Playroom and Front-Hall Railroad system. This, though, is not real story-telling. The toys practically tell the story for him and are no stimulant to the imagination. However, the child goes beyond the toys. He dramatizes every object of his surroundings. The books of the library shelves are files of soldiers, the rugs are islets in the seaway of the floor, the easy chair is a comfortable old gentleman holding out his arms, the sofa a private brig or a Baldwin locomotive, and the child creates of his surroundings an entire and complex work of fiction of which he is at one and the same time hero, author and public.

Within the heart of every mature human being, not a writer of fiction, there is the withered remains of a little story-teller who died very young. And the love of good fiction and the appreciation of a fine novel in the man of the world of riper years is—I like to think—a sort of memorial tribute which he pays to his little dead playmate of so very long ago, who died very quietly with his little broken tin locomotive in his hands on the cruel day when he woke to the realization that it had outlived its usefulness and its charm.

Even in the heart of some accepted and successful fiction-writer you shall find this little dead story-teller. These are the novelists of composition, whose sense of fiction, under stress of circumstances, has become so blunted that when come at last to full maturity and to the power of using the faculty, they can no longer command it. These are novelists rather of intellect than of spontaneous improvisation; and all the force of their splendid minds, every faculty other than the lost fiction-faculty, must be brought into play to compensate for the lack. Some more than compensate for it, so prodigal in resource, so persistent in effort, so powerful in energy and in fertility of invention, that—as it were by main strength—they triumph over the other writer, the natural story-teller, from whose pen the book flows with almost no effort at all.

Of this sort—the novelists of intellect, in whom the born story-teller is extinct, the novelists of composition in a word—the great example, it would seem, is George Eliot. It was by taking thought that the author of *Romola* added to her stature. The result is superb, but achieved at what infinite pains, with what colossal labor—of head rather than of the heart! She did not *feel,* she *knew,* and to attain that knowledge, what effort had to be expended! Even all her art cannot exclude from her pages evidences of the labor, of the superhuman toil. And it was labor and toil for what? To get back, through years of sophistication, of solemn education, of worldly wisdom, back again to the point of view of the little lost child of the doll-house days.

But sometimes the little story-teller does not die, but lives on and grows with the man, increasing in favor with God, till at last he dominates the man himself and the play-room of the old days simply widens its walls till it includes the street outside, and the street beyond and other streets, the whole city, the whole world and the story-teller discovers a set of new toys to play with, and new objects of a measureless environment to dramatize about, and in exactly, *exactly* the same spirit in which he trundled his tin train through the halls and shouted boarding orders from the sofa he moves now through the world's play-room "making up stories"; only now his heroes and his public are outside himself and he alone may play the author.

For him there is but little effort required. He has a *sense of fiction.* Every instant of his day he is dramatizing. The cable-car has for him a distinct personality. Every window in the residence quarters is an eye to the soul of the house behind. The very lamp-post on the corner, burning on through the night and through the storm, is a soldier, dutiful, vigilant in stress. A ship is Adventure. An engine a living brute; and the easy-chair of his library is still the same comfortable and kindly old gentleman holding out his arms.

The men and women of his world are not apt to be—to him—so important in themselves as in relation to the whirl of things in which he chooses to involve them. They cause events, or else events happen to them, and by an unreasoned instinct the story-teller preserves the consistencies (just as the child would not have run the lines of the hall railway across the sea-way of the floor between the rugs). Much thought is not necessary to him. Production is facile, a constant pleasure. The story runs from his pen almost of itself, it takes this shape or that, he knows not why, his people do this or that and by some blessed system of guesswork they are somehow always plausible and true-to-life. His work is haphazard, yet in the end and in the main tremendously probable. Devil-may-care, slipshod, melodramatic, but invincibly persuasive he uses his heart, his senses, his emotions, every faculty but that of the intellect. He does not *know,* he *feels.*

Dumas was this, and *The Three Musketeers,* different from *Romola* in kind but not in degree, is just as superb as Eliot at her best. Only the Frenchman had a sense of fiction which the Englishwoman had not. Her novels are character studies, are portraits, are portrayals of emotions, or pictures of certain times and certain events, are everything you choose but they are not stories and no stretch of the imagination, no liberalness of criticism can make them such. She succeeded by dint of effort where the Frenchman—merely wrote.

George Eliot compensated for the defect artificially and succeeded eminently and conclusively, but there are not found wanting cases—in modern literature—where "novelists of composition" have *not* compensated beyond a very justifiable doubt, and where had they but rejoiced in a very small modicum of this dowry of the gods their work would have been—to one's notion—infinitely improved.

As for instance Tolstoy; incontestably great though he be, all his unquestioned power has never yet won for him that same vivid sense of fiction enjoyed by so (comparatively) unimportant a writer as the author of *Sherlock Holmes*. And of the two, judged strictly upon their merits as *story-tellers,* one claims for Mr. Doyle the securer if not the higher place, despite the magnificent genius of the novelist.

In the austere Russian—gloomy, sad, acquainted with grief—the child died irrevocably long, long ago; and no power however vast, no wisdom however profound, no effort however earnest, can turn one wheel on the little locomotive of battered tin or send it one inch along the old right of way between the nursery and the front room. One cannot but feel that the great author of *Anna Karenina* realizes as much as his readers the limitations that the loss of this untainted childishness imposes. The power was all his, the wonderful intellectual grip, but not the fiction spirit—the child's knack and love of "making up stories." Given *that,* plus the force already his own, and what a book would have been there! The perfect novel! No doubt, clearer than all others, the great Russian sees the partial failure of his work, and no doubt keener and deeper than all others sees that unless the child-vision and the child-pleasure be present to guide and to stimulate the entrances of the kingdom must stay forever shut to those who would enter, storm they the gates never so mightily and beat they never so clamorously at the doors.

Whatever the end of fiction may be, whatever the reward and recompense bestowed, whatever object is gained by good work, the end will not be gained, nor the reward won, nor the object attained by force alone—by strength of will or of mind. Without the auxiliary of the little playmate of the old days the great doors that stand at the end of the road will stay forever shut. Look once, however, with the child's eyes, or for once touch the mighty valves with the child's hand and Heaven itself lies open with all its manifold wonders.

So that in the end, after all trial has been made and every expedient tested, the simplest way is the best and the humblest means the surest. A little child stands in the midst of the wise men and the learned, and their wisdom and their learning are set aside and they are taught that unless they become as one of these they shall in nowise enter into the Kingdom of Heaven.

Definitions

INTRODUCTION

Norris placed realism, romanticism, and naturalism in a dialectic, in which realism and romanticism were opposing forces, and naturalism was transcending synthesis. Realism was the method of "accuracy," and was therefore limited to the surface commonplaces of life. Romanticism, on the other hand, probed life for "truth," and therefore dealt with the sensational, violent energies at the heart of life. Howells was Norris' archetypal realist, Hugo his romanticist. Naturalism incorporated both the concern for surface detail of realism and the sensationalism and depth of romanticism. It differed from both, however, in occupying itself with all levels of contemporary life, particularly the low, rather than confining itself to one class or to the past. Although Norris at times called Zola a romantic, in order to stress that Zola's fiction was not realistic,[1] he distinguished between Zola's and traditional romanticism, and frequently named him a naturalist.

The importance of Norris' definition of naturalism is that it tells us a great deal about his own concept and practice of fiction, and also about the naturalistic movement in America. His definition obviously attempts to embody in one formula both his entire critical system and his fictional technique at its best. It thus defines primarily his own practice of combining detailed verisimilitude ("accuracy") with vast themes ("truth"), or the extraordinary and the sensational ("life") with a dramatic didacticism ("sincerity"). Most of all, it defines the technique of *The Octopus*, though it is also applicable to much of his other fiction.

What is particularly absorbing in this definition is that it is limited entirely to subject matter and method. It does not mention materialistic determinism or any other philosophical idea, and thus differs from the philosophical orientation of Zola's discussions of naturalism and of those by modern critics of the movement.[2] Norris conceived of naturalism as a fictional mode which illustrated some fundamental truth of life within a detailed presentation of the sensational and low. Unlike Zola, how-

[1] It was not uncommon throughout Zola's career for critics to call him a romanticist because of his sensational plots, though such critics usually intended disparagement rather than praise. See Max Nordau, *Degeneration* (New York: D. Appleton & Company, 1895), pp. 494–497, and F. W. J. Hemmings, *Émile Zola* (Oxford: Clarendon Press, 1953), p. 74.

[2] See Émile Zola's *The Experimental Novel and Other Essays* (New York: Cassell & Co., 1893), pp. 17–18; and Lars Åhnebrink, *The Beginnings of Naturalism in American Fiction* (Cambridge, Massachusetts: Harvard University Press, 1950), pp. vi–vii, and Charles C. Walcutt, *American Literary Naturalism, A Divided Stream* (Minneapolis: University of Minnesota Press, 1956), pp. vii–viii.

ever, he did not specify the exact nature of the truth to be depicted, and it is clear that he believed that Hugo's "truth" was just as naturalistic as Zola's. With Norris' definition in mind, then, we can perhaps understand his remark to Marcosson that *The Octopus* was going to be a return to the "style" of *McTeague*—"straight naturalism."[3] Although the first novel is consciously deterministic in its treatment of human action and the second dramatizes a complex intermingling of free will and determinism, this contradiction is nonexistent within the philosophical vacuum of Norris' definition.

Norris' definition, however, not only has significance for his own fictional practice. It also clarifies some fundamental characteristics of the naturalistic movement in America. It suggests that for most Americans influenced by European naturalistic currents, the naturalistic mode involved primarily the contemporary, low, and sensational, elaborately documented within some large thematic framework. The writer might give his work a philosophical center or foundation—indeed, the naturalistic mode encouraged such a practice. But the core ideas or values present in particular works tended to be strikingly diverse from author to author, as each writer approached his material from a highly individual direction rather than the direction of an ideological "school." American naturalism, in short, has been primarily a movement characterized by similarities in material and method, not by philosophical coherence. And perhaps this very absence of a philosophical center to the movement has been one of the main reasons for its continuing strength in this country, in contrast to its decline in Europe. For writers as different as Dreiser and Crane, or Farrell and Faulkner, have responded to the exciting possibilities of a combination of romantic grandioseness, detailed verisimilitude, and didactic sensationalism, and yet, like Norris, have been able to shape these possibilities into works expressing, most of all, their own distinctive temperaments.

[3] Norris to Isaac Marcosson, November, 1899, *Letters,* p. 48.

ZOLA AS A ROMANTIC WRITER[4]

It is curious to notice how persistently M. Zola is misunderstood. How strangely he is misinterpreted even by those who conscientiously admire the novels of the "man of the iron pen." For most people Naturalism has a vague meaning. It is a sort of inner circle of realism—a kind of diametric opposite of romanticism, a theory of fiction wherein things are represented "as they really are," inexorably, with the truthfulness of a camera. This idea can be shown to be far from right, that Naturalism, as understood by Zola, is but a form of romanticism after all.

Observe the methods employed by the novelists who profess and call themselves "realists"—Mr. Howells, for instance. Howells's characters live across the street from us, they are "on our block." We know all about them, about their affairs, and the story of their lives. One can go even further. We ourselves are Mr. Howells's characters, so long as we are well behaved and ordinary and bourgeois, so long as we are not adventurous or not rich or not unconventional. If we are otherwise, if things commence to happen to us, if we kill a man or two, or get mixed up in a tragic affair, or do something on a large scale, such as the amassing of enormous wealth or power or fame, Mr. Howells cuts our acquaintance at once. He will none of us if we are out of the usual.

This is the real Realism. It is the smaller details of every-day life, things that are likely to happen between lunch and supper, small passions, restricted emotions, dramas of the reception-room, tragedies of an afternoon call, crises involving cups of tea. Every one will admit there is no romance here. The novel is interesting—which is after all the main point—but it is the commonplace tale of commonplace people made into a novel of far more than commonplace charm. Mr. Howells is not uninteresting; he is simply not romantic. But that Zola should be quoted as a realist, and as a realist of realists, is a strange perversion.

Reflect a moment upon his choice of subject and character and episode. The Rougon-Macquart live in a world of their own; they are not of our lives any more than are the Don Juans, the Jean Valjeans, the Gil Blases, the Marmions, or the Ivanhoes. We, the bourgeois, the commonplace, the ordinary, have no part nor lot in the *Rougon-Macquart*, in *Lourdes,* or in *Rome*; it is not our world, not because our social position is different, but because we are *ordinary*. To be noted of M. Zola we must leave the rank and the file, either run to the forefront of the marching world, or fall by the roadway; we must separate ourselves; we must become individual, unique. The naturalist takes no note of common people, common in so far as their interests, their lives, and the things that occur in them

4 *Wave*, XV, (June 27, 1896), 3.

are common, are ordinary. Terrible things must happen to the characters of the naturalistic tale. They must be twisted from the ordinary, wrenched out from the quiet, uneventful round of every-day life, and flung into the throes of a vast and terrible drama that works itself out in unleashed passions, in blood, and in sudden death. The world of M. Zola is a world of big things; the enormous, the formidable, the terrible, is what counts; no teacup tragedies here. Here Nana holds her monstrous orgies, and dies horribly, her face distorted to a frightful mask; Étienne Lantier, carried away by the strike of coal miners of *Le Voreux,* (the strike that is almost war), is involved in the vast and fearful catastrophe that comes as a climax of the great drama; Claude Lantier, disappointed, disillusioned, acknowledging the futility of his art after a life of effort, hangs himself to his huge easel; Jacques Lantier, haunted by an hereditary insanity, all his natural desires hideously distorted, cuts the throat of the girl he loves, and is ground to pieces under the wheels of his own locomotive; Jean Macquart, soldier and tiller of the fields, is drawn into the war of 1870, passes through the terrible scenes of Sedan and the Siege of Paris only to bayonet to death his truest friend and sworn brother-at-arms in the streets of the burning capital.[5]

Everything is extraordinary, imaginative, grotesque even, with a vague note of terror quivering throughout like the vibration of an ominous and low-pitched diapason. It is all romantic, at times unmistakably so, as in *Le Rêve* or *Rome,* closely resembling the work of the greatest of all modern romanticists, Hugo. We have the same huge dramas, the same enormous scenic effects, the same love of the extraordinary, the vast, the monstrous, and the tragic.

Naturalism is a form of romanticism, not an inner circle of realism. Where is the realism in the *Rougon-Macquart?* Are such things likely to happen between lunch and supper? That Zola's work is not purely romantic as was Hugo's, lies chiefly in the choice of Milieu. These great, terrible dramas no longer happen among the personnel of a feudal and Renaissance nobility, those who are in the fore-front of the marching world, but among the lower—almost the lowest—classes; those who have been thrust or wrenched from the ranks, who are falling by the roadway. This is not romanticism—this drama of the people, working itself out in blood and ordure. It is not realism. It is a school by itself, unique, somber, powerful beyond words. It is naturalism.

[5] The novels referred to are, in order, *Nana, Germinal, L'Oeuvre, La Bête Humaine,* and *La Débâcle.*

FRANK NORRIS' WEEKLY LETTER[6]

It is not more than a week ago since the present writer, in going through the daily batch of volunteer manuscripts submitted to a certain firm of New York publishers, came across a letter pinned to the typewritten draft of a novel. The letter was, in a way, a note and commentary upon the novel, and its writer declared with some vehemence, and more than once, that the events in the novel were true—were taken from real life—actually occurred, etc., etc. The inference was plain as paint. The author believed his story to be better by just so much, because the things in it were taken from actual life, were based on fact—must, therefore, be true to life. Now, here is the point. Is an event that is taken from actual life, true to life? Let us consider now. Suppose one had overlooked this author's letter, and had written to him to say that one of the faults of his story lay in the fact that it was not true to life. What a chance! How that author would have countered! How he would have forever demolished the critic, or the reader, with the one phrase, "But, sir, it actually happened." Therefore, it must be true.

Well, I say no. Let us talk about this Truth in Fiction, and with a certain provincial magistrate ask—in the name of American literature— "What is Truth?" A thing has actually happened; that is the proposition. Given to prove that it is not necessarily true when told as fiction— not necessarily true even when told with the most scrupulous adherence to fact, even when narrated with the meticulous science of the phonograph or pictured with the incontestable precision of the photograph.

Perhaps we will get a good grip of the problem at the outset if we make a difference, a wide difference, between Accuracy and Truth. A story can be accurate and yet lamentably—even wickedly—untrue. As, for instance, let us suppose that you have never seen a sheep, and that it devolves upon me to give you an idea of the animal—describe it, in fact. I go out into the fields and select a sheep. In size, build, habits, weight, wool-producing qualities and the like it is precisely like other sheep—but it is black. To you, then I bring this sheep. I call your attention to the characteristics. I falsify nothing, conceal nothing. I present the creature fairly in every detail, in every particular. I am, in a word, accurate. But what is the result? To your notion all sheep are black, which is an untruth.

So that Accuracy is not necessarily Truth, and the novelist who relies upon the accurate presentation of a crisis in life, hoping by this means to create the impression of Truth, is leaning upon a broken reed.

For further—Life itself is not necessarily True—not necessarily True

[6] *Chicago American*, August 3, 1901, p. 5.

to life. I admit that this is much easier to assert than to prove, and the sound of it is that of a flippant paradox. Let us try an illustration or two. How many times—how almost invariably, especially with us stoical Anglo-Saxons—do men or women confronted suddenly with great tragedy or great joy fail to "rise to the occasion." How seldom is it that their actions or words at the moment are adequate, are interpretive of their emotions, give an expression of themselves. Mr. Davis tells of a condemned murderer who received the news of his pardon with the words: "That's good. That's good."

Death-bed scenes are notoriously tame; heroic rescuers are most frequently silent at their work; the soldier receiving a mortal wound, when not struck unconscious, shouts "Gee!" and sits down suddenly with straddled legs. Wellington, at Waterloo, never cried "Up guards and at 'em!" Louis Napoleon's tame eagle refused to fly at the fortress of Ham; and Newton, when his little dog, by overturning a lamp, had irreparably destroyed fifty years of work, could only exclaim, "Ah, Flo, Flo, thou little knowest the ruin thou hast wrought!" Suppose Newton had acted and spoken in proportion to the poignancy of his grief, what a noble, heroic strain of tragedy would have been given to the world. But if we all gave true expression to our feelings under stress there would be no need nor place for fiction.

And here comes the dividing line. Here stands the crux. Is it too much to say that fiction can be truer than Life itself? I take it that we can say this and yet be well within conservatism. For fiction must not be judged by standards of real life, but both life and fiction referred to a third standard. The expression "true to life" is false, is inadequate, for life itself is not always true.

To what, then, should the truth of a novel be referred—to what standard? By what touchstone may we recognize the true metal?

Difficult question. Standards vary for different works of fiction. We must not refer Tolstoy to the same standard as Victor Hugo—the one a realist, the other a romanticist. We can conceive of no standard which would be large enough to include both, unless it would be one so vague, so broad, so formless as to be without value. Take the grand scene in *Hernani*. How would Tolstoy have done it? He would have brought it home as close to the reader as possible. Hugo has elevated it as far as he could in the opposite direction. Tolstoy would have confined himself to probabilities only. Hugo is confined by nothing save the limitations of his own imagination. The realist would have been accurate—only in this case he would not have chosen a black sheep. The romanticist aims at the broad truth of the thing—puts into his people's mouths the words they would have spoken if only they could have given expression to his thoughts.

Then the conclusion. Is it permissible to say that Accuracy is realism and Truth romanticism? I am not so sure, but I feel that we come close to a solution here. The divisions seem natural and intended. It is not difficult to be accurate, but it is monstrously difficult to be True; at best the romanticists can only aim at it, while on the other hand, mere accuracy as an easily obtainable result is for that reason less worthy.

Does Truth after all "lie in the middle"? And what school, then, is midway between the Realists and Romanticists, taking the best from each? Is it not the school of Naturalism, which strives hard for accuracy and truth? The nigger is out of the fence at last, but must it not be admitted that the author of *La Débâcle* (not the author of *La Terre* and *Fécondité*)[7] is up to the present stage of literary development the most adequate, the most satisfactory, the most just of them all?

A PLEA FOR ROMANTIC FICTION[8]

Let us at the start make a distinction. Observe that one speaks of Romanticism and not of sentimentalism. One claims that the latter is as distinct from the former as is that other form of art which is called Realism. Romance has been often put upon and overburdened by being forced to bear the onus of abuse that by right should fall to sentiment; but the two should be kept very distinct, for a very high and illustrious place will be claimed for Romance, while sentiment will be handed down the scullery stairs.

Many people today are composing mere sentimentalism, and calling it and causing it to be called Romance, so with those who are too busy to think much upon these subjects, but who none the less love honest literature, Romance too has fallen into disrepute. Consider now the cut-and-thrust stories. They are all labelled Romances, and it is very easy to get the impression that Romance must be an affair of cloaks and daggers, or moonlight and golden hair. But this is not so at all. The true Romance is a more serious business than this. It is not merely a conjurer's trick box, full of flimsy quackeries, tinsel and clap traps, meant only to amuse, and relying upon deception to do even that. Is it not something better than this? Can we not see in it an instrument, keen, finely tempered, flawless —an instrument with which we may go straight through the clothes and tissues and wrappings of flesh down deep into the red, living heart of things?

---

[7] This choice of novels is not entirely clear, but perhaps it can be explained by the contemporary reputation of the three works and by the fact that Norris was writing for a newspaper supplement. *La Débâcle* was well received in America, whereas *La Terre* was attacked for its gross sexuality and *Fécondité* was almost universally criticized for its excessive polemicism.

[8] *Boston Evening Transcript,* December 18, 1901, p. 14.

Is all this too subtle, too merely speculative and intrinsic, too *précieuse* and nice and "literary"? Devoutly one hopes the contrary. So much is made of so-called Romanticism in present day fiction, that the subject seems worthy of discussion, and a protest against the misuse of a really noble and honest formula of literature appears to be timely—misuse, that is, in the sense of limited use. Let us suppose for the moment that a Romance can be made out of the cut-and-thrust business. Good Heavens, are there no other things that are romantic, even in this—falsely, falsely called—humdrum world of today? Why should it be that so soon as the novelist addresses himself—seriously—to the consideration of contemporary life he must abandon Romance and take up that harsh, loveless, colorless, blunt tool called Realism?

Now, let us understand at once what is meant by Romance and what by Realism. Romance—I take it—is the kind of fiction that takes cognizance of variations from the type of normal life. Realism is the kind of fiction that confines itself to the type of normal life. According to this definition, then, Romance may even treat of the sordid, the unlovely—as for instance, the novels of M. Zola. (Zola has been dubbed a Realist, but he is, on the contrary, the very head of the Romanticists.) Also, Realism, used as it sometimes is as a term of reproach, need not be in the remotest sense or degree offensive, but on the other hand respectable as a church and proper as a deacon—as, for instance, the novels of Mr. Howells.

The reason why one claims so much for Romance, and quarrels so pointedly with Realism, is that Realism stultifies itself. It notes only the surface of things. For it Beauty is not even skin-deep, but only a geometrical plane, without dimensions of depth, a mere outside. Realism is very excellent so far as it goes, but it goes no farther than the Realist himself can actually see, or actually hear. Realism is minute, it is the drama of a broken teacup, the tragedy of a walk down the block, the excitement of an afternoon call, the adventure of an invitation to dinner. It is the visit to my neighbor's house, a formal visit, from which I may draw no conclusions. I see my neighbor and his friends—very, oh, such very! probable people—and that is all. Realism bows upon the doormat and goes away and says to me, as we link arms on the sidewalk: "That is life." And I say it is not. It is not, as you would very well see if you took Romance with you to call upon your neighbor.

Lately you have been taking Romance a weary journey across the water —ages and the flood of years—and haling her into the fubsy, musty, worm-eaten, moth-riddled, rust-corroded "Grandes Salles" of the Middle Ages and the Renaissance, and she has found the drama of a bygone age for you there. But would you take her across the street to your neighbor's front parlor (with the bisque fisher boy on the mantel and the photograph of Niagara Falls on glass hanging in the front window); would you introduce her there? Not you. Would you take a walk with her on Fifth avenue, or Beacon street, or Michigan avenue? No indeed. Would you choose her for a companion of a morning spent in Wall Street, or an afternoon in the Waldorf-Astoria? You just guess you would not.

She would be out of place, you say, inappropriate. She might be awkward in my neighbor's front parlor, and knock over the little bisque fisher boy. Well, she might. If she did, you might find underneath the base of the statuette, hidden away, tucked away—what? God knows. But something which would be a complete revelation of my neighbor's secretest life.

So you think Romance would stop in the front parlor and discuss medicated flannels and mineral waters with the ladies? Not for more than five minutes. She would be off upstairs with you, prying, peeping, peering into the closets of the bedroom, into the nursery, into the sitting-room; yes, and into that little iron box screwed to the lower shelf of the closet in the library; and into those compartments and pigeon-holes of the *secrétaire* in the study. She would find a heartache (may-be) between the pillows of the mistress's bed, and a memory carefully secreted in the master's deedbox. She would come upon a great hope amid the books and papers of the study table of the young man's room, and—perhaps— who knows—an affair, or, great heavens, an intrigue, in the scented ribbons and gloves and hairpins of the young lady's bureau. And she would pick here a little and there a little, making up a bag of hopes and fears, and a package of joys and sorrows—great ones, mind you—and then come down to the front door, and stepping out into the street, hand you the bags and package, and say to you—"That is Life!"

Romance does very well in the castles of the Middle Ages and the Renaissance chateaux, and she has the entrée there and is very well received. That is all well and good. But let us protest against limiting her to such places and such times. You will find her, I grant you, in the chatelaine's chamber and the dungeon of the man-at-arms; but, if you choose to look for her, you will find her equally at home in the brownstone house on the corner and in the office building downtown. And this very day, in this very hour, she is sitting among the rags and wretchedness, the dirt and despair of the tenements of the East Side of New York.

"What?" I hear you say, "look for Romance—the lady of the silken robes and golden crown, our beautiful, chaste maiden of soft voice and gentle eyes—look for her among the vicious ruffians, male and female, of Allen street and Mulberry Bend?" I tell you she is there, and to your shame be it said you will not know her in those surroundings. You, the aristocrats, who demand the fine linen and the purple in your fiction; you, the sensitive, the delicate, who will associate with your Romance only so long as she wears a silken gown. You will not follow her to the slums, for you believe that Romance should only amuse and entertain you, singing you sweet songs and touching the harp of silver strings with rosy-tipped fingers. If haply she should call to you from the squalor of a dive, or the awful degradation of a disorderly house, crying: "Look! listen! This, too, is life. These, too, are my children, look at them, know them and, knowing, help!" Should she call thus, you would stop your ears; you would avert your eyes, and you would answer, "Come from there, Romance. Your place is not there!" And you would make of her a harlequin, a tumbler, a sword dancer, when, as a matter of fact, she should be by right divine a teacher sent from God.

She will not always wear the robe of silk, the gold crown, the jeweled shoon, will not always sweep the silver harp. An iron note is hers if so she choose, and coarse garments, and stained hands; and, meeting her thus, it is for you to know her as she passes—know her for the same young queen of the blue mantle and lilies. She can teach you, if you will be humble to learn. Teach you by showing. God help you, if at last you take from Romance her mission of teaching, if you do not believe that she has a purpose, a nobler purpose and a mightier than mere amusement, mere entertainment. Let Realism do the entertaining with its meticulous presentation of teacups, rag carpets, wall paper and haircloth sofas, stopping with these, going no deeper than it sees, choosing the ordinary, the untroubled, the commonplace.

But to Romance belongs the wide world for range, and the unplumbed depths of the human heart, and the mystery of sex, and the problems of life, and the black, unsearched penetralia of the soul of man. You, the indolent, must not always be amused. What matter the silken clothes, what matter the prince's houses? Romance, too, is a teacher, and if— throwing aside the purple—she wears the camel's hair and feeds upon the locusts, it is to cry aloud unto the people, "Prepare ye the way of the Lord; make straight his path."

PART TWO
THE WRITER AND SOCIETY

The Responsibilities of the Novelist

INTRODUCTION

Norris' views on the social responsibilities of the novelist have two major sources—the general literary scene at the turn of the century, and his own basic frame of mind, particularly his intense moralism.

During the 1890's there emerged a large new reading public, a group formed by increased public education and by popular emphasis upon cultural self-improvement. Its growth was aided also by the generally prosperous condition of the country and by improved means of cheap publication. This new public—or at least this greatly augmented public—added to the demand for various kinds of easily digestible news and literature: for yellow journalism and the Sunday supplements, for the large circulation ten-cent magazine (such as *McClure's* and the *Saturday Evening Post*), and for "light" fiction. It was thus a period of vogues in popular novels. Such works as *Trilby, The Prisoner of Zenda, When Knighthood Was in Flower,* and *David Harum* sold in the hundreds of thousands, and the best-seller lists were dominated by historical and pastiche romances, by folksy tales of small-town life, and by novels of high adventure—in short, by what we today call "escape" literature.[1]

There is, of course, a parallel between the situation in the novel at that time, particularly after 1898, and that existing in television since World War II. In both instances, those realizing the power of mass media have been much concerned with the opportunities for both good and evil which exist in the public's preoccupation with a particular form of entertainment. Norris revealed his concern by calling for the novelist to recognize his responsibility as a molder of the public mind. The novelist, he believed, must have a literary conscience which leads him to write novels that guide the people by "proving something" about life or by exposing some of the evils of life. The novelist who fulfills these demands may not make his fortune, but he will have the "true reward" of knowing he has been faithful to himself and to his duty. The operative word in these requirements is "sincerity." Norris meant by sincerity most of all that the writer be a novelist of "life, not literature"—that he avoid books (that is, in this case, popular vogues) and rather cultivate his own response to the teeming modern world. He called, in short, for the writer to pursue the method of naturalism, and thereby to penetrate to the "true romance" of contemporary life. By this method, the novelist will demonstrate both the vast

---

[1] See James D. Hart, *The Popular Book* (New York: Oxford University Press, 1950), pp. 180–200, and Frank L. Mott, *Golden Multitudes* (New York: The Macmillan Company, 1947), pp. 183–193.

forces and the particular faults of society, a revelation which should play a role in social progress. Norris' demand for social responsibility is thus not distinct from his ideas concerning the proper content and form of the novel. Rather, that demand both stems from and embodies his basic aesthetic position. Like so many writers with primitivistic values, Norris' call for a literature of "life" is counterbalanced and partially motivated by an actively engaged social conscience, though in Norris' case this engagement took several years to mature.

But also present in Norris' cry for responsibility is an aspect of his nature as deep as his primitivistic anti-intellectualism—that is, his moralism. Several elements in his call for the responsible writer derive from this quality. For example, his moral intensity underlies his emphasis upon the chivalric code of "truth to oneself" of Robert Louis Stevenson and Kipling, and it is present as a major force in the puritan stress on conscience which runs through much of his thinking. Norris' demand for the committed writer is therefore not only the product of his rationally derived belief, similar to Howells' and Zola's, that critical realism can play a major social role. It is also the result of his emotional need, similar to Tolstoy's, to affirm the moral role of literature and the positive morality of the responsible writer.

Norris' conception of the social importance of fiction is implicit in many of his *Wave* editorials of 1896–1897. The explicit expression of this idea, however, did not occur until 1901–1902, as he planned and wrote his epic of the wheat. For in this series, written at the height of the rage for historical romance, Norris himself was engaged in "proving something" about contemporary life rather than in reaping the easy reward of a literature of "clothes"—that is, of historical paraphernalia. Some of the force of these essays, then, is conditioned by an element of self-righteous, but not unjustified, pride which Norris felt in his own role as a responsible writer.

So in the permanent debate on the function of the popular arts in a democracy—and at the end of the last century the novel was perhaps even more of a popular art than the stage—Norris takes a definite stand.[2] He refutes the conventional objections, conventional then as now, that people have enough trouble in their "real" lives and deserve "pure" entertainment, and that the work which "preaches" cannot be art. He rejects, above all, the excuse that the responsibility for improving popular art lies with the people. Norris believed that since these arts shape the mind of the public, whether the public wanted its mind shaped or not, control is the

---

[2] In the nineties this debate is best represented by W. D. Howells' support of the novel with a purpose in his *Criticism and Fiction* (1891) and F. M. Crawford's attack on "purpose fiction" in his *The Novel: What It Is* (1893).

duty of those originating these arts. It is up to the television station to attempt the possible task of bettering its programs, Norris would say, rather than for the viewer to attempt the almost impossible task of turning off his set. And in a larger sphere than the problem of mass culture, Norris appeals for the fully committed writer—for the writer conscious of the social involvement of art and of its function as an instrument of social control and improvement.

THE TRUE REWARD OF THE NOVELIST[3]

Not that one quarrels with the historical novel as such; not that one does not enjoy good fiction wherever found, and in whatever class. It is the method of attack of the latter-day copyists that one deplores—their attitude, the willingness of so very, very many of them to take off the hat to Fashion, and then hold the same hat for Fashion to drop pennies in.

Ah, but the man must be above the work or the work is worthless, and the man better off at some other work than that of producing fiction. The eye never once should wander to the gallery, but be always and with single purpose turned *inward* upon the work, testing it and retesting it that it rings true.

What one quarrels with is the perversion of a profession, the detestable trading upon another man's success. No one can find fault with those few good historical novels that started the fad. There was good workmanship in these, and honesty. But the copyists, the fakirs—they are not novelists at all, though they write novels that sell by the hundreds of thousands. They are business men. They find out—no, they allow *someone else* to find out—what the public wants, and they give it to the public cheap, and advertise it as a new soap is advertised. Well, they make money; and, if that is their aim—if they are content to prostitute the good name of American literature for a sliding scale of royalties—let's have done with them. They have their reward. But the lamentable result will be that these copyists will in the end so prejudice the people against an admirable school of fiction—the school of Scott—that for years to come the tale of historic times will be discredited and many a great story remain unwritten, and many a man of actual worth and real power hold back in the ranks for very shame of treading where so many fools have rushed in.

For the one idea of the fakir—the copyist—and of the public which for the moment listens to him, is Clothes, Clothes, Clothes, first, last and always Clothes. Not Clothes only in the sense of doublet and gown, but Clothes of speech, Clothes of manners, Clothes of customs. Hear them expatiate over the fashion of wearing a cuff, over a trick of speech, over the architecture of a house, the archaeology of armor and the like. It is all well enough in its way, but so easily dispensed with if there be flesh and blood underneath. Veronese put the people of his "Marriage at Cana" into the clothes of his contemporaries. Is the picture any less a masterpiece?

Do these Little People know that Scott's archaeology was about one thousand years "out" in *Ivanhoe,* and that to make a parallel we must conceive of a writer describing Richelieu—say—in small clothes and a

[3] *World's Work,* II (October, 1901), 1337–39.

top hat? But is it not Richelieu we want, and Ivanhoe, not their clothes, their armor? And in spite of his errors Scott gave us a real Ivanhoe. He got beneath the clothes of an epoch and got the heart of it, and the spirit of it (different essentially and vitally from ours or from every other, the spirit of feudalism); and he put forth a masterpiece.

The Little People so very precise in the matter of buttons and *bacinets* do not so. Take the clothes from the people of their Romances and one finds only wooden manikins. Take the clothes from the epoch of which they pretend to treat and what is there beneath? It is only the familiar, well-worn, well-bethumbed nineteenth or twentieth century after all. As well have written of Michigan Avenue, Chicago, as "La Rue de la Harpe," "The Great North Road" or the "Appian Way."

It is a masquerade, the novel of the copyists; and the people who applaud them—are they not the same who would hold persons in respect because of the finery on their bodies? A poor taste, a cheap one; the taste of servingmen, the literature of chambermaids.

To approach the same subject by a different radius: why must the historical novel of the copyists always be conceived of in the terms of Romance? Could not the formula of Realism be applied at least as well, not the Realism of mere externals (the copyists have that), but the Realism of motives and emotions? What would we not give for a picture of the fifteenth century as precise and perfect as one of Mr. James's novels? Even if that be impossible the attempt, even though half-way successful, would be worth while, would be better than the wooden manikin in the tin-pot helmet and baggy hose. At least we should get somewhere, even if no farther than Mr. Kingsley took us in *Hereward,* or Mr. Blackmore in *Lorna Doone.*

How about the business life and the student life, and the artisan life and the professional life, and above all, the home life of historic periods? Great Heavens! There was something else sometimes than the soldier life. They were not always cutting and thrusting, not always night riding, escaping, venturing, posing.

Or suppose that cut-and-thrust must be the order of the day, where is the "man behind," and the heart in the man and the spirit in the heart and the essential vital, elemental, all-important true life within the spirit? We are all Anglo-Saxons enough to enjoy the sight of a fight, would go a block or so out of the way to see one, or be a dollar or so out of pocket. But let it not be these jointed manikins worked with a thread. At least let it be Mr. Robert Fitzsimmons or Mr. James Jeffries.

Clothes, paraphernalia, panoply, pomp and circumstance, and the copyist's public and the poor be-deviled, ink-corroded hack of an overdriven, underpaid reviewer on an inland paper speak of the "vivid coloring" and "the fine picture of a by-gone age"—it is easy to be vivid with a pot of vermilion at the elbow. Any one can scare a young dog with a falseface and a roaring voice, but to be vivid and use grays and browns, to scare the puppy with the lifted finger, that's something to the point.

The difficult thing is to get at the life immediately around you, the very life in which you move. No romance in it? No romance in *you,* poor fool. As much romance on Michigan Avenue as there is realism in King Arthur's court. It is as you choose to see it. The important thing to decide is which formula is the best to help you grip the Real Life of this or any other age. Contemporaries always imagine that theirs is the prosaic age, and that chivalry and the picturesque died with their forbears. No doubt Merlin mourned for the old time of romance. Cervantes held that romance was dead. Yet most of the historical romances of the day are laid in Cervantes's time, or even after it.

Romance and Realism are constant qualities of every age, day and hour. They are here today. They existed in the time of Job. They will continue to exist till the end of time, not so much in things as in the point of view of the people who see things.

The difficulty then is to get at the immediate life, immensely difficult, for you are not only close to the canvas, but are yourself part of the picture.

But the historic age is almost done to hand. Let almost any one shut himself in his closet with a history and Viollet-le-Duc's *Dictionnaire du Mobilier* and, given a few months' time, he can evolve an historical novel of the kind called popular. He need not know men—just clothes and the lingo, the "what-ho-without-there" gabble. But if he only chose he could find romance and adventure in Wall street or Bond street. But romance there does not wear the gay clothes and the showy accouterments, and to discover it—the real romance of it—means hard work and close study, not of books, but of people and actualities.

Not only this, but to know the life around you, you must live—if not *among* people then *in* people. You must be something more than a novelist if you can, something more than just a writer. There must be that nameless sixth sense or sensibility in you that great musicians have in common with great inventors and great scientists, the thing that does not enter into the work, but that is back of it, the thing that would make of you a good *man* as well as a good novelist, the thing that differentiates the mere business man from the financier (for it is possessed of the financier and poet alike—so only they be big enough).

It is not genius, for genius is a lax, loose term so flippantly used that its expressiveness is long since lost. It is more akin to sincerity. And there once more we halt upon the great word—sincerity, sincerity, and again sincerity. Let the writer attack his historical novel with sincerity and he cannot then do wrong. He will see then the man beneath the clothes, and the heart beneath both, and he will be so amazed at the wonder of that sight that he will forget the clothes. His public will be small, perhaps, but he will have the better reward of the knowledge of a thing well done. Royalties on editions of hundreds of thousands will not pay him more to his satisfaction than that. To make money is not the province of a novelist. If he is the right sort he has other responsibilities, heavy ones. He of all men cannot think only of himself or for himself. And when the last page is written and the ink crusts on the pen-point and the hungry presses go clashing after another writer, the "new man" and the new fashion of the hour, he will think of the grim long grind of the years of his life that he has put behind him and of his work that he has built up volume by volume, sincere work, telling the truth as he saw it, independent of fashion and the gallery gods, holding to these with gripped hands and shut teeth—he will think of all this then, and he will be able to say: "I never truckled, I never took off the hat to Fashion and held it out for pennies. By God, I told them the truth. They liked it or they didn't like it. What had that to do with me? I told them the truth; I knew it for the truth then, and I know it for the truth now."

And that is his reward—the best that a man may know; the only one really worth the striving for.

THE NEED OF A LITERARY CONSCIENCE[4]

"Pilate saith unto them: what is truth?" and it is of record that he received no answer—and for very obvious reasons. For is it not a fact, that he who asks that question must himself find the answer and that not even one sent from Heaven can be of hope or help to him, if he is not willing to go down into his own heart and into his own life to find it?

To sermonize, to elaborate a disquisition on nice distinctions of metaphysics is not appropriate here. But it is—so one believes—appropriate to consider a certain very large class of present day novelists of the United States who seldom are stirred by that spirit of inquiry that for a moment disturbed the Roman, who do *not* ask what is truth, who do not in fact care to be truthful at all, and who—and this is the serious side of the business—are bringing the name of American literature perilously near to disrepute.

One does not quarrel for one instant with the fact that certain books of the writers in question have attained phenomenally large circulations. This is as it should be. There are very many people in the United States, and compared with such a figure as seventy million, a mere hundred thousand of books sold is no great matter.

[4] *World's Work*, III (December, 1901), 1559–60.

But here—so it seems—is the point. He who can address a hundred thousand people is, no matter what his message may be, in an important position. It is a large audience one hundred thousand, larger than any roofed building now standing could contain. Less than one one-hundredth part of that number nominated Lincoln. Less than half of it won Waterloo.

And it must be remembered that for every one person who buys a book there are three who will read it and half a dozen who will read what someone else has written about it, so that the sphere of influence widens indefinitely, and the audience that the writer addresses approaches the half-million mark.

Well and good; but if the audience is so vast, if the influence is so far-reaching, if the example set is so contagious, it becomes incumbent to ask, it becomes imperative to demand that the half-million shall be told the truth and not a lie.

And this thing called truth—"what is it?" says Pilate, and the average man conceives at once of an abstraction, a vague idea, a term borrowed from the metaphysicians, certainly nothing that has to do with practical, tangible, concrete work-a-day life.

Error! If truth is not an actual work-a-day thing, as concrete as the lamp-post on the corner, as practical as a cable-car, as real and homely and work-a-day and commonplace as a boot-jack, then indeed we are of all men most miserable and our preaching vain.

And truth in fiction is just as real and just as important as truth anywhere else—as in Wall Street, for instance. A man who does not tell the truth there, and who puts the *un*truth upon paper over his signature will be very promptly jailed. In the case of the Wall Street man the sum of money in question may be trivial, a hundred dollars, fifty dollars. But the untruthful novelist who starts in motion something like half a million dollars invokes not fear nor yet reproach. If truth in the matter of the producing of novels is not an elusive, intangible abstraction, what then is it? Let us get at the hard nub of the business, something we can hold in the hand. It is the thing that is one's own, the discovery of a subject suitable for fictitious narration that has never yet been treated, and the conscientious study of that subject and the fair presentation of results. Not a difficult matter it would appear, not an abstraction, not a philosophical kink. Newspaper reporters, who are not metaphysicians, unnamed, unrewarded, despised even and hooted and hounded, are doing this every day. They do it on a meagre salary, and they call the affair a "scoop." Is the standard of the novelist—he who is entrusted with the good name of his nation's literature—lower than that of a reporter?

"Ah, but it is so hard to be original," "ah, but it is so hard to discover anything new." Great Heavens! when a new life comes into the world for every tick of the watch in your pocket—a new life with all its complications, and with all the thousand and one other complications it sets in motion!

Hard to be original! when of all of those billion lives your own is as distinct, as individual, as "original," as though you were born out of season in the Paleozoic age and yours the first human face the sun ever shone upon.

Go out into the street and stand where the ways cross and hear the machinery of life work clashing in its grooves. Can the utmost resort of your ingenuity evolve a better story than any one of the millions that jog your elbow? Shut yourself in your closet and turn your eyes inward upon yourself—deep *into* yourself, down, down into the heart of you; and the tread of the feet upon the pavement is the systole and diastole of your own being—different only in degree. It is life; and it is that which you must have to make your book, your novel—life, not other people's novels.

Or look from your window. A whole Literature goes marching by, clamoring for a leader and a master hand to guide it. You have but to step from your doorway. And instead of this, instead of entering into the leadership that is yours by right divine, instead of this, you must toilfully, painfully endeavor to crawl into the armor of the chief of some other cause, the harness of the leader of some other progress.

But you will not fit into that panoply. You may never brace that buckler upon your arm, for by your very act you stand revealed as a littler man than he who should be chief—a little man and a weaker; and the casque will fall so far over your face that it will only blind you, and the sword will trip you, and the lance, too ponderous, will falter in your grip, and all that life which surges and thunders behind you, will in time know you to be the false leader, and as you stumble will trample you in its onrush, and leave you dead and forgotten upon the road.

And just as a misconception of the truth makes of this the simplest and homeliest of things, a vagary, an abstraction and a bugbear, so it is possible that a misconception of the Leader creates the picture of a great and dreadful figure wrapped in majesty, solemn and profound. So that perhaps for very lack of self-confidence, for very diffidence, one shrinks from lifting the sword of him and from enduing one's forehead with the casque that seems so ponderous.

In other causes no doubt the leader must be chosen from the wise and great. In science and finance one looks to him to be a strong man, a swift and a sure man. But the literature that today shouts all in vain for its chief needs no such a one as this. Here the battle is not to the strong nor yet the race to the swift. Here the leader is no vast, stern being, profound, solemn, knowing all things, but, on the contrary, is as humble as the lowliest that follow after him. So that it need not be hard to step into that place of eminence. Not by arrogance, nor by assumption, nor by the achievement of the world's wisdom, shall you be made worthy of the place of high command. But it will come to you, if it comes at all, because you shall have kept yourself young and humble and pure in heart, and so unspoiled and unwearied and unjaded that you shall find joy in the mere rising of the sun, a wholesome, sane delight in the sound of the wind at night, a pleasure in the sight of the hills at evening, shall see God in a little child and a whole religion in a brooding bird.

THE NOVEL WITH A "PURPOSE"[5]

After years of indoctrination and expostulation on the part of the artists, the people who read appear at last to have grasped this one precept—"the novel must not preach," but "the purpose of the story must be subordinate to the story itself." It took a very long time for them to understand this, but once it became apparent they fastened upon it with a tenacity comparable only to the tenacity of the American schoolboy to the date "1492." "The novel must not preach," you hear them say.

As though it were possible to write a novel without a purpose, even if it is only the purpose to amuse. One is willing to admit that this savors a little of quibbling, for "purpose" and purpose to amuse are two different purposes. But every novel, even the most frivolous, must have some reason for the writing of it, and in that sense must have a "purpose."

Every novel must do one of three things—it must (1) tell something, (2) show something or (3) prove something. Some novels do all three of these; some do only two; all must do at least one.

The ordinary novel merely tells something, elaborates a complication, devotes itself primarily to *things*. In this class comes the novel of adventure, such as *The Three Musketeers*.

The second and better class of novel shows something, exposes the workings of a temperament, devotes itself primarily to the minds of human beings. In this class falls the novel of character, such as *Romola*.

The third, and what we hold to be the best class, proves something, draws conclusions from a whole congeries of forces, social tendencies, race impulses, devotes itself not to a study of men but of man. In this class falls the novel with the purpose, such as *Les Misérables*.

And the reason we decide upon this last as the highest form of the novel is because that, though setting a great purpose before it as its task, it nevertheless includes, and is forced to include, both the other classes.

[5] *World's Work*, IV (May, 1902), 2117–19.

It must tell something, must narrate vigorous incidents and must show something, must penetrate deep into the motives and character of type-men, men who are composite pictures of a multitude of men. It must do this because of the nature of the subject, for it deals with elemental forces, motives that stir whole nations. These cannot be handled as abstractions in fiction. Fiction can find expression only in the concrete. The elemental forces, then, contribute to the novel with a purpose to provide it with vigorous action. In the novel, force can be expressed in no other way. The social tendencies must be expressed by means of analysis of the characters of the men and women who compose that society, and the two must be combined and manipulated to evolve the purpose—to find the value of x.

The production of such a novel is probably the most arduous task that the writer of fiction can undertake. Nowhere else is success more difficult; nowhere else is failure so easy. Unskilfully treated the story may dwindle down and degenerate into mere special pleading, and the novelist become a polemicist, a pamphleteer, forgetting that, although his first consid-eration is to prove his case, his *means* must be living human beings, not statistics, and that his tools are not figures, but pictures from life as he sees it. The novel with a purpose *is,* one contends, a preaching novel. But it preaches by telling things and showing things. Only, the author selects from the great storehouse of actual life the things to be told and the things to be shown, which shall bear upon his problem, his purpose. The preaching, the moralizing, is the result not of direct appeal by the writer, but is made—should be made—to the reader by the very incidents of the story.

But here is presented a strange anomaly, a distinction as subtle as it is vital. Just now one has said that in the composition of the kind of novel under consideration the *purpose* is for the novelist the all-important thing, and yet it is impossible to deny that the *story,* as a mere story, is to the story writer the one great object of attention. How reconcile then these two apparent contradictions?

For the novelist, the purpose of his novel, the problem he is to solve, is to his story what the keynote is to the sonata. Though the musician cannot exaggerate the importance of the keynote, yet the thing that interests him is the sonata itself. The keynote simply coördinates the music, systematizes it, brings all the myriad little rebellious notes under a single harmonious code.

Thus, too, the purpose in the novel. It is important as an end and also as an ever-present guide. For the writer it is as important only as a note to which his work must be attuned. The moment, however, that the writer becomes really and vitally interested in his purpose his novel fails.

Here is the strange anomaly. Let us suppose that Hardy, say, should be engaged upon a story which had for purpose to show the injustices under which the miners of Wales were suffering. It is conceivable that he could write a story that would make the blood boil with indignation. But he himself, if he is to remain an artist, if he is to write his novel successfully, will, as a novelist, care very little about the iniquitous labor system of the Welsh coal mines. It will be to him as impersonal a thing as the key is to the composer of a sonata. As a man Hardy may or may not be vitally concerned in the Welsh coal miner. That is quite unessential. But as a novelist, as an artist, his sufferings must be for him a matter of the mildest interest. They are important, for they constitute his keynote. They are *not* interesting for the reason that the working out of his *story*, its people, episodes, scenes and pictures, is for the moment the most interesting thing in all the world to him, exclusive of everything else. Do you think that Mrs. Stowe was more interested in the slave question than she was in the writing of *Uncle Tom's Cabin?* Her book, her manuscript, the page-to-page progress of the narrative, were more absorbing to her than all the Negroes that were ever whipped or sold. Had it not been so that great purpose-novel never would have succeeded.

Consider the reverse,—*Fécondité* for instance. The purpose for which Zola wrote the book ran away with him. He really did care more for the depopulation of France than he did for his novel. Result—sermons on the fruitfulness of women, special pleading, a farrago of dry, dull incidents, overburdened and collapsing under the weight of a theme that should have intruded only indirectly.

This is preëminently a selfish view of the question, but it is assuredly the only correct one. It must be remembered that the artist has a double personality, himself as a man, and himself as an artist. But, it will be urged, how account for the artist's sympathy in his fictitious characters, his emotion, the actual tears he sheds in telling of their griefs, their deaths, and the like?

The answer is obvious. As an artist his sensitivesness is quickened because they are characters in his novel. It does not at all follow that the same artist would be moved to tears over the report of parallel catastrophes in real life. As an artist, there is every reason to suppose he would welcome the news with downright pleasure. It would be for him "good material." He would see a story in it, a good scene, a great character. Thus the artist. What he would do, how he would feel as a man is quite a different matter.

To conclude, let us consider one objection urged against the novel with a purpose by the plain people who read. For certain reasons, difficult to explain, the purpose novel always ends unhappily. It is usually a record of suffering, a relation of tragedy. And the plain people say, "Ah, we see so much suffering in the world, why put it into novels? We do not want it in novels."

One confesses to very little patience with this sort. "We see so much suffering in the world already!" Do they? Is this really true? The people who buy novels are the well-to-do people. They belong to a class whose whole scheme of life is concerned solely with an aim to avoid the unpleasant. Suffering, the great catastrophes, the social throes, that annihilate whole communities, or that crush even isolated individuals—all these are as far removed from them as earthquakes and tidal waves. Or, even if it were so, suppose that by some miracle these blind eyes were opened and the sufferings of the poor, the tragedies of the house around the corner, really were laid bare. If there is much pain in life, all the more reason that it should appear in a class of literature which, in its highest form, is a sincere transcription of life.

It is the complaint of the coward, this cry against the novel with a purpose, because it brings the tragedies and griefs of others to notice. Take this element from fiction, take from it the power and opportunity to prove that injustice, crime and inequality do exist and what is left? Just the amusing novels, the novels that entertain. The juggler in spangles with his balancing pole and gilt ball does this. You may consider the modern novel from this point of view. It may be a flippant paper-covered thing of swords and cloaks, to be carried on a railway journey and to be thrown out the window when read, together with the sucked oranges and peanut shells. Or it may be a great force, that works together with the pulpit and the universities for the good of the people, fearlessly proving that power is abused, that the strong grind the faces of the weak, that an evil tree is still growing in the midst of the garden, that undoing follows hard upon unrighteousness, that the course of Empire is not yet finished, and that the races of men have yet to work out their destiny in those great and terrible movements that crush and grind and rend asunder the pillars of the houses of the nations.

Fiction may keep pace with the Great March, but it will not be by dint of amusing the people. The muse is a teacher not a trickster. Her rightful place is with the leaders, but in the last analysis that place is to be attained and maintained not by cap-and-bells but because of a serious and sincere interest, such as inspires the great teachers, the great divines, the great philosophers, a well-defined, well-seen, courageously sought-for purpose.

THE RESPONSIBILITIES OF THE NOVELIST[6]

It is not here a question of the "unarrived," the "unpublished"; these are the care-free irresponsibles whose hours are halcyon and whose endeavors have all the lure, all the recklessness of adventure. They are not recognized; they have made no standards for themselves, and if they play the *saltimbanque* and the charlatan nobody cares and nobody (except themselves) is affected.

But the writers in question are the successful ones who have made a public and to whom some ten, twenty or a hundred thousand people are pleased to listen. You may believe if you choose that the novelist of all workers is independent, that he can write what he pleases, and that certainly, certainly he should never "write down to his readers," that he should never consult them at all.

On the contrary, I believe it can be proved that the successful novelist should be more than all others limited in the nature and character of his work; more than all others he should be careful of what he says; more than all others he should defer to his audience; more than all others—more even than the minister and the editor—he should "feel his public" and watch his every word, testing carefully his every utterance, weighing with the most relentless precision his every statement; in a word, possess a sense of his responsibilities.

For the novel is the great expression of modern life. Each form of art has had its turn at reflecting and expressing its contemporaneous thought. Time was when the world looked to the architects of the castles and great cathedrals to truly reflect and embody its ideals. And the architects—serious, earnest men—produced such "expressions of contemporaneous thought" as the castle of Coucy and the church of Notre Dame. Then with other times came other customs, and the painters had their day. The men of the Renaissance trusted Angelo and da Vinci and Velásquez to speak for them, and trusted not in vain. Next came the age of the drama. Shakespeare and Marlowe found the value of *x* for the life and the times in which they lived. Later on contemporary life had been so modified that neither painting, architecture, nor drama was the best vehicle of expression, the day of the longer poems arrived, and Pope and Dryden spoke for their fellows.

Thus the sequence. Each age speaks with its own peculiar organ, and has left the Word for us moderns to read and understand. The castle of Coucy and the church of Notre Dame are the spoken words of the Middle Ages. The Renaissance speaks—and intelligibly—to us through the sibyls of the Sistine chapel and the "Mona Lisa." *Macbeth* and *Tamburlaine* ré-

[6] *Critic*, XLI (December, 1902), 537–540.

sumé the whole spirit of the Elizabethan age, while the "Rape of the Lock" is a wireless message to us straight from the period of the Restoration.

To-day is the day of the novel. In no other way and by no other vehicle is contemporaneous life so adequately expressed; and the critics of the twenty-second century, reviewing our times, striving to reconstruct our civilization, will look not to the painters, not to the architects nor dramatists, but to the novelists to find our idiosyncrasy.

I think this is true. I think if the matter could in any way be statisticized, the figures would bear out the assumption. There is no doubt the novel will in time "go out" of popular favor as irrevocably as the long poem has gone, and for the reason that it is no longer the right mode of expression.

It is interesting to speculate upon what will take its place. Certainly the coming civilization will revert to no former means of expressing its thought or its ideals. Possibly music will be the interpreter of the life of the twenty-first and twenty-second centuries. Possibly one may see a hint of this in the characterization of Wagner's operas as the "Music of the Future."

This, however, is parenthetical and beside the mark. Remains the fact that to-day is the day of the novel. By this one does not mean that the novel is merely popular. If the novel was not something more than a simple diversion, a means of whiling away a dull evening, a long railway journey, it would not, believe me, remain in favor another day.

If the novel then is popular it is popular with a reason, a vital inherent reason; that is to say, it is essential. Essential—to resume once more the proposition—because it expresses modern life better than architecture, better than painting, better than poetry, better than music. It is as necessary to the civilization of the twentieth century as the violin is necessary to Kubelik, as the piano is necessary to Paderewski, as the plane is necessary to the carpenter, the sledge to the blacksmith, the chisel to the mason. It is an instrument, a tool, a weapon, a vehicle. It is that thing which, in the hand of man, makes him civilized and no longer savage, because it gives him a power of durable, permanent expression. So much for the novel—the instrument.

Because it is so all-powerful to-day, the people turn to him who wields this instrument with every degree of confidence. They expect—and rightly—that results shall be commensurate with means. The unknown archer who grasps the bow of Ulysses may be expected by the multitude to send his shaft far and true. If he is not true nor strong he has no business with the bow. The people give heed to him only because he bears a great weapon. He himself knows before he shoots whether or no he is worthy.

It is all very well to jeer at the People and at the People's misunderstanding of the arts, but the fact is indisputable that no art that is not in the end understood by the People can live or ever did live a single generation. In the larger view, in the last analysis, the People pronounce the final judgment. The People, despised of the artist, hooted, caricatured, and vilified, are after all, and in the main, the real seekers after Truth. Who is it after all, whose interest is liveliest in any given work of art? It is not now a question of *aesthetic* interest; that is the artist's, the amateur's, the *cognoscente's*. It is a question of *vital* interest. Say what you will, Maggie Tulliver—for instance—is far more a living being for Mrs. Jones across the street than she is for your sensitive, fastidious, keenly critical artist, litterateur, or critic. The People—Mrs. Jones and her neighbours—take the life history of these fictitious characters, these novels, to heart with a seriousness that the aesthetic cult have no conception of. The cult consider them almost solely from their artistic sides. The People take them into their innermost lives. Nor do the People discriminate. Omnivorous readers as they are to-day, they make little distinction between Maggie Tulliver and the heroine of the last "popular novel." They do not stop to separate true from false, they do not care.

How necessary it becomes, then, for those who, by the simple act of writing, can invade the heart's heart of thousands, whose novels are received with such measureless earnestness—how necessary it becomes for those who wield such power to use it rightfully. Is it not expedient to act fairly? Is it not in Heaven's name essential that the People hear, not a lie, but Truth?

If the novel were not one of the most important factors of modern life, if it were not the completest expression of our civilization, if its influence were not greater than all the pulpits, than all the newspapers between the oceans, it would not be so important that its message should be true.

But the novelist to-day is the one who reaches the greatest audience. Right or wrong the People turn to him the moment he speaks, and what he says they believe.

For the million, Life is a contracted affair, is bounded by the walls of the narrow channel of affairs in which their feet are set. They have no horizon. They look to-day as they never have looked before, as they never will look again, to the writer of fiction to give them an idea of Life beyond their limits, and they believe him as they never have believed before and never will again.

This being so, is it not difficult to understand how certain of these successful writers of fiction—these favored ones into whose hands the gods have placed the great bow of Ulysses—can look so frivolously upon their craft? It is not necessary to specify. One speaks of those whose public is measured by "one hundred and fifty thousand copies sold." We know them, and because the gods have blessed us with wits beyond our deserving we know their work is false. But what of the "hundred and fifty thousand" who are not discerning and who receive this falseness as Truth, who believe this topsy-turvy picture of Life beyond their horizons is real and vital and sane?

There is no gauge to measure the extent of this malignant influence. Public opinion is made no one can say how, by infinitesimal accretions, by a multitude of minutest elements. Lying novels, surely, surely in this day and age of indiscriminate reading contribute to this more than all other influences of present-day activity.

The Pulpit, the Press and the Novel—these indisputably are the great moulders of Public opinion and Public morals to-day. But the Pulpit speaks but once a week; the Press is read with lightning haste and the morning news is wastepaper by noon. But the novel goes into the home to stay. It is read word for word, is talked about, discussed; its influence penetrates every chink and corner of the family.

Yet novelists are not found wanting who write for money. I do not think this is an unfounded accusation. I do not think it asking too much of credulity. This would not matter if they wrote the Truth. But these gentlemen who are "in literature for their own pocket every time" have discovered that for the moment the People have confounded the Wrong with the Right, and prefer that which is a lie, to that which is true. "Very well then," say these gentlemen. "If they want a lie they shall have it"; and they give the People a lie in return for royalties.

The surprising thing about this is that you and I and all the rest of us do not consider this as disreputable, do not yet realize that the novelist has responsibilities. We condemn an editor who sells his editorial columns, and we revile the Pulpit attainted of venality. But the venal novelist,—he whose influence is greater than either the Press or Pulpit,—*him* we greet with a wink and the tongue in the cheek.

This should not be so. Somewhere the protest should be raised, and those of us who see the practice of this fraud should bring home to ourselves the realization that the selling of one hundred and fifty thousand books is a serious business. The People have a right to the Truth as they have a right to life, liberty, and the pursuit of happiness. It is *not* right that they be exploited and deceived with false views of life, false characters, false sentiment, false morality, false history, false philosophy, false emotions, false heroism, false notions of self-sacrifice, false views of religion, of duty, of conduct, and of manners.

The man who can address an audience of one hundred and fifty thousand people who—unenlightened—*believe what he says* has a heavy duty to perform, and tremendous responsibilities to shoulder; and he should address himself to his task not with the flippancy of the catchpenny juggler at the county fair, but with earnestness, with soberness, with a sense of his limitations, and with all the abiding sincerity that by the favor and mercy of the gods may be his.

The Novelist as American

INTRODUCTION

In the following six essays Norris replies to the question inherent in his discussion of the sincere, responsible writer: If the American novelist is to deal with the vital realities of contemporary American life, what requirements and limitations are imposed upon him by the characteristics of American life? Norris' answer to this question was influenced both by the contemporary debate over the Great American Novel and by the quality of local-color fiction.

The demand for the Great American Novel was a manifestation of that pervasive nineteenth-century American critical nationalism which sought to stimulate works of literary greatness commensurate with our sense of national greatness.[1] The Great American Novel, by capturing the essence of the American spirit, would be such a work. Norris, however, argued that such a novel was possible only after a homogeneous national spirit had developed, and that America was still a nation of sections, each with its distinctive quality. He therefore joined in the critical position taken by such supporters of local color as Garland, Howells, and Eggleston. But despite this allegiance, Norris was dissatisfied with much local-color fiction. He believed that its overdependence upon detailed surface verisimilitude in matters of custom, dress, and accent resembled what he elsewhere called "accuracy." Rejecting, then, these extremes of the overgrandiose and the overdetailed, Norris asked for a balancing of the two by means of a regionalism in depth. The responsible American writer, he believed, should attempt to capture the "truth" of his area, its essence, its underlying distinctiveness, while still dealing with the particulars of the contemporary life of that area.[2]

Norris' own region, of course, was the West, and in his essays he pointed out that its permanent reality was the spirit of adventure and robust energy derived from the conquest of a vast new land. This immense act of conquest, the true epic material of American literature, had been neglected by American writers while it was occurring. But its spirit remained as the primary reality of western life, and was the distinctive quality which Norris believed the western writer should attempt to dramatize despite the surface similarities between the West and other areas.

Norris' conception of the West, however, can be fully understood only

[1] See Herbert R. Brown, "The Great American Novel," *American Literature,* VII (March, 1935), 1–14, and Benjamin T. Spencer, *The Quest for Nationality* (Syracuse: Syracuse University Press, 1957), pp. 328–331.

[2] Benjamin T. Spencer describes these three viewpoints—the national, local-color, and regional—in his "Nationality During the Interregnum (1892–1912)" (*American Literature,* XXXII [January, 1961], 434–445).

in relation to his belief that the conquest of the West was the most recent forward thrust of the "long march"—that is, that Germany, England, and America were basically similar in institutions and values because of their similar racial stock, and that the western United States was the latest victory of a restless, fighting people who had begun their journey in the swamps of Friesland. This theory, which American historians had adopted from German and English scholars, was the dominant interpretation of American life throughout the late nineteenth century.[3] It received its greatest support from Herbert B. Adams at Johns Hopkins, and from there spread to the history departments of most universities and to the widely read works of the popular historians. During the 1880's, for example, John Fiske constantly emphasized the Germanic origins of American institutions, while Theodore Roosevelt examined *The Winning of the West* as a triumph of Anglo-Saxon strength and courage, and as part "of a work that began with the conquest of Britain."[4] At the turn of the century American expansionism was often defended by combining the Anglo-Saxon idea of advance through struggle with a social application of the Darwinian struggle for existence.[5]

Norris had accepted Anglo-Saxon historicism early in his career.[6] As a confirmed evolutionist, he readily assented to the Teutonic historians' emphasis upon heredity and upon progress through conflict. Moreover, the racist possibilities of the theory—the Anglo-Saxons were strongest and therefore other races were inferior—were easily adaptable to the intense xenophobia of many Californians.[7] Most of all, Norris responded to the idea that national greatness was the product not of intellect or learning but of the primitive virtues of courage and strength.

[3] See Edward N. Saveth, "Race and Nationalism in American Historiography: The Late Nineteenth Century," *Political Science Quarterly*, LIV (September, 1939), 421–441, and Howard Mumford Jones, "The Arms of the Anglo-Saxons," *The Theory of American Literature* (Ithaca: Cornell University Press, 1948), pp. 79–117.

[4] Theodore Roosevelt, *The Winning of the West* (New York: G. P. Putnam's Sons, 1889), I, 30.

[5] For a study of the relationship between Darwinism, racism, and imperialism, see Richard Hofstadter, *Social Darwinism in American Thought* (New York: George Braziller, 1959), pp. 170–200. Josiah Strong's *Our Country* (New York: The Baker & Taylor Company, 1885), pp. 159–180, contains a popular contemporary amalgam of these movements.

[6] He probably encountered Teutonic ideas in his history courses at Berkeley, if not during his first two years, then almost certainly during his last two, when he took courses from Bernard Moses, chairman of the department. (History was one of his favorite subjects; he had seven courses in the subject while at California.) Moses, who had received his Ph.D. at Heidelberg, supported American expansionism and later served on the Philippine Commission. For a characteristic statement of the "long march" idea, see Moses' "Data of Mexican and United States History," *Papers of the California Historical Society*, I (1887), 17. Norris may also have encountered Anglo-Saxon ideas in the *Argonaut* and the *Overland Monthly*, two San Francisco magazines which were militantly racist and to which he contributed.

[7] See John Higham, "The American Party, 1886–1891," *Pacific Historical Review*, XIX (February, 1950), 37–46.

Both racism and praise of pugnacious strength—two applications of Anglo-Saxon historicism—appear in Norris' early work. Maria Macapa and Zerkow, in *McTeague*, are aspects of the first, while the second produced the following defense in the *Wave* of class rushes at Berkeley:

Fighting is a good thing. We Anglo-Saxons are a fighting race; have fought our way from the Swamps of Holland to the shore of the Pacific Coast at the expense of worse things than smashed faces and twisted knees. Civilization is far from that time when the fighting man can be dispensed with. The strongest nations of today are the fighting nations. . . .[8]

A number of his early stories also firmly endorse the Anglo-Saxon chauvinism of Richard Harding Davis and Kipling. They present a young San Francisco Anglo-Saxon "thoroughbred" who successfully demonstrates the racial virtues of strength and courage against drunken Irish hooligans (they are desecrating the flag!) and treacherous Chinese thugs.[9]

In his discussions of western literature, therefore, Norris stressed the Anglo-Saxon qualities of western life. In addition, *The Octopus* is both a sermon on western literary regionalism and an example of it. The sermon exists in the character of Presley, a sincere writer, but one whose over-literary background prevents him from seeing that the conflict between the railroad and the ranchers is a modern, western approximation of a Homeric struggle, and could serve as the basis for an epic work. Presley in this respect is a kind of anti-Norris; unlike Norris, he fails to perceive the romance beneath the commonplaces of modern life. Moreover, though Norris attempted in *The Octopus* to strike what he called the "world-note," he combined with his large social themes much regional "romance" in which his Anglo-Saxon ideas are prominent. They are present, for example, in the rabbit drive, where the "degenerate" Mexicans commit the final slaughter, while the Anglo-Saxons, who love a good but fair fight, hold back. They appear in Cedarquist's plan to ship wheat to Asia because " 'the Anglo-Saxon started from there at the beginning of everything and it's manifest destiny that he must circle the globe and fetch up where he began'."[10] Most of all, they play a major role in the characterization of Magnus Derrick, who illustrates Norris' thesis that if you scratch a western farmer or businessman you will find an Anglo-Saxon forty-niner. Magnus is adventurer in the guise of farmer. He struggles to possess all he can as quickly as he can, and he is ready to take chances or to fight. He is also, however, the easy victim of "modern" subterfuge and treachery.

8 "Ethics of the Freshman Rush," *Wave*, XVI (September 4, 1897), 2.

9 "A Defense of the Flag," *Argonaut*, XXXVII (October 28, 1895), 4, and "Outward and Visible Signs. V. Thoroughbred," *Overland Monthly*, 2nd Ser., XXV (February, 1895), 196–201.

10 *The Complete Edition of Frank Norris* (Garden City, New York: Doubleday, Doran & Company, 1928), II, 356.

He is very much like Grettir, the outlaw Icelandic folk hero whom Norris dealt with in several stories of this period. Both are heroic fighters who have conquered by boldness and force but who are defeated by treachery.[11]

Although Norris' Anglo-Saxon ideas persisted, they were not static. Rather, they underwent the same social orientation of much of his thought. By 1901–1902, for example, he no longer expressed his earlier sheer delight in "that fine, reckless arrogance, that splendid, brutal, bullying spirit that is the Anglo-Saxon's birthright."[12] The true hero of the West, he now believes, is the Anglo-Saxon fighter as law-bringer and peacemaker, as hero of law and order. In this description, Norris anticipates Owen Wister's *The Virginian* (1902) and much of the myth of the lawman as he appears in the modern "western."[13] Moreover, Norris adopts in his later criticism the American middle-class version of Anglo-Saxonism, as he substitutes trade competition for war and emphasizes the world-wide benefits of this rivalry. Lastly, Norris combined with the "long march" theme the idea that increased social complexity produces a widening social allegiance, from the family, to clan, to city, to nation, and—in the future —to humanity at large. Since the "long march" and this growth in social interdependence occurred simultaneously, Norris implies that the first has caused the second. He thus finds a moral justification for Anglo-Saxonism because its goal is human brotherhood. So the annexation of the Philippines or the sending of troops to Peking are but steps toward that goal.

Norris, in other words, like many late nineteenth-century figures who found the Anglo-Saxon theory useful or emotionally appealing, also had to placate a Christian conscience. Some achieved this appeasement by relying upon the white man's burden of increased world prosperity, others by stressing that the brotherhood or man was the ultimate product of conquest. But whether the attempt to reconcile Anglo-Saxon and Christian ethics was hypocritical or not (and Norris' was honest), the attempt was essentially part of a larger need to reconcile the values of traditional humanism with popular beliefs about Darwinism. Although Norris evades the problem by placing its solution in the future—meanwhile, by all means let us keep the Philippines—his response is little different from the generic evasion of the age: that strife was still the present mode of progress, though man was advancing toward love.[14]

---

[11] Norris explicitly associated Grettir with the western adventurer in his "The Literature of the West," p. 107 below.

[12] "Ethics of the Freshman Rush," *Wave*, XVI (September 4, 1897), 2.

[13] Norris first described the western hero as law-bringer in his "Literature of the West" (*Boston Evening Transcript*, January 8, 1902) some months before the publication of *The Virginian*. However, his fullest presentation of the idea occurs in "A Neglected Epic," which was published after he read *The Virginian*. (Jeannette Norris recalled his reading the novel, FWC.)

[14] This was essentially the widely accepted position of both Herbert Spencer and his

Norris' Anglo-Saxonism also illustrates, in conjunction with his ideas on the responsibilities of the novelist, that a primitivistic ethic can lead to contradictory social beliefs. On the one hand, a writer's affirmation of the "natural" and instinctive is often complemented, as I have suggested, by his sense of involvement in the quest for social justice. This interaction between primitivism and social commitment occurs in Norris' idea of the sincere, responsible writer and in the fiction of a Steinbeck or a Faulkner. On the other hand, a writer's obsession with the "natural" and instinctive may reflect his social alienation, the possibility of which exists in Norris' "fine, reckless arrogance," and which actually occurs in the later work of D. H. Lawrence. Norris' ideas contain both potentials.[15] It is a sign of his growing maturity that in his later work he either replaces his earlier militant Anglo-Saxonism with a call for responsibility or at least provides for it socially beneficial goals.

In all, Norris' conception of the writer as American has major strengths and flaws. His discussions of his own region are often fuzzy and contradictory. For example, his idea of the West tries to combine two irreconcilable theories. First, he seems to be a follower of Frederick Jackson Turner's thesis that the frontier is the unique American experience and is responsible for our distinctively American characteristics. Thus, the American western hero to Norris is a unique type. But he is also a follower of the Teutonic school and its belief that the West is a continuation of the "long march," and that the Westerner is basically an Anglo-Saxon, little different from his Friesland forefathers. Thus, the American West could have produced epic heroes and an epic literature similar to those of other nations. In addition, Norris is inconsistent in his beliefs concerning the possibility of an epic literature in America. At one point he argues that we never went through a primitive stage, and therefore could not have produced a genuine epic. At another point, we are berated for neglecting our genuine epic material, the conquest of the West.

Norris' conception of American regionalism in general, however, is significant and revelatory. He calls for American local color to come of age—the American writer should ignore the chimera of the Great American Novel, but should not fall victim to a fiction of surface local eccentricities and details. He is therefore one of our first writers to describe and practice local color in a way which distinguishes between the short-story miniatures of the late nineteenth century and the important work of our modern regionalists.

American disciple John Fiske. (Fiske was, interestingly enough, an avowed expansionist. His 1885 essay on "Manifest Destiny" was one of the period's most popular restatements of that idea.) T. H. Huxley's refusal to accept this solution, in his 1893 Romanes Lecture, dramatizes and clarifies the uneasy nature of the attempt.

[15] Richard Chase makes this point, though in another context, in his *The American Novel and Its Tradition* (Garden City, New York: Doubleday & Company, 1957), p. 198.

"THE LITERATURE OF THE WEST": A REPLY TO W. R. LIGHTON[16]

In the issue of the *Transcript* dated Dec. 28 Mr. William R. Lighton publishes an article under the title, "The Literature of the West." The contribution is important, the matter is carefully arranged and the points ingeniously brought out. Furthermore, Mr. Lighton writes from certain knowledge, and in this field is "one having authority."[17]

One can but applaud his serious protest against the "red shirt" literature of Western life, his deprecation of the sensationalism that has been foisted upon the country and the conditions that prevail west of the Mississippi; but at the same time it may be permitted to take issue with some of his statements and to deny some of his conclusions.

In the first place, Mr. Lighton says: "The literature of the West has been only the literature of the mining camp and the cowboy." He deprecates this; he exclaims, "Will they (the people) never get enough of the Buffalo Bill style of entertainment, and think to ask how the West is really living?" and he calls for a saner, soberer literature, one that shall ignore the desperado, the cow puncher, the prospector and miner. He pleads for the fiction that shall picture the West as a quiet, well-ordered country wherein the people are peaceful, tranquil, rational and contented. He claims that the wild life is no longer the true life of the West.

But the West is yet in the transitional period. There was a time when the wild life was the only life. There will come a time when the quiet life will be the only life. But as yet the West is midway of the two extremes. It is true that the West is a place of banks, of schools, of policemen and law courts, but it is equally true that as yet the Desert is a tremendous immovable fact, that the Apache and the Sioux are just where they were when we found them seventy years ago, and that the expression of personal physical courage is more often and to a greater degree called upon in Arizona, Montana, Idaho, New Mexico and Nevada than anywhere else in the United States.

Understand the distinction; we are quite ready to relegate the red shirt fellow with his stock lingo, his make-up, his swagger and his gallery plays, to the lumber room and the county jail. We are done with him. He was a characteristic once, but now he is only a very bad actor who dresses the part according to the illustrated weeklies, and who, *pour épater les bour-*

---

[16] *Boston Evening Transcript*, January 8, 1902, p. 7.

[17] William R. Lighton (1866–1923), a Kansas lawyer, was the author of *Sons of Strength, A Romance of the Kansas Border Wars* (1899) and *Lewis and Clark* (1901). Norris' defense of an "adventurous" western fiction was a defense not only of *The Octopus* but also of many of his short stories of 1901–1902. Several of these stories, for example, deal with "The Three Black Crows," a group of adventurers working out of San Francisco.

geois, wears "chaps" on the plains. We distinctly do not want him to speak of his local habitation as "These 'ere diggin's," or to address us as "pard," or to speak of death as the passing in of checks, or the kicking of the bucket. He would not be true to Western life.

But because of this, are we ready to accept as typical of our Far West the prosaic farming folk of Iowa or the city-bred gentleman of the office buildings of Denver or San Francisco, who pays his pew-rent regularly and who has never been out of whistling distance of a police officer? These would not be true to Western life. They exist, no question or doubt about it; so does the red-shirt man, but neither is characteristic.

Let us even concede Mr. Lighton's point that today in the West the undramatic, the unadventurous is oftenest to be met with, is in fact almost universal. That this is so is urged by Mr. Lighton as a reason for a calm, uneventful, sober-hued fiction. He says it is a true reflex of conditions.

It would seem so upon first consideration. But in the fictitious presentation of an epoch of a people, the writer must search for the idiosyncrasy, the characteristic, that thing, that feature, element or person that distinguishes the times or place treated of from all other times and all other places. He must address himself to the task of picturing the peculiarity, the specialized product of conditions that obtain in that locality and nowhere else. Thus if one were telling a story of a Southern plantation one would not choose as the main feature of the narrative a pirate captain of the Caribbean, but rather the typical planter. If the story were of Wall Street it would be inappropriate to introduce as chief actor a Maine Yankee.

One must observe the typical. It is all very well for Mr. Lighton to urge that the peaceable citizens, the city-bred men of the Denver office blocks, are in overwhelming majority to the cowboys, the miners, and frontiersmen. They are not typical of the West; the West did not produce them. They are in no way different from the peace loving, law-abiding citizens of New York or Chicago. Not so very different from the same class of man the world over.

New York produced the financier, Maine the trader, the South the planter, Boston the litterateur, Chicago the business man, but the product of the West from the very first and up to this very hour of writing has always been, through every varying condition, occupation or calling, the adventurer. You cannot get away from him. Long since he has put off the red shirt, he has even abandoned his revolver. Meet him and for all you would know he is a man of sober mind, decorous even, the kind to whom you would suppose adventures never came. A man who very possibly drinks little, who gambles less, who wears the bowler hat and pressed trousers of convention.

But scratch the surface ever so little and behold—there is the Forty-niner. There just beneath the veneer is the tough fibre of the breed, whose work since the beginning of the nineteenth century has been the subjugating of the West.

In all history I do believe there is no more splendid achievement than this conquering of the wilderness that began with Lewis and Clark and that—all asseveration to the contrary notwithstanding—still is going on. In years—centuries—to come, perhaps, these men, this epoch, this phase of our civilization will receive a just and adequate appreciation. The work these men have done—are yet doing—is nothing short of colossal. We who see it so continually, who are so close to the canvas are all too apt to underrate it. Remember that only sixty years ago this Western country was an unfenced wilderness, as untamed as the Arctic, unknown, unknowable, a region of terrors.

Other nations, other peoples, have put century after century to the reclaiming and subduing of their hinterlands. Some take as long as that to build one single cathedral. A scattering advance line of hard-grained, hard-riding, hard-working fellows, Anglo-Saxons, Americans, dash into this country, with its gigantic sweep of deserts, its inhospitable sands, its forbidding mountains, and in less than a generation have all but civilized it.

Then when the deserts are crossed by railroads, when the sands are irrigated, when the mountains are mined, the cañons bridged, and the Indian driven off, when in fact, the country is rendered habitable, along comes the quiet unadventurous farmer and city-bred fellow to settle in the policed and protected country. And it is these men, cast in a mould as common as the lamppost on the corner, that Mr. Lighton would put forward as the typical, distinctive Westerner.

Mr. Lighton permits himself a prophecy. He looks forward to a writer who shall "offer to the world a Western book that shall come from and relate to the prairies and their people, for that is where the vital life of the West is throbbing. These are the men and women who are to shape Western destiny. It is in the mountains," he continues, "that Western men are doing the theatrical things, keeping up the fire and fury of morbid overwrought excitement, fancying themselves thrilled with deep purposes, yet at the bottom irreclaimably narrow."

I do not believe the story of the West, the epic of this wonder work of the nineteenth century, will confine itself to any one section. I do not believe that a chronicle of uneventful, unperturbed life will truly present the character of the region. No doubt there is beauty, poetry even to be found, just as Mr. Lighton claims, in the dull, prosaic farm labor of the prairies. No doubt there are thousands upon thousands of people beyond the Missouri who lead uneventful, unperturbed lives. No doubt of it. Equally there is no doubt that simultaneously with the siege of Troy there was to be found in vast tracts of the old Greek world a quiet, beautiful bucolic life. No doubt there were thousands of people who never saw a spear hurled, except at the games. But the expression of the general life of that time, its idiosyncrasy, is not to be found in bucolic verse, or unadventurous chronicle, but in Homer's *Iliad*, an epic of strife, of conquest.

Exactly the same conditions prevailed within the past half century in the West as prevailed in Trojan times. It was the beginning of an epoch, the dawn of a new civilization, and the man of deeds, the man of action, the adventurer, the pioneer, was the great figure, the true figure.

Hector, however, had his Homer, Roland, Siegfried and Robin Hood had their poets, but the conquerors of the West have gone to their graves unsung, save in the traducing, falsifying dime-novels which have succeeded only in discrediting our one great chance for distinctive American literature. We had the material, Homer found no better, the heroes, the great fights, the play of unleashed, unfettered passionate humanity, and we let it all go, this national epic of America, the only one we shall ever have, to the wretched "Deadwood Dicks" and Buffalo Bills of the yellow backs, while we niggled and pottered and puddled about with a faked, half-baked imported semi-English school whose followers went to Florence and Rome for their backgrounds or to ante-revolutionary days for their characters, or who lied and tricked and strutted in Pathfinder and Leather-Stocking series.

We would not see it while it was working out its tremendous battle at our very doors, and now when the great fight is almost over—when even yet there may be a chance to note the passing phase by actual vision, and to speak first hand—now already there are many like Mr. Lighton who would have us forget our fighters and be ashamed of them as "sensational swashbucklers," putting forward instead the second generation, who, undisturbed, have sunk to the level of the commonplace, claiming that these are the true Westerners.

Mr. Lighton is justified in a prophecy. The Epic of the West will some day, in years to come, be written, but it will not confine itself to the prairie country, it will not deal with the present-day farmer of Iowa, nor the present-day merchant of Denver or San Francisco. It will be a universal theme that shall sing of no one locality but of the huge conglomerate West; and the true knight of the song shall be the fighter, rescued from the hands of the blackmailers and liars and set in his true place at last, dignified, heroic, indomitable, blood brother to Roland and Grettir the Strong, the one distinctive and romantic figure of American life.

AN AMERICAN SCHOOL OF FICTION? A DENIAL[18]

It seems to me that it is a proposition not difficult of demonstration that the United States of America has never been able to boast of a school of fiction distinctively its own. And this is all the more singular when one considers that in all other activities Americans are peculiarly independent in thought and in deed, and have acquired, abroad, a reputation—even a notoriety—for being original.

In the mechanical arts, in the industries, in politics, in business methods, in diplomacy, in ship-building, in war, even in dentistry, if you please —even in the matter of riding race horses—Americans have evolved their own methods, quite different from European methods.

Hardy and adventurous enough upon all other lines, disdainful of conventions, contemptuous of ancient custom, we yet lag behind in the arts— slow to venture from the path blazed long ago by Old World masters.

It is preëminently so in the fine arts. No sooner does an American resolve upon a career of painting, sculpture or architecture than straight he departs for Paris, the Beaux-Arts and the Julian atelier; and, his education finished, returns to propagate French ideas; French methods; and our best paintings today are more French than American; French in conception, in composition, in technique and treatment.

I suppose that the nearest we ever came to an organized school of native-born Americans, writing about American things from an American point of view, was in the days of Lowell, Longfellow, Holmes, Whittier and the rest of that illustrious company. But observe: How is this group spoken of and known to literature? Not as the American school, but as the New England school. Even the appellation "New" England as differentiated from "old" England is significant. And New England is not America.

Hawthorne, it will be urged, is a great name among American writers of fiction. Not peculiarly American, however. Not so distinctively and unequivocally as to lay claim to a vigorous original Americanism. *The Scarlet Letter* is not an American story, but rather a story of an English colony on North American soil. *The Marble Faun* is frankly and unreservedly foreign. Even the other novels were pictures of a very limited and circumscribed life—the life of New England again.

Cooper, you will say, was certainly American in attitude and choice of subject; none more so. None less, none less American. As a novelist he is saturated with the romance of the contemporary English story tellers. It is true that his background is American. But his heroes and heroines talk like the characters out of Bulwer in their most vehement moods, while his Indians stalk through all the melodramatic tableaux of Byron, and de-

[18] *Boston Evening Transcript*, January 22, 1902, p. 17.

claim in the periods of the border noblemen in the pages of Walter Scott.

Poe we may leave out of classification; he shone in every branch of literature but that of novel-writing. Bret Harte was a writer of short stories and—oh, the pity of it, the folly of it!—abandoned the field with hardly more than a mere surface-scratching.

There can be no doubt that had Mr. Henry James remained in America he would have been our very best writer. If he has been able to seize the character and characteristics so forcibly of a people like the English, foreign to him, different, unfamiliar, what might he not have done in the very midst of his own countrymen, into whose company he was born, reared and educated. All the finish of style, the marvelous felicity of expression would still have been his and at the same time, by the very nature of the life he lived and wrote about, the concrete, the vigorous, the simple direct action would have become a part of his work, instead of the present ultimate vagueness and indecision that so mars and retards it.

Of all the larger names remain only those of Mr. Howells and Mr. Clemens. But as the novelists, as such, are under consideration, even Mark Twain may be left out of the discussion. American to the core, posterity will yet know him not as a novel writer, but as a humorist. Mr. Howells alone is left then, after the elimination is complete. Of all producers of American fiction he has had the broadest vision, at once a New Englander and a New Yorker, an Easterner and—in the Eastern sense—a Westerner. But one swallow does not make a summer, nor does one writer constitute a "school." Mr. Howells has had no successors. Instead, just as we had with *Lapham* and the *Modern Instance* laid the foundation of fine, hardy literature, that promised to be our very, very own, we commence to build upon it a whole confused congeries of borrowed, faked, pilfered romanticisms, building a crumbling gothic into a masonry of honest brown stone, or foisting colonial porticos upon façades of Montpelier granite, and I cannot allow this occasion to pass without protest against what I am sure every serious minded reader must consider a lamentable discrowning.

Of the latter-day fiction writers Miss Wilkins had more than all others convinced her public of her sincerity. Her field was her own, the place was ceded to her. No other novelist could invade her domain and escape the censure that attaches to imitation. Her public was loyal to her, because it believed in her, and it was a foregone conclusion that she would be loyal to it.

More than this: A writer who occupies so eminent a place as Miss Wilkins, who has become so important, who has exerted and still can exert so strong an influence, cannot escape the responsibilities of her position. She cannot belong wholly to herself, cannot be wholly independent. She owes a duty to the literature of her native country.

Yet in spite of all this, and in spite of the fact that those who believe in the future of our nation's letters look to such established reputations as hers to keep the faith, to protest, though it is only by their attitude, silently and with dignity, against corruptions, degradations; in spite of all this and in the hey-day of her power, Miss Wilkins chooses to succumb to the momentary, transitory set of the tide, and forsaking her own particular work, puts forth, one of a hundred others, a "Colonial Romance."[19] It is a discrowning. It can be considered as no less. A deliberate capitulation to the clamor of the multitude. Possibly the novelist was sincere, but it is perilously improbable that she would have written her "Colonial Romance" had not "colonial romances" been the fashion. On the face of it Miss Wilkins has laid herself open to a suspicion of disingenuousness that every honest critic can only deplore. Even with all the sincerity in the world she had not the right to imperil the faith of her public, to undermine its confidence in her. She was one of the leaders. It is as if a captain —during action—had deserted to the enemy.

It could not have been even for the baser consideration of money. With her success assured in advance Miss Wilkins can be above such influences. Nor of fame. Surely no great distinction centres upon writers of "colonial romances" of late. Only the author herself may know her motives, but we who looked to her to keep the standard firm—and high—have now to regret the misfortune of a leader lost, a cause weakened.

However, it is a question after all if a "school," understood in the European sense of the word, is possible for America just yet. France has had its schools of romance and naturalism. Russia its schools of realism, England its schools of psychologists. But France, Russia and England now, after so many centuries of growth, may be considered as units. Certain tendencies influence each one over its whole geographical extent at the same time. Its peoples have been welded together to a certain homogeneousness. It is under such conditions that "schools" of fiction, of philosophy, of science and the like arise.

But the United States are not yet, in this European sense, united. We have existed as a nation hardly more than a generation and during that time our peoples have increased largely by emigration. From all over the globe different races have been pouring in upon us. The North has been settled under one system, the South under another, the Middle West under another, the East under another. South Central and Far West under still others. There is no homogeneousness among us as yet. The Westerner thinks along different lines from the Easterner and arrives at different conclusions. What is true of California is false of New York. Mr. Cable's picture of life is a far different thing than that of Mr. Howells.

---

[19] Mary E. Wilkins, *The Heart's Highway: A Romance of Virginia in the Seventeenth Century* (1900). Sarah Orne Jewett, another distinguished New England local color writer, had also "succumbed" with *The Tory Lover* (1901).

The "school" implies a rallying of many elements under one standard. But no such thing is possible today for American writers. Mr. Hamlin Garland could not merge his personality nor pool his ideals with Edith Wharton. Their conceptions of art are as different as the conditions of life they study in their books.

The school of fiction American in thought, in purpose and in treatment will come in time—inevitably. Meanwhile the best we can expect of the leaders is to remain steadfast, to keep unequivocably to the metes and bounds of the vineyards of their labors; no trespassing, no borrowing, no filching of the grapes of another man's vines. The cultivation of one's own vine is quite sufficient for all energy. We want these vines to grow— in time—to take root deep in American soil so that by and by the fruit shall be all of our own growing.

We do not want—distinctly and vehemently we do not want the vine-grower to leave his own grapes to rot while he flies off to the gathering of—what? The sodden lees of an ancient crushing.

THE FRONTIER GONE AT LAST[20]

Suddenly we have found that there is no longer any Frontier. Until the day when the first United States marine landed in China we had always imagined that out yonder somewhere in the West was the borderland where civilization disintegrated and merged into the untamed.[21] Our skirmish-line was there, our posts that scouted and scrimmaged with the wilderness, a thousand miles in advance of the steady march of civilization.

And the Frontier has become so much an integral part of our conception of things that it will be long before we shall all understand that it is gone. We liked the Frontier; it was romance, the place of the poetry of the Great March, the firing-line where there was action and fighting, and where men held each other's lives in the crook of the forefinger. Those who had gone out came back with tremendous tales, and those that stayed behind made up other and even more tremendous tales.

When we—we Anglo-Saxons—busked ourselves for the first stage of the march, we began from that little historic reach of ground in the midst of the Friesland swamps, and we set our faces Westward, feeling no doubt the push of the Slav behind us. Then the Frontier was Britain and the sober peacefulness of land where are the ordered, cultivated English farm-yards of today was the Wild West of the Frisians of that century; and for the little children of the Frisian peat cottages, Hengist was the Apache

[20] *World's Work*, III (February, 1902), 1728–31.
[21] Norris refers here (and on p. 112 below) to the Boxer rebellion of mid-1900, which had led the United States to send a detachment of marines to China for the relief of our Peking legation.

Kid and Horsa Deadwood Dick—freebooters, law-defiers, slayers-of-men, epic heroes, blood brothers if you please to Boone and Bowie.

Then for centuries we halted and the van closed up with the firing-line, and we filled all England and all Europe with our clamor because for a while we seemed to have gone as far Westward as it was possible; and the checked energy of the race reacted upon itself, rebounded as it were, and back we went to the Eastward again—crusading, girding at the Mahommedan, conquering his cities, breaking into his fortresses with mangonel, siege engine and catapult—just as the boy shut indoors finds his scope circumscribed and fills the whole place with the racket of his activity.

But always, if you will recall it, we had a curious feeling that we had not reached the ultimate West even yet, and there was still a Frontier. Always that strange sixth sense turned our heads toward the sunset; and all through the Middle Ages we were peeking and prying at the Western horizon, trying to reach it, to run it down, and the queer tales about Vineland and that storm-driven Viking's ship would not down.

And then at last a naked savage on the shores of a little island in what is now our West Indies, looking Eastward one morning, saw the caravels, and on that day the Frontier was rediscovered, and promptly a hundred thousand of the more hardy rushed to the skirmish-line and went at the Wilderness as only the Anglo-Saxon can.

And then the skirmish-line decided that it would declare itself independent of the main army behind and form an advance column of its own, a separate army corps, and no sooner was this done than again the scouts went forward, went Westward, pushing the Frontier ahead of them, scrimmaging with the wilderness, blazing the way. At last they forced the Frontier over the Sierra Nevadas down to the edge of the Pacific. And here it would have been supposed that the Great March would have halted again as it did before the Atlantic, that here at last the Frontier ended.

But on the first of May, eighteen hundred and ninety-eight, a gun was fired in the Bay of Manila, still further Westward, and in response the skirmish-line crossed the Pacific, still pushing the Frontier before it. Then came a cry for help from Legation Street in Peking and as the first boat bearing its contingent of American marines took ground on the Asian shore, the Frontier—at last after so many centuries, after so many marches, after so much fighting, so much spilled blood, so much spent treasure, dwindled down and vanished; for the Anglo-Saxon in his course of empire had circled the globe and brought the new civilization to the old civilization, had reached the starting point of history, the place from which the migrations began. So soon as the marines landed there was no longer any West, and the equation of the horizon, the problem of the centuries for the Anglo-Saxon was solved.

So, lament it though we may, the Frontier is gone, an idiosyncrasy that has been with us for thousands of years, the one peculiar picturesqueness of our life is no more. We may keep alive for many years yet the idea of a Wild West, but the hired cowboys and paid rough riders of Mr. William Cody are more like "the real thing" than can be found today in Arizona, New Mexico or Idaho. Only the imitation cowboys, the college-bred fellows who "go out on a ranch" carry the revolver or wear the poncho. The Frontier has become conscious of itself, acts the part for the Eastern visitor; and this self-consciousness is a sign, surer than all others, of the decadence of a type, the passing of an epoch. The Apache Kid and Deadwood Dick have gone to join Hengist and Horsa and the heroes of the *Magnusson Saga*.

But observe. What happened in the Middle Ages when for awhile we could find no Western Frontier? The race impulse was irresistible. March we must, conquer we must, and checked in the Westward course of empire we turned Eastward and expended the resistless energy that by blood was ours in conquering the Old World behind us.

Today we are the same race, with the same impulse, the same power and, because there is no longer a Frontier to absorb our overplus of energy, because there is no longer a wilderness to conquer and because we still must march, still must conquer, we remember the old days when our ancestors before us found the outlet for their activity checked and, rebounding, turned their faces Eastward, and went down to invade the Old World. So we. No sooner have we found that our path to the Westward has ended than, reacting Eastward, we are at the Old World again, marching against it, invading it, devoting our overplus of energy to its subjugation.

But though we are the same race, with the same impulses, the same blood-instincts as the old Frisian marsh people, we are now come into a changed time and the great word of our century is no longer War but Trade.

Or if you choose it is only a different word for the same race-characteristic. The desire for conquest—say what you will—was as big in the breast of the most fervid of the Crusaders as it is this very day in the most peacefully-disposed of American manufacturers. Had the Lion-Hearted Richard lived today he would have become a "leading representative of the Amalgamated Steel Companies," and doubt not for one moment that he would have underbid his Manchester rivals in the matter of bridge girders. Had Mr. Andrew Carnegie been alive at the time of the preachings of Peter the Hermit he would have raised a company of *gens d'armes* sooner than all of his brothers-in-arms, would have equipped his men better and more effectively, would have been first on the ground before Jerusalem, would have built the most ingenious siege engine and have hurled the first cask of Greek-fire over the walls.

Competition and conquest are words easily interchangeable, and the whole spirit of our present commercial crusade to the Eastward betrays itself in the fact that we cannot speak of it but in terms borrowed from the glossary of the warrior. It is a commercial "invasion," a trade "war," a "threatened attack" on the part of America; business is "captured," opportunities are "seized," certain industries are "killed," certain former monopolies are "wrested away." Seven hundred years ago a certain Count Baldwin, a great leader in the attack of the Anglo-Saxon Crusaders upon the Old World, built himself a siege engine which would help him enter the beleaguered city of Jerusalem. Jerusalem is beleaguered again today, and the hosts of the Anglo-Saxon commercial crusaders are knocking at the gates. And now a company named for another Baldwin—and for all we know a descendant of the count—leaders of the invaders of the Old World, advance upon the city, and, to help in the assault, build an engine —only now the engine is no longer called a mangonel, but a locomotive.[22]

The difference is hardly of kind and scarcely of degree. It is a mere matter of names, and the ghost of Saladin watching the present engagement might easily fancy the old days back again.

So perhaps we have not lost the Frontier, after all. A new phrase, reversing that of Berkeley's, is appropriate to the effect that "Eastward the course of commerce takes its way," and we must look for the lost battle-line not toward the sunset, but toward the East. And so rapid has been the retrograde movement that we must go far to find it, that scattered firing-line, where the little skirmishes are heralding the approach of the Great March. We must already go further afield than England. The main body, even to the reserves, are intrenched there long since, and even continental Europe is to the rear of the skirmishers.

Along about Suez we begin to catch up with them where they are deepening the great canal, and we can assure ourselves that we are fairly abreast of the most distant line of scouts only when we come to Khiva, to Samarcand, to Bokhara and the Trans-Baikal country.

Just now one hears much of the "American commercial invasion of England."[23] But adjust the field glasses and look beyond Britain and search for the blaze that the scouts have left on the telegraph poles and mile posts of Hungary, Turkey, Turkey in Asia, Persia, Baluchistan, India

---

[22] Baldwin of Edessa, later King of Jerusalem, was a leader in the first crusade and the fall of Jerusalem (1099). Matthias W. Baldwin (1795–1866) founded the great Baldwin Locomotive Company of Philadelphia.

[23] A frequent magazine topic during 1900–1901. See, for example, B. Waldron, "Europe's Peril from Yankeeism," *Chautauquan*, XXXIV (October, 1901), 21–26, and Paul S. Reinsch, "New Conquest of the World," *World's Work*, I (February, 1901), 425–431.

and Siam. You'll find the blaze distinct and the road, though rough hewn, is easy to follow. Prophecy and presumption be far from us, but it would be against all precedent that the Grand March should rest forever upon its arms and its laurels along the Thames, the Mersey and the Clyde, while its pioneers and Frontiersmen are making roads for it to the Eastward.

Is it too huge a conception, too inordinate an idea to say that the American conquest of England is but an incident of the Greater Invasion, an affair of outposts preparatory to the real manoeuver that shall embrace Europe, Asia, the whole of the Old World? Why not? And the blaze is ahead of us, and every now and then from far off there in the countries that are under the rising sun we catch the faint sounds of the skirmishing of our outposts. One of two things invariably happens under such circumstances as these: either the outposts fall back upon the main body or the main body moves up to the support of its outposts. One does not think that the outposts will fall back.

And so goes the great movement, Westward, then Eastward, forward and then back. The motion of the natural forces, the elemental energies, somehow appear to be thus alternative—action first, then reaction. The tides ebb and flow again, the seasons have their slow vibrations, touching extremes at periodic intervals. Not impossibly, in the larger view, is the analogy applicable to the movements of the races. First Westward with the great migrations, now Eastward with the course of commerce, moving in a colossal arc measured only by the hemispheres, as though upon the equator a giant dial hand oscillated, in gradual divisions through the centuries, now marking off the Westward progress, now traveling proportionately to the reaction toward the East.

Races must follow their destiny blindly, but is it not possible that we can find in this great destiny of ours something a little better than mere battle and conquest, something a little more generous than mere trading and underbidding? Inevitably with constant change of environment comes the larger view, the more tolerant spirit, and every race movement, from the first step beyond the Friesland swamp to the adjustment of the first American theodolite on the Himalayan watershed, is an unconscious lesson in patriotism. Just now we cannot get beyond the self-laudatory mood, but is it not possible to hope that, as the progress develops, a new patriotism, one that shall include all peoples, may prevail? The past would indicate that this is a goal toward which we trend.

In the end let us take the larger view, ignoring the Frieslanders, the Anglo-Saxons, the Americans. Let us look at the peoples as a people and observe how inevitably as they answer the great Westward impulse the true patriotism develops. If we can see that it is so with all of them we can assume that it must be so with us, and may know that mere victory in battle as we march Westward, or mere supremacy in trade as we react to the East is not after all the great achievement of the races but patriotism. Not our selfish present-day conception of the word, but a new patriotism, whose meaning is now the secret of the coming centuries.

Consider then the beginnings of patriotism. At the very first, the seed of the future nation was the regard of family; the ties of common birth held men together and the first feeling of patriotism was the love of family. But the family grows, develops by lateral branches, expands and becomes the clan. Patriotism is the devotion to the clan, and the clansmen will fight and die for its supremacy.

Then comes the time when the clans, tired of the roving life of herders, halt a moment and settle down in a chosen spot; the tent becoming permanent evolves the dwellinghouse, and the encampment of the clan becomes at last a city. Patriotism now is civic pride, the clan absorbed into a multitude of clans is forgotten; men speak of themselves as Athenians not as Greeks, as Romans not as Italians. It is the age of cities.

The city extends its adjoining grazing fields, they include outlying towns, other cities, and finally the State comes into being. Patriotism no longer confines itself to the walls of the city, but is enlarged to encompass the entire province. Men are Hanoverians or Wurtemburgers not Germans; Scots or Welsh not English; are even Carolinians or Alabamans rather than Americans.

But the States are federated, pronounced boundaries fade, State makes common cause with State and at last the nation is born. Patriotism at once is a national affair, a far larger, broader, truer sentiment than that first huddling about the hearthstone of the family. The word "brother" may be applied to men unseen and unknown, and a countryman is one of many millions.[24]

We have reached this stage at the present, but if all signs are true, if all precedent may be followed, if all augury may be relied on and the tree grow as we see the twig is bent, the progress will not stop here.

By war to the Westward the family fought its way upward to the dignity of the nation, by reaction Eastward the nation may in patriotic effect merge with other nations, and others and still others, peacefully, the bitterness of trade competition may be lost, the business of the nations seen as a friendly *quid pro quo,* give and take arrangement, guided by a generous reciprocity. Every century the boundaries are widening, patriotism widens with the expansion, and our countrymen are those of different race, even different nations.

---

[24] Norris expressed this idea of a gradually expanding range of patriotism as early as 1891. See his "The Son of a Sheik," *Argonaut*, XXVIII (June 1, 1891), 6. (Republished in *The Third Circle*.)

Will it not go on, this epic of civilization, this destiny of the races, until at last and at the ultimate end of all, we who now arrogantly boast ourselves as Americans, supreme in conquest, whether of battle-ship or of bridge-building, may realize that the true patriotism is the brotherhood of man and know that the whole world is our nation and simple humanity our countrymen?

THE NATIONAL SPIRIT AS IT RELATES TO THE "GREAT AMERICAN NOVEL"[25]

With us, on this side of the Atlantic, this one subject, the great American novel, seems inexhaustible. Also by implication, the fact that there is no great American novel is deplored, lamented. It seems to be considered a vague reflection upon our literature.

On the whole, it does not appear that this should be so. It seems, on the contrary, that the difficulty of adjusting the novelists' conception of American life, their ideas of art, their definition of the word "novel" to fit this sounding phrase is practically insurmountable. Who is to say what is meant by "great"? Who is to formulate just what is meant by "American"? Who is even to decide upon the kind and school of novel writing best adapted to a presentation of the subject in hand?

A national literature, distinctive, excellent, is one of the last things acquired by a people. Observe one says "distinctive." An early literature is almost invariably characterized by universal sentiments, is a presentation of characteristics common to humanity in general. The *Iliad* could have been written as well of Romulus and Remus as of Agamemnon and Priam. The *Chanson de Roland* is in sentiment as much German as French. Grettir of Iceland and Robin Hood of England are much the same. In the primitive stages, in the primitive ideals all peoples, all races are alike, and it is only after thousands of years of geographical isolation, after generations of action and government independent of and separated from the mass that the national spirit, the distinctive national spirit, discloses itself. It is not a question of "patriotism." Patriotism and a national spirit are two very different conceptions. Patriotism is an impulse, whereas "nationalism" is an attitude. Patriotism produces the great epics, the *Iliad*, the *Nibelungen Lied*, the *Saga*, the *Zend Avesta*. The national spirit is at the root of Notre Dame de Paris, of *Anna Karenina*, of *Adam Bede*.

There is no such thing as a national American epic, in the strictest sense of the term. Unlike all other nations, we Americans have never been a primitive people. Very possibly it is to our disadvantage. At all events as a distinct people primitive life has never been ours. We did not evolve

[25] *Boston Evening Transcript*, February 5, 1902, p. 11.

through centuries of growth. We simply declared our independence and came into the world already half-grown. If Americans have any national epics at all they must not be looked for in the early days of the United States, but in the beginnings of English life. To all ends and purposes *Beowulf* and the *Romance of the Rose* are American epics. But the Declaration of Independence relegated those to a nation which our forbears decided to call foreign.

We had patriotism enough in those early days, but it was not the patriotism of the young new people, not the kind that produces epics. We were born too late for that. If we had that kind of spirit we should have found our national epic in the "Winning of the West," in the "Frontier Life." But we neglected it and overlooked it, and abandoned the one great field for American epic literature to the yellow-backs and dime-novels.

Remains then the national spirit? As was said above, the national spirit is the inspiration and opportunity of the national novel, just as the early fiery patriotism is the inspiration and opportunity of the national epic.

But patriotism is not national spirit, nor is it even the beginnings of it; for the two, it seems to me, are as different in kind as in degree. The latter comes only after centuries of race specialization, when a given people by virtue of independent government, hard and fast localization of physical boundaries, aloofness, separateness, all prevailing for generation after generation, have been moulded together, welded together to form a single, distinct, homogeneous unit, different from all others. Then under such conditions comes the national literature, and from that literature issues at last the few great novels that express in one word the national life, résumé in one theme the characteristics of an entire people.

So that it seems almost conclusive that the great American novel will not be written until the development of the great American national spirit. And have we this spirit among us as yet?

By expressing a doubt as to its prevalence one realizes that one sheers perilously close to a misunderstanding. We are a patriotic people. None more so. Proud of our country and the clearer-minded among us believe in its great destiny and know that our feet are even now set in the way of righteousness. That the national spirit is not strong among us as yet is small discredit. It took 2000 years and a Bismarck to inspire it in federated Germany, 2000 years and a Garibaldi to spread it over united Italy. We of the new land toward the west have had, God knows and God be thanked, our Bismarcks and our Garibaldis, but the 2000 years are almost all ahead of us yet. True we began the cause with a fine impetus from the mother country; we began, as was said, our career, half-grown, but even allowing for that, we have not yet lived long enough as a nation to have a national spirit so strong and so inherent as the nations of the Old World. There is no fault in this, only the disadvantage of being very young.

The national spirit, say what we will, does not yet exist among us Americans. What we believe to be national spirit is a fine and healthy patriotism. We are tremendously sectional even yet. In certain cafes of New York where an orchestra plays during dinner one will hear "Dixie" cheered to the echo, while "The Star Spangled Banner" is received almost in silence. Such things are significant, you cannot argue them away. We may have fine novels, even "great American" novelists, but so long as there is one man in all the United States who thrills more to the strain of "Dixie" than to the notes of the "Star Spangled Banner" just so long will there be no universal national spirit in the United States, and just so long —one of many small results of a single noble cause—just so long will there be no great American novel.

A NEGLECTED EPIC[26]

As I have tried to point out once before in these pages, the Frontier has disappeared.[27] The westward-moving course of empire has at last crossed the Pacific Ocean. Civilization has circled the globe and has come back to its starting point, the vague and mysterious East.

The thing has not been accomplished peacefully. From the very first it has been an affair of wars—of invasions. Invasions of the East by the West, and of raids north and south—raids accomplished by flying columns that dashed out from both sides of the main army. Sometimes even the invaders have fought among themselves, as for instance the Trojan War, or the civil wars of Italy, England and America; sometimes they have turned back on their tracks and, upon one pretext or another, reconquered the races behind them, as for instance Alexander's wars to the eastward, the Crusades, and Napoleon's Egyptian campaigns.

Retarded by all these obstacles, the march has been painfully slow. To move from Egypt to Greece took centuries of time. More centuries were consumed in the campaign that brought empire from Greece to Rome, and still more centuries passed before it crossed the Alps and invaded northern and western Europe.

But observe. Once across the Mississippi, the West—our Far West— was conquered in about forty years. In all the vast campaign from east to west here is the most signal victory, the swiftest, the completest, the most brilliant achievement—the wilderness subdued at a single stroke.

Now all these various fightings to the westward, these mysterious race-movements, migrations, wars and wanderings have produced their litera-ture, distinctive, peculiar, excellent. And this literature we call epic. The Trojan War gave us the *Iliad*, the *Odyssey* and the *Aeneid*; the campaign

26 *World's Work*, V (December, 1902), 2904–2906.
27 "The Frontier Gone at Last," *World's Work*, February, 1902 (pp. 111–117 above).

of the Greeks in Asia Minor produced the *Anabasis*; a whole cycle of literature grew from the conquest of Europe after the fall of Rome—*The Song of Roland, The Nibelungenlied, The Romance of the Rose, Beowulf, Magnusson, The Scotch Border Ballads, The Poem of the Cid, The Heimskringla, Orlando Furioso, Jerusalem Delivered,* and the like.

On this side of the Atlantic, in his clumsy, artificial way, but yet recognized as a producer of literature, Cooper has tried to chronicle the conquest of the eastern part of our country. Absurd he may be in his ideas of life and character, the art in him veneered over with charlatanism; yet the man was solemn enough and took his work seriously, and his work is literature.

Also a cycle of romance has grown up around the Civil War. The theme has had its poets to whom the public have been glad to listen. The subject is vast, noble; is in a word epic, just as the Trojan War and the Retreat of the Ten Thousand were epic.

But when at last one comes to look for the literature that sprang from and has grown up around the last great epic event in the history of civilization, the event which in spite of stupendous difficulties was consummated more swiftly, more completely, more satisfactorily than any like event since the westward migration began—I mean the conquering of the West, the subduing of the wilderness beyond the Mississippi—What has this produced in the way of literature? The dime novel! The dime novel and nothing else. The dime novel and nothing better.

The Trojan War left to posterity the character of Hector; the wars with the Saracens gave us Roland; the folklore of Iceland produced Grettir; the Scotch border poetry brought forth the Douglas; the Spanish epic the Cid. But the American epic, just as heroic, just as elemental, just as important and as picturesque, will fade into history leaving behind no finer type, no nobler hero than Buffalo Bill.

The young Greeks sat on marble terraces overlooking the Aegean Sea and listened to the thunderous roll of Homer's hexameter. In the feudal castles the minstrel sang to the young boys, of Roland. The farm folk of Iceland to this very day treasure up and read to their little ones handwritten copies of the Grettla Saga chronicling the deeds and death of Grettir the Strong. But the youth of the United States learn of their epic by paying a dollar to see the "Wild West Show."

The plain truth of the matter is that we have neglected our epic—the black shame of it be on us—and no contemporaneous poet or chronicler thought it worth his while to sing the song or tell the tale of the West, because literature in the day when the West was being won was a cult indulged in by certain well-bred gentlemen in New England who looked eastward to the Old World, to the legends of England and Norway and Germany and Italy for their inspiration, and left the great, strong, honest, fearless, resolute deeds of their own countrymen to be defamed and defaced by the nameless hacks of the "yellow back" libraries.

One man,—who wrote "How Santa Claus Came to Simpson's Bar,"—one poet, one chronicler did, in fact, arise for the moment, who understood that wild, brave life and who for a time gave promise of bearing record of things seen.

One of the requirements of an epic—a true epic—is that its action must devolve upon some great national event. There was no lack of such in those fierce years after '49. Just that long and terrible journey from the Mississippi to the ocean is an epic in itself. Yet no serious attempt has ever been made by an American author to render into prose or verse this event in our history as "national" in scope, in origin and in results as the Revolution itself. The prairie schooner is as large a figure in the legends as the black ship that bore Ulysses homeward from Troy. The sea meant as much to the Argonauts of the fifties as it did to the ten thousand.

And the Alamo! There is a trumpet-call in the word; and only the look of it on the printed page is a flash of fire. But the very histories slight the deed, and to many an American, born under the same flag that the Mexican rifles shot to ribbons on that splendid day, the word is meaningless. Yet Thermopylae was less glorious, and in comparison with that siege the investment of Troy was mere wanton riot. At the very least the Texans in that battered adobe church fought for the honor of their flag and the greater glory of their country, not for loot or the possession of the person of an adultress. Young men are taught to consider the *Iliad*, with its butcheries, its glorification of inordinate selfishness and vanity, as a classic. Achilles, murderer, egoist, ruffian and liar, is a hero. But the name of Bowie, the name of the man who gave his life to his flag at the Alamo, is perpetuated only in the designation of a knife. Crockett is the hero only of a "funny story" about a sagacious coon; while Travis, the boy commander who did what Gordon with an empire back of him failed to do, is quietly and definitely ignored.

Because we have done nothing to get at the truth about the West, because our best writers have turned to the old country folklore and legends for their inspiration, because "melancholy harlequins" strut in fringed leggings upon the street corners, one hand held out for pennies, we have come to believe that our West, our epic, was an affair of Indians, road agents and desperadoes, and have taken no account of the brave men who stood for law and justice and liberty, and for those great ideas died by the hundreds, unknown and unsung; died that the West might be subdued, that the last stage of the march should be accomplished, that the Anglo-Saxon should fulfil his destiny and complete the cycle of the world.

The great figure of our neglected epic, the Hector of our ignored *Iliad*, is not, as the dime novels would have us believe, a lawbreaker, but a law-

maker; a fighter, it is true, as is always the case with epic figures, but a
fighter for peace, a calm, grave, strong man who hated the lawbreaker as
the hound hates the wolf.

He did not lounge in barrooms; he did not cheat at cards; he did not
drink himself to maudlin fury; he did not "shoot at the drop of the hat."
But he loved his horse, he loved his friend, he was kind to little children;
he was always ready to side with the weak against the strong, with the
poor against the rich. For hypocrisy and pretense, for shams and subter-
fuges, he had no mercy, no tolerance. He was too brave to lie and too
strong to steal. The odds in that lawless day were ever against him; his
enemies were many and his friends were few; but his face was always set
bravely against evil, and fear was not in him even at the end. For such a
man as this could die no quiet death in a land where law went no further
than the statute books and life lay in the crook of my neighbor's forefinger.

He died in defense of an ideal, an epic hero, a legendary figure, formidable, sad. He died facing down injustice, dishonesty and crime; died "in
his boots"; and the same world that has glorified Achilles and forgotten
Travis finds none so poor to do him reverence. No literature has sprung
up around him—this great character native to America. He is of all the
world-types the one distinctive to us—peculiar, particular and unique. He
is dead and even his work is misinterpreted and misunderstood. His very
memory will soon be gone, and the American epic, which, on the shelves
of posterity, should have stood shoulder to shoulder with *The Heimskringla* and *The Tales of the Nibelungen* and *The Song of Roland*, will
never be written.

THE GREAT AMERICAN NOVELIST[28]

Of all the overworked phrases of overworked book reviewers, the
phrase, the "Great American Novelist," is beyond doubt worn the thinnest from much handling—or mishandling. Continually the little literary
middlemen who come between the producers and the consumers of fiction
are mouthing the words with a great flourish of adjectives, scareheading
them in Sunday supplements or placarding them on posters, crying out,
"Lo, he is here!" or "lo, there!" But the heathen rage and the people
imagine a vain thing. The G. A. N. is either as extinct as the Dodo or as
far in the future as the practical aeroplane. He certainly is not discoverable
at the present.

The moment a new writer of fiction begins to make himself felt he is
gibbeted upon this elevation—upon this *false,* insecure elevation, for the
underpinning is of the flimsiest, and at any moment is liable to collapse

[28] Syndicated, January 19, 1903.

under the victim's feet and leave him hanging in midair by head and hands, a fixture and a mockery.

And who is to settle the title upon the aspirant in the last issue? Who is to determine what constitutes the G. A. N? Your candidate may suit *you,* but your neighbor may have a very different standard to which he must conform. It all depends upon what you mean by *Great,* what you mean by *American.* Shakespeare has been called great, and so has Mr. Stephen Phillips.[29] Oliver Wendell Holmes was *American,* and so is Bret Harte. Who is to say?

And many good people who deplore the decay of American letters are accustomed to refer to the absence of a G. A. N. as though there were a Great English Novelist or a Great French Novelist. But do these two people exist? Ask any dozen of your friends to mention the Great English Novelist, and out of the dozen you will get at least a half-dozen different names. It will be Dickens or Scott or Thackeray or Bronte or Eliot or Stevenson, and the same with the Frenchman. And it seems to me that if a novelist were great enough to be universally acknowledged to be the Great one of his country, he would cease to belong to any particular geographical area and would become a heritage of the whole world; as for instance Tolstoy; when one thinks of him it is—is it not?—as a novelist first and as a Russian afterward.

But if one wishes to split hairs, one might admit that while the Great American Novelist is yet to be born, the possibility of *A*—note the indefinite article—*A* Great American Novel is not too remote for discussion. But such a novel will be sectional. The United States is a Union, but not a unit, and the life in one part is very, very different from the life in another. It is as yet impossible to construct a novel which will represent all the various characteristics of the different sections. It is only possible to make a picture of a single locality. What is true of the South is not true of the North. The West is different, and the Pacific Coast is a community by itself.

Many of our very best writers are working on this theory. Bret Harte made a study of the West as he saw it, and Mr. Howells has done the same for the East. Cable has worked the field of the Far South, and Eggleston has gone deep into the life of the Middle West.

But consider a suggestion. It is an argument on the other side, and to be fair one must present it. It is a good argument, and if based on fact is encouraging in the hope that the *Great* man may yet appear. It has been said that "what is true—vitally and inherently true—for any one man is true for all men." Accordingly, then, what is vitally true of the Westerner

[29] Phillips (1868–1915), an English poet and playwright, had a much inflated popular reputation at the turn of the century.

is true of the Bostonian—yes, and of the creole. So that if Mr. Cable, say, should only go *deep enough* into the hearts and lives of his creoles, he would at last strike the universal substratum and find the elemental thing that is common to the creole and to the Puritan alike—yes, and to the Cowboy and Hoosier and Greaser and Buckeye and Jay Hawker, and that, once getting hold of *that*, he could produce the Great American Novel that should be a picture of the entire nation.

Now, that is a very ingenious argument and sounds very plausible. But it won't do, and for this reason: If an American novelist should go so deep into the lives of the people of any one community that he would find the thing that is common to another class of people a thousand miles away, he would have gone *too* deep to be exclusively American. He would not only be American, but English as well. He would have sounded the world-note; he would be a writer not national, but international, and his countrymen would be all humanity, not the citizens of any one nation. He himself would be a heritage of the whole world, a second Tolstoy, which brings us back to the very place from which we started.

And the conclusion of the whole matter? That fiction is very good or very bad—there is no middle ground; that writers of fiction in their points of view are either limited to a circumscribed area or see humanity as a tremendous conglomerate whole; that it must be either Mary Wilkins or George Eliot, Edward Eggleston or William Shakespeare; that the others do not weigh very much in the balance of the world's judgment; and that the Great American Novel is not extinct like the Dodo, but mythical like the Hippogriff, and the thing to be looked for is not the Great American Novelist, but the Great Novelist who shall also be an American.

Popular Fiction

INTRODUCTION

Many intellectuals of Norris' day felt that the untrained appetite of a mass-reading public was causing a degeneration of literary taste. Norris accepted the premise that this new public encouraged the production of superficial popular novels. But to Norris, this immense body of readers, whatever its deficiencies, was a promise rather than a threat. He believed that when men begin to read, they gradually improve their taste. The public would slowly educate itself to appreciate better works, and a reciprocal faith would develop between public and writer. The responsible writer would believe in the public's ability to recognize his integrity and to accept his work; the public would believe in the sincerity of the responsible writer; and from this reciprocal confidence would come a vital literature. Norris argued that though at present neither faith prevailed—most writers catered to the worst in public taste, and the public gorged itself on the worst fiction—this great new public represented a mass seeding from which would rise a substantial number of readers seeking honest literature. The land might look bleak and barren, but spring would come.[1]

Norris' faith in the ability of the public to advance its literary taste can be attacked as illustrating that naïve confidence in the common man which often accompanies a primitivistic ethic. One can note that the public, rather than "advancing" from *Trilby* to *The Sound and the Fury*, still prefers *Trilby* in the form of a *Forever Amber* or a *Peyton Place*. But despite the continuing vast market for superficial fiction, Norris' confidence in the beneficent effects of this new public was not entirely misplaced. When in the 1920's there did appear a group of "responsible" authors—that is, outspoken, rebellious writers—they were supported by a large enough portion of the public to be encouraged and to flourish. And their success differs markedly from that of a Whitman or a Melville at an earlier period when the book-buying public was insufficient to support such writers. In other words, the contemporaneous readers of novels like *Moby Dick* or *The Sound and the Fury* will perhaps always be a minority of the reading public, but that minority can be adequate if the public be large enough. Though not all Norris' *Old Sleuth* readers grew up to be admirers of Faulkner, perhaps enough did to represent at least one factor in the literary renaissance of the 1920's and 1930's.

---

[1] Although the two essays in this section were published in 1903, Norris expressed their basic theme as early as May 25, 1901, in his "Weekly Letter" in the *Chicago American*, and frequently in his "Salt and Sincerity" columns of mid-1902.

THE AMERICAN PUBLIC AND "POPULAR" FICTION[2]

The American people judged by Old World standards—even sometimes according to native American standards—have always been considered a practical people, a material people.

We have been told and have also told ourselves that we are hardheaded, that we rejoiced in facts and not in fancies, and as an effect of this characteristic were not given to books. We are not literary, we assumed, were not fond of reading. We, who were subjugating a continent, who were inventing machinery and building railroads, left it to the older and more leisurely nations—to France and to England—to read books.

On the face of it this would seem a safe assumption. As a matter of fact, the American people are the greatest readers in the world. That is to say, that, count for count, there are more books read in the United States in one year than in any other country of the globe in the same space of time.

Nowhere do the circulations attain such magnitude as they do with us. A little while ago—ten years ago—the charge that we did not read was probably true. But there must exist some mysterious fundamental connection between this recent sudden expansion of things American—geographic, commercial and otherwise—and the demand for books. Imperialism, Trade Expansion, the New Prosperity and the Half Million Circulation all came into existence at about the same time.

Merely the fact of great prosperity does not account for the wider reading. Prosperous periods, good prices, easy credit and a mobile currency have occurred often before without producing the demand for books. Something more than prosperity has suddenly swept across the continent and invaded the spirit of the times. Something very like an awakening, something very like a renaissance and the 70,000,000 have all at once awakened to the fact that there are books to be read.[3] As with all things sudden, there is noticeable with this awakening a lack of discrimination, the 70,000,000 are so eager for books that, *faute de mieux,* anything printed will pass current for literature. It is a great animal, this American public, and having starved for so long, it is ready, once aroused, to devour anything. And the great presses of the country are for the most part merely sublimated sausage machines that go dashing along in a mess of paper and printer's ink turning out the meat for the monster.

[2] Syndicated, February 2, 1903.

[3] Many magazine and newspaper editorials of this period commented on the great increase in novel reading. A typical editorial, "Growth of Novel Reading" (*Independent,* LII [November 8, 1900], 2701–2702), attributed this growth to increased literacy and education, to the work of literary clubs, and to the church's withdrawal of its opposition to novel reading.

There are not found wanting many who deplore this and who black-guard the great brute for his appetite. Softly, softly. If the Megatherium has been obliged to swallow wind for sustenance for several hundred years, it would be unkind to abuse him because he eats the first lot of spoiled hay or over-ripe twigs that is thrust under the snout of him. Patience and shuffle the cards. Once his belly filled, and the pachyderm will turn to the new-mown grass and fruit trees in preference to the hay and twigs.

So the studios and the Browning classes need not altogether revile the great American public. Better bad books than no books; better half a loaf of hard bread than *no* frosted wedding-cake. The American people, unlike the English, unlike the French and other Europeans, have not been edu-cated and refined and endoctrinated for 2,000 years, and when you re-member what they have done in *one hundred* years, tamed an entire continent, liberated a race, produced a Lincoln, invented the telegraph, spanned the plains—when you remember all this, do not spurn the 70,-000,000 because they do not understand Henry James, but be glad that they even care for "The Duchess" and "Ouida."[4] The wonder of it is not that they do not read or appreciate the best, but that they have set apart any time at all in the struggle of civilizing the wilderness and forging steel rivets to so much as pick up any kind or description of a book.

Consider the other nations, France for instance—the very sanctum of Art, the home and birthplace of literature. Compare the rural districts of France with the rural districts of the United States, and in the comparison allow, if you like, for all the centuries of quiet uninterrupted growth, the wilderness tamed, life domesticated, reduced to routine that modern France enjoys. Do you suppose for one moment that a bourgeois family of —say—Tours is on the same level in the matter of its reading as the house-hold of a contractor's family in—for example—Martinez, California, or Cheyenne, Wyoming?

I tell you there is no comparison whatever. The West may be wild even yet, may be what Boston would call uncultured, but it *reads*. There are people in Cheyenne and Martinez who can express an opinion—and a more intelligent opinion, mark you—on Maeterlinck and Bourget, better than the same class of readers in Belgium and France. And quite as likely as not the same class of people in the native countries of the two writers named have never so much as heard of these writers.

This, admittedly, is the exception, but if our exceptional Martinez and Cheyenne people are so far advanced in literary criticism, we may reason-ably expect that the rank and file below them are proportionately well on.

---

[4] The Duchess (Margaret Hungerford) and Ouida (Louise de la Ramée) were pro-lific writers of popular romances.

Maeterlinck and Bourget are closed books to those rank-and-file readers yet. But again I say, this is not the point. The point is, that they are readers at all. Let them—in the name of future American literature—read their Duchesses and Ouidas and Edna Lyalls and Albert Rosses.[5] What are their prototypes in France, Germany and Russia reading? They simply are not reading at all, and as often as not it is not because of the lack of taste, but because of the lack of sheer downright ability, because they do not know how to read.

A very great man once said that "books never have done harm,"[6] and under this sign let us conquer. There is hardly a better to be found. Instead, then, of deploring the vast circulation of mediocre novels, let us take the larger view and find in the fact not a weakness, but a veritable strength. The more one reads—it is a curious consolatory fact—the more one is apt to discriminate. The ten-year-old who reads *Old Sleuth* to-day, in a little while will find Scott more to his liking.[7] Just now the 70,000,- 000 is ten years old. But it is started right. Patience. Books have never done harm, and in the end let us be certain that the day will come when the real masterpiece, the real literature, will also be selling in its "five hundredth thousand."

CHILD STORIES FOR ADULTS[8]

There was a time, none too remote at this date of writing, when juvenile and adult fiction were two separate and distinct classifications. Boys read stories for boys and girls stories for girls, and the adults contented themselves with the wise lucubrations of their equals in years. But the last few years have changed all that—have changed everything in American literature, in fact.

Some far-distant day, when the critics and litterateurs of the twenty-second and twenty-third centuries shall be writing of our day and age, they will find a name for the sudden and stupendous demand for reading matter that has penetrated to all classes and corners since 1890. A great deal could be said upon this sudden demand in itself, and I think it can be proved to be the first effects of a genuine awakening—a second Renaissance. But the subject would demand an article by itself, and in the meanwhile we may use the term awakening as a self-evident fact and consider not so much the cause as the effects.

[5] Edna Lyall (pseudonym of Ellen Bayly) and Albert Ross (pseudonym of Linn Porter) also wrote popular novels of adventure and love.

[6] Norris elsewhere (p. 199) attributes this statement to Hugo, though I fail to find it in Hugo's work.

[7] George Munro's Old Sleuth's Library, established in 1882, rivaled Beadle's Dime Library in the publication of juvenile detective and adventure fiction.

[8] Syndicated, February 9, 1903.

One of the effects, as has been already suggested, is the change in classifications. Old forms and formulas are, or are being, rapidly broken up, and one school and style merging into others, till now what was once amusement for the children has become entertaining for the elders. And vice versa. The abruptness of the awakening has disjointed and inverted all the old fabric. *Robinson Crusoe*, written for adults, is now exclusively a "juvenile," while *Treasure Island*, written for boys, has been snapped up by the parents.

Simultaneously with this topsy-turvy business, and I am sure in some way connected with it, comes the craze for stories about very young children for adult reading. A boy's story must now be all about the doings of men, fighters preferably, man-slayers, terrible fellows full of blood and fury, stamping on their quarter-decks or counting doubloons by torch-light on unnamed beaches. Meanwhile the boy's father with a solemn interest is following the fortunes of some terrible infant of the kindergarten, or the vagaries of a ten-year-old of a country town, or the teacup tragedy of "The Very Little Girl," or "The Indiscretion of Pinky Trevethan," or "The Chastening of Skinny McCleave," etc., etc.

It is interesting to try to account for this. It may either be a fad or a phase. It is almost too soon to tell, but in either case the matter is worth considering.

Roughly speaking, the Child's Stories for Adults fall into three classes. First there is "The Strange Child Story." This is a very old favorite, and was pretty well installed long before the more recent developments. In "The Strange Child Story" the bid for the reader's pity and sympathy fairly clamored from between the lines. Always and persistently The Strange Child was misunderstood. He had "indefinable longings" that were ridiculed, budding talents that were nipped, heartaches—terrible, tear-compelling heartaches—that were ignored; and he lived in an atmosphere of gloom, hostility and loneliness that would have maddened an eremite.

But as his kind declined in popular estimate the country boy, the ten-year-old—who always went in swimmin' and lost his tow—appeared in the magazines. There is no sentiment about him. Never a tear need be shed over the vicarious atonements of Pinky Trevethan or Skinny Mc-Cleave.

It is part of the game to pretend that the Pinkys and Skinnys and Peelys and Mickeys are different individuals. Error. They are merely different names of the boy that perennially and persistently remains the same. Do you know who he is? He is the average American business man before he grew up. That accounts for his popularity. The average business man had clean forgotten all about those early phases of primitive growth, and it amuses him immensely to find out that the scribe has been making a study of him and bringing to light the forgotten things that are so tremendously familiar when presented to the consideration. It is not fiction nor yet literature in the straightest sense of the word, this rehabilitation of Skinny McCleave. It has a value vaguely scientific, the same value that a specimen, a fossil insect, has when brought to the attention of the savant. It is the study of an extinct species, a report upon the American boy of thirty years ago.

Then lastly—the latest development—there is the cataclysm of the kindergarten, the checked apron drama, the pigtail passion, the epic of the broken slate-pencil. This needs a delicacy of touch that only a woman can supply, and as a matter of fact it is for the most part women who sign the stories. The interest in these is not so personal and retrospective as in the Skinny McCleave circle, for the kindergarten is too recent to be part of the childhood memories of the present generation of adult magazine readers. It is more informative, a presentation of conditions hitherto but vaguely known, and at the same time it is an attempt to get at and into the heart and head of a little child.

And in this last analysis it would seem as if here existed the barrier insurmountable. It is much to be doubted if ever a genius will arise so thoughtful, so sensitive that he will penetrate into more than the merest outside integument of a child's heart. Certain phases have been guessed at with beautiful intention, certain rare insights have been attained with exquisite nicety, but somehow even the most sympathetic reader must feel that the insight is as rare as the interest is misguided.

Immanuel Kant conceived of, and, in the consummate power of his intellect, executed the *Critique of Pure Reason*; Darwin had taken the adult male and female human and tracked down their every emotion, impulse, quality and sentiment.[9] The intellectual powers and heart-beats of a Napoleon or a Shakespeare have been reduced to mere commonplace corner gossip, but after thousands of years of civilization, with the subject ever before us, its workings as near to us as air itself, the mind of a little child is as much a closed book, as much an enigma, as much a blank space upon the charts of our intellectual progress as at the very first.

Volumes have been written about the child, and stories for and of the child, and very learned men have lectured and other very eminent and noble men have taught, and it has all been going on for nineteen hundred and two years. And yet, notwithstanding all this, there lurks a mystery deep down within the eye of the five-year-old, a mystery that neither you nor I may know. You may see and understand what he actually does, but

---

[9] Charles Darwin, *The Expression of the Emotions in Man and Animals* (1872).

the thinking part of him is a second hidden nature that belongs to him and to other children, not to adults, not even to his mother. Once the older person invades the sphere of influence of this real undernature of the child and it congeals at once. It thaws and thrives only in the company of other children, and at the best we older ones may see it from a distance and from the outside. Between us and them it would appear that a great gulf is bridged; there is no knowing the child as he really is, and until the real child can be known the stories about him and the fiction and literature about him can at best be only a substitute for the real knowledge that probably never shall be ours.

PART THREE
THE WRITER AS BUSINESSMAN

INTRODUCTION

Although Norris often attacked the writer "who is in literature for his own pocket every time," he himself was much interested in the economics of authorship and was not reluctant to express that interest in his essays. He had been involved in publishing affairs since his *Wave* days, when as a member of a small staff he did everything on the magazine from reporting to last-minute proofreading. But the realities of publishing and authorship were perhaps not completely driven home to him until he left San Francisco for New York. There, for the first time, he was entirely dependent on his writing, and there he first experienced the inner workings of large publishing organizations.

The five essays which follow thus represent a firsthand account of authorship as a business—from the submission of a book to the sale of its final copy. In them Norris relies on concrete details from his experiences as a *Wave* reporter, as a reader for Doubleday, Page, and as an author aware of the delusion of "royalties." In several of the essays he adopts the device of explaining a "mystery" from the "inside," thereby appealing to the almost universal desire to know how some unusual activity "really works," particularly if money is involved in its operation.

But other motives are present in these essays besides Norris' obvious attempt to make salable copy out of his experiences as an author. Norris probably equated his frank interest in literature as a business with an attack on the aesthete or gentleman–scholar, both of whom would supposedly greet with horror any association of art with cash. To Norris, however, this association was a part of the "life" of a man of letters. The business affairs of an author are an inevitable result of his participation in the world of men outside his study and are as much a matter of concern as the "life" activities of any group. Norris discussed the writer as businessman, therefore, not only without the embarrassment with which Howells approached the subject in 1893,[1] but also with the tone of one performing a service for the public at large as well as for the fledgling author.

Moreover, the essays constitute a defense of publishing practices, a defense epitomized by the long anecdote about the indigent Frenchman and his lost manuscript. Though the publisher could have sent the Frenchman away, it would have been bad business to have done so, and he instead rewarded him with a position. So Norris implied throughout these essays that though the economics of publishing caused some hardship and injustice, in general they resulted in the publication of the best manuscripts,

---

[1] W. D. Howells, "The Man of Letters as a Man of Business," *Scribner's Magazine*, XIV (October, 1893), 429–445. After some introductory quibbling, however, Howells went on to describe the state of the "market" in great detail.

in the ultimate reward of the sincere writer, and in the downfall of the copyist. This defense perhaps stems from Norris' satisfactory relations with the publishing industry during 1901–1902, when he was being partially subsidized by Doubleday and when he was finding a ready market for his stories and essays. But there is something anomalous in it, nevertheless, given another range of his experience—that involving publishers' suppression of the more outspoken work of "sincere" writers. Norris' own *McTeague* had been held by Doubleday and McClure for over a year before publication, and his *Vandover and the Brute* had been rejected outright.[2] And Norris had been as close as anyone to the throttling of Dreiser's *Sister Carrie* by Doubleday, Page.[3] In his capacity as reader he had highly recommended the novel, and had later publicly proclaimed it the best work of American realism since Howells' *A Modern Instance*.[4] There is no duplicity, however, in Norris' neglect of these experiences. There is rather (to use his own critical terms) his selection of those details which would most effectively communicate his general idea, and his general response to the publishing industry had been favorable.

Though Norris omitted some aspects of his personal experience, he used his articles as fully as possible to express his personal critical ideas. One finds in them his pleas for "life, not literature," for sincerity, and for faith in the public. Like the work of most critics with a cohesive body of ideas, Norris' essays, whatever their ostensible subject, almost always return to a reaffirmation of his primary beliefs.

[2] John S. Phillips, an editor of Doubleday and McClure, noted in a letter to Franklin Walker, April 18, 1932 (FWC), that *McTeague* was "held up by Doubleday's hesitancy because of the realistic contents," and that *Vandover* was rejected for the same reason.

[3] The fullest accounts of this well-known incident are in Dreiser's "The Early Adventures of Sister Carrie" (*Colophon*, Part V [1931], n.p.) and *Letters* (pp. 57–64).

[4] "Frank Norris' Weekly Letter," *Chicago American*, May 25, 1901, p. 8.

THE UNKNOWN AUTHOR AND THE PUBLISHER[5]

"There," says the author as yet unpublished; "the manuscript is finished, is even type-written, 'tied-up, ticketed, and labelled' and forwarded to the publisher, with directions as to its return, but I am a nobody as yet. *My* manuscript will not be read. It will be returned, possibly without being unwrapped. To get anything read these days one must have influence."

So he gets this influence—or thinks he does—through a letter of introduction written by some one who has "influence" with the publisher.

The result is that the letter carries not the slightest weight, and the chances are that the letter and not the manuscript is the unread contribution.

For the Great Unpublished should believe this of all things: *Every manuscript submitted is given a chance*; never a one is returned unconsidered, and read often several times. The house for which the writer of these confessions spends himself has the invariable rule that each manuscript be read by two persons, and if one of these gives hint of merit, it is passed to a third. It should be apparent to every one in these days why this should be so. There have been too many instances where publishers have made small fortunes from "first books,"—books whose manuscripts have been submitted without preliminary introductions, unsought and unheralded. Indeed, there is more chance of financial success with "first books" than with those written by authors of established reputations, for these latter are justified in demanding heavy royalties, which cut deep into the profits.

The numerous instances of the great success of "first" books, written by "new men," have established admirable precedents. Considering the matter strictly from the financial point of view, one can never say when, in looking through the day's batch, one is to come upon a second *David Harum*, a second *Peter Sterling*, or a second *Eben Holden*.[6] If the unpublished author will reflect upon the matter, he will soon realize that the publisher *must* look for him with *more* eagerness than he is looking for the publisher; because, if the author fails to "place" his manuscript, he loses no more, financially, than the price of paper and ink, and he can try other publishers. He is not limited to this one chance; whereas the publisher has only this one chance on this manuscript, and if he fails to accept a *David Harum*, loses, we will say, something in the neighborhood of a quarter of a million dollars.

[5] *World's Work,* I (April, 1901), 663–665.
[6] Edward N. Westcott's *David Harum* (1898), Paul L. Ford's *The Honorable Peter Stirling* (not *Sterling*) (1894), and Irving Bacheller's *Eben Holden* (1900) were all highly popular novels.

So the possibility of being neglected should never discourage even the most diffident, the least self-confident. Remember an axiom: If you submit a manuscript, it will be read; if it is good enough, it will be published, —published whether your name be Rudyard Kipling or Sarah Brown.

It is *not* the men of established reputations who are sought for so painfully; these already have found their publisher and in a great majority of cases are bound to one particular House. They are for all other Houses out of the market. The "New Man" is the free lance; he is drifting hither and thither, ready to be snapped up by the first bidder; then, too, the arrived author's limit of success can be pretty well gauged,—so-and-so will sell 5000, so-and-so 10,000,—but who shall say how far the "New Man" will go? "A first book by a new author, and a good book at that!" The average bookseller will order more copies than of a new novel by Henry James.

It would interest and surprise the pessimists, could they but know how the game goes in the editorial office; could they but understand how easy —and *not* how difficult—it is for even fair work to pass muster. It is true that it is easier to induce the publisher to accept a novel than it is to get the public to buy it. As a matter of course, the Reader for the House must have his standard. The public, too, has its own; but the public's standard is determined only by *published* books—books that have been deemed good enough to print. On the other hand, the Reader must pass in review hundreds upon hundreds of manuscripts that are—ninety-nine out of a hundred of them—impossible. How easy it is, then, for even the moderately good book to stand forth resplendent from the sombre background of worthlessness! How easy it is to judge it not by standards of real actual excellence, but by those of the "unavailables" in whose company it is found.

All volunteer manuscripts, then, have their chance—are considered. But it does not follow that each and every one is read from cover to cover. Some can be pronounced unavailable after a reading of a few pages or chapters; a larger number hold out illusive hopes of better ahead through the first chapter; a few do not prove hopeless till the middle of the story; still fewer are read to the very end before decision is reached.

However, long experience developes a certain instinct, a certain *flair*. If the author has a good story to tell, there will be an unmistakable sense of mastery of words in his very introduction; a convincing feeling of power of presentation in the very first page. The unpublished will never know, can never understand, the infinite relief, the sensation of actual exhilaration, that invades the Reader of Many Many Manuscripts when he realizes that here at last is something good—not merely popular necessarily, but a book earnestly done and with a knowledge of the tools. Nor could the author's dearest friend labor so diligently to get the book accepted than does the Reader in such case.

More people are writing to-day than ever before; constantly the "New Man" is coming to the front with his thousands and tens of thousands of copies sold. While these lines are being written, there is very little doubt that somewhere between the Oceans an unknown and unpublished author is at work upon a story that will soon be "the literary sensation of the year." It stands to all good reason that it behooves the publisher to discover him. Obviously this is so. Was not *The Red Badge of Courage* thus written and *The Gentleman from Indiana* and *Plain Tales*, and others, and still others, and still others? The history of publishing teems with just such "finds."

So remembering all these things and possibly remembering "finds" of his own, the Reader attacks his pile of manuscript in much the same spirit as the miner his work of prospecting, disappointed from hour to hour, yet hoping always that the next wrapper removed, the next stone turned, may uncover the chef-d'oeuvre or the mine; or if not the next, why, then, the next, or the next after that, or the next after that, and so on to the end, —always cheerfully expectant and almost always disappointed.

For so many—so very, very many—of the manuscripts are so very—so very, very—bad.[7] The great difficulty seems to be that the writers confuse literature and life, and hold to the foolish mistake that the first is of more importance than the last. They have believed that the way to equip themselves for their profession is to read and study other novels; that they must—in a word—be literary. Error, hopeless and complete, and resulting in stories that at the very best and by the most elastic stretch of charity can be only mediocrities. The great bulk of declined manuscripts falls under this head, and the author, seeing that his work is like that of others who are published and successful, fails to understand the reason for the refusal to publish.

In these manuscripts you shall find the stock incidents, the stock characters, the stock episodes that have done duty since the days of Hawthorne and Cooper. Is it a novel of the South? Behold the General with his inevitable "damme, sir" and mint julep; behold the young man, newly arrived from "up North" and falling in love with the one available girl of the community; behold the complication brought about by the young girl's brother and the catastrophe precipitated by conflicting sectional instincts! Invariably does this kind begin with the expected arrival of the Northern stranger, and no sooner does the wearied Reader of Many Manuscripts discover in the first chapter the old negro hitching up the decrepit horse

[7] For Norris' reader's report on such a novel—entitled *Aida of the Coal Mines*—see *Letters*, pp. 51–52.

to the broken-down conveyance, when promptly the entire panorama of the story rises up—a ghost of other long-dead stories—and stands despairing in the eye of the mind.

Is it a story of Colonial Virginia? So, in the opening paragraphs the "gentle" Reader is ungently transported to the market place of the town on the morning of a public event. Behold the old familiar "Burgess" with his old familiar, "Why, how now, Mistress Nancy, and whither away so bravely bedecked?" as the heroine "trips lightly"—they always trip lightly in the colonial romance—upon the scene.

But ah—most frequent of all, it is the novel of Cavalier and Roundhead. Alas for the naïvete of it, alas for the guilelessness of it; with its "beshrew me's" and its "and thou lovest me's"; its Puritan maiden in love with the Cavalier, or its Cavalier damsel in love with the Puritan stalwart; and, as if for the first time in the world, upon the title page, inevitably *inevitably*, this inscription: *"From the memoirs of one Perkyn Warbeck* (or whatever the name), *Sometime Field Cornet in his Majesty's Troop of Horse."*

It is hard to read this kind; one knows what is to follow. How easy it is to foretell the vicissitudes of the romance. How surely it can be prophesied that the $\begin{bmatrix} \text{Cavalier} \\ \text{Puritan} \end{bmatrix}$ in love with the $\begin{bmatrix} \text{Puritan} \\ \text{Cavalier} \end{bmatrix}$ will get into trouble because of that fatal passion, and be misunderstood and misjudged as a traitor. How accurately can that battle, which will occur in Chapter XV, be foreseen, how positive from the very start may one be of the little imitation strut of the little imitation manikin—copied from those literary Godey books of the historical romancers, Scott and Weyman.[8] How certain one is of the demureness of the Puritan maid, how positive of the "roystering" swagger of the Cavalier blade.

Fustian, stuffing, sawdust, rhetoric, "damme, sir," "what ho there," "beshrew me," and all the rest of it,—what a labor lost, what effort unconsciously misdirected!

One pities this kind, but there are some at whom one can afford to be indignant. These are they who know better, who are *not* unpublished, but, "watching the market," pilfer from former successes.

There is quick work with this kind, for their insincerity is apparent from the very first. The petty thief stealing an overcoat risks at least the thirty days of the law. But these literary pickpockets are lower even than he, for they know no law can reach them, and they write with the avowed object of selling,—selling stolen goods,—and they forfeit the right to be resentful when the publisher refuses to act as their pawnbroker or

---

[8] Stanley J. Weyman was a writer of popular historical romances in the 1890's. *Godey's Lady's Book* was famous for its patterns of women's clothes.

"fence." A case in point came to hand not sixty days since, where a publishing house was asked to consider an "historical romance," signed by a name known to every magazine reader in the United States. Before the end of the first chapter, the thief had embroiled his hero in a duel and had presented him, while at sword's play with his adversary, composing a set of verses, pinking his foe at the close of the envoy.[9]

The Reader of Many Manuscripts, it may be believed, disposes of these gentlemen in short order, preferring to put his time to the better purpose of considering blundering, clumsy originality, so only it be conceived in a spirit of sincerity.

That is the word to end upon, *sincerity*, sincerity, and again and again sincerity. If the unpublished is sincere, if he takes his profession seriously, if honestly he tries to present life as he sees it (not as the public have pretended to like to see it), then he is the "New Man" for whom a hundred clashing presses are waiting, for whom every House is searching. He may not be accepted at once, but his work is watched, he himself is kept in view and in mind. Encouragement, even to the advancing of royalty upon work yet to be written, is awaiting him; and not only will his manuscripts be read as earnestly and seriously as he has written them, but in the end his work will be published, and with all the energy and resource of which the House is capable pushed to the extremest limits of its circulation.

THE "VOLUNTEER MANUSCRIPT": PLAIN TALK TO THE AMBITIOUS AMATEUR[10]

At a conservative estimate there are 70,000,000 people in the United States. At a liberal estimate 100,000 of these have lost the use of both arms; remain then 69,900,000—who write novels. Indeed, many are called, but few—oh, what a scanty, skimped handful that few represent —are chosen.

The work of choosing these few, or rather of rejecting these many, devolves upon the manuscript readers for the baker's dozen of important New York publishing houses, and a strange work it is, and strange are the contributions that pass under their inspection. As one not unfamiliar with the work of "reading" the present writer may offer a little seasonable advice.

1. First have your manuscript typewritten. The number of manuscripts is too great and the time too short to expect the reader to decipher script, and, besides, ideas presented or scenes described in type are infinitely more

---

[9] Norris alludes to the famous dueling scene in Edmond Rostand's *Cyrano de Bergerac* (1897).

[10] *Boston Evening Transcript,* December 11, 1901, p. 25.

persuasive, more plausible than those set down in script. A good story typewritten will appear to better advantage; a poor one similarly treated seems less poverty stricken.

2. Do not, by any manner of means, announce in a prefatory note that you "lay no claim to literary excellence," with the intention thereby of ingratiating yourself with regard to the "reader," winning him over by a parade of modesty. Invariably the statement is prejudicial, producing an effect exactly contrary to the one desired. It will make the mildest of "readers" angry. If you have no claims upon literary excellence, why in heaven's name are you bothering him to read your work?

3. Enclose a forwarding address in case of rejection. This, seemingly, is superfluous advice. But it is astonishing how many manuscripts come in innocent even of the authors' names, with never a scrap nor clue as to their proper destination.

4. Don't ask for criticism. The reader is not a critic. He passes only upon the availability of the manuscript for the uses of the publisher who employs him. And a manuscript of paramount literary quality may be rejected for any number of reasons, none of which have anything to do with its literary worth—or accepted for causes equally outside the domain of letters. Criticism is one thing, professional "reading" quite another.

5. Don't bother about "enclosing stamps for return." The manuscript will go back to you by c.o.d. express.

6. Don't submit a part of a manuscript. It is hard enough sometimes to judge the story as a whole, and no matter how discouraging the initial chapter may be, the publisher will always ask to see the remaining portions before deciding.

7. Don't write to the publisher beforehand asking him if he will consider your manuscript. If it is a novel he will invariably express his willingness to consider it. How can he tell whether he wants it or not until he, through his "reader," has seen it?

8. Don't expect to get an answer much before a month. Especially if your story has merit, it must pass through many hands and be considered by many persons before judgment is rendered. The better it is the longer you will wait before getting a report.

9. Don't, in Heaven's name, enclose commendatory letters written by your friends, favorable reviews by your pastor, or by the president of the local college. The story will speak for itself more distinctly than any of your acquaintances.

10. Don't say you will revise or shorten to suit the tastes or judgment of the publisher. At best that's a servile humility that in itself is a confession of weakness, and that will make you no friends at court.

11. Don't forward a letter of introduction no matter from how near a

friend of the publisher. The publisher will only turn the MS. over to his "readers," and with them the letter from a stranger carries no weight.

12. Don't write a colonial novel.

13. Don't write a Down East novel.

14. Don't write a *Prisoner of Zenda* novel.

15. Don't write a novel.

16. Try to keep your friends from writing novels. And of all the rules one is almost tempted to declare that the last two are the most important. For to any one genuinely interested in finding "good stuff" in the ruck and run of volunteer manuscripts nothing is more discouraging, nothing more apparently hopeless of ultimate success than the consistent and uniform trashiness of the day's batch of submitted embryonic novels. Infinitely better for their author had they never been written; infinitely better for him had he employed his labor—at the very least it is a labor of three months—upon the trade or profession to which he was bred. It is very hard work to write a good novel, but it is much harder to write a bad one. Its very infelicity is a snare to the pen, its very clumsiness a constant demand for laborious boosting and propping.

And consider another, and further word of advice—number 17, if you please. Don't go away with that popular idea that your manuscript will [not] be considered, or if really and undeniably good will be heedlessly rejected. Bad manuscripts are not read from cover to cover. The reader has not the right to waste his employer's time in such unremunerative diligence. Often a page or two will betray the hopelessness of the subsequent chapters, and no one will demand of the "reader" a perusal of a work that he knows will be declined in the end.

Nor was there ever a sincere and earnest effort that went unappreciated in a publisher's place of business. I have seen an entire office turned upside down by a "reader" who believed he had discovered among the batch of voluminous MS. something "really good, you know," and who almost forced a reading of the offering in question upon every member of the firm from the senior partner down to the assistant salesman.

As a rule all manuscripts follow the same routine. From the clerk who receives them at the hands of the expressman they go to the recorder, who notes the title, address and date of arrival, and also, after turning them over to the junior reader, the fact of the transfer. The junior reader's report upon the manuscript is turned in to one of the members of the firm, whose decision is final. The manuscript itself goes up to the senior reader, who also reports upon it to the firm member. If both reports are unfavorable, this latter directs the manuscript to be returned with or without a personal letter, as he deems proper. If both the readers' reports are favorable, or even if one is sufficiently laudatory, he calls for the manuscript and reads it himself. If he disagrees with the readers' reports, the manuscript is declined. If not, he passes the manuscript on to one of the partners of the house, who also reads it. The two "talk it over," and out of the conference comes the ultimate decision in the matter.

Sometimes the circulation manager and head salesman are consulted to decide whether or not—putting all questions of the book's literary merits aside—the "thing will sell." And doubt not for a moment that their counsel carries weight.

Another feature of the business which it is very well to remember is that all publishers cannot be held responsible for the loss of or damage to unsolicited manuscripts. If you submit the MS. of a novel you do it at your own risk, and the carelessness of an office boy may lose for you the work of many months—years, even; work that you could never do over again. You could demand legally no reparation. The publishers are not responsible. Only in case where a letter signed by one of the "heads" has been sent to the author requesting that the manuscript be forwarded does the situation become complicated. But in the case of an unknown writer the monetary value of his work in a court of law would be extremely difficult to place, and even if an award of damages could be extorted it would hardly more than pay the typewriter's bill.

But the loss of manuscript may be of serious import to the publisher for all that. That reputation for negligence in the matter of handling unsolicited matter fastens upon a firm with amazing rapidity. Bothersome as the number of volunteer manuscripts are they do—to a certain extent— gauge the importance of a given concern. And as they arrive in constantly increasing quantities, the house may know that it is growing in favor and in reputation, and so a marked falling off reverses the situation. Writers will be naturally averse to submitting manuscripts to offices which are known to be careless. And I know of at least one instance where the loss of a couple of manuscripts within a month produced a marked effect upon the influx of the volunteers. Somehow the news of the loss always gets out, and spreads by some mysterious means till it is heard of from strangely remote quarters. The author will, of course, tell his friends of the calamity, and will make more ado over the matter than if his story was accepted. Of course, this particular story is the one great masterpiece of his career; the crass stupidity of the proud and haughty publisher has ruined his chance of success, and the warning "Don't send your stuff to that firm. It will be lost," is passed on all along the line. So that repeated instances of the negligence may in the end embarrass the publisher, and the real masterpiece, the first novel of a New Man, goes to a rival.

I have in mind one case where a manuscript was lost under peculiarly distressing circumstances. The "reader," who had his office in the editorial rooms of a certain important house of New York, was on a certain day called to the reception-room to interview one of the host of writers who came daily to submit their offerings in person.

In this case the "reader" confronted a little gentleman in the transition period of genteel decay. He was a Frenchman. His moustache, tight, trim and waxed, was white. The frock coat was buttoned only at the waist; a silk handkerchief puffed from the pocket, and a dried carnation, lamentably faded, that had done duty for many days, enlivened with a feeble effort the worn silk lapel.

But the innate French effervescence, debonair, insouciant, was not gone yet. The little gentleman presented a card. Of course, the name boasted that humblest of titles—baron. The baron, it appeared, propitiated destiny by "Instruction in French, German and Italian," but now instruction was no longer propitious. With a deprecating giggle this was explained, the Baron did not wish to make the "reader" feel bad, to embarrass him.

"I will probably starve very soon," he observed, still with the modifying little giggle, and, of course, the inevitable shrug, "unless—my faith— something turns up."

It was to be turned up, evidently, by means of an attenuated manuscript which he presented. He had written—during the intervals of instruction —a series of articles on the character of Americans as seen by a Frenchman, and these had been published by the newspaper of the town in which he instructed—an absolutely obscure town, lost and forgotten, away up among the New Hampshire hills.

The articles, he insinuated, might be made into a book—a book that might be interesting to the great American public. And, with a naïvete that was absolutely staggering, he assumed without question that the firm would publish his book—that it was really an important contribution to American literature.

He would admit that he had not been paid very liberally by the country papers for the articles as they appeared. He was not Émile Zola. If he was he might have sold his articles at fifteen or twenty dollars each.

He said just that. Think of it! The poor little Instructor-Baron Zola! fifteen dollars! Well!

He left the articles—neatly cut out and pasted in a copybook—with the "reader" and gave as his address a dreadfully obscure hotel.

The "reader" could not make up his mouth to tell him, even before looking over the first paragraph of the first article, that as a book the commercial value of the offering was absolutely, irrevocably and hopelessly nil, and so the little manuscript went into the mill—and in two days was lost.

I suppose that never in the history of that particular firm was the search for a missing manuscript prosecuted with half the energy or ardor that ensued upon the discovery of this particular loss. From the desk files of the senior partner to the shipping slips of the packer's assistant the hunt proceeded—and all in vain.

Meanwhile the day approached on which the baron was to come for his answer and at last it arrived, and promptly at the appointed hour the poor little card with the hyphenated titled name written carefully and with beautiful flourishes in diluted ink was handed in.

Do you know what the publisher did? He wrote the absurd, pompous name across the order line of a check and signed his own name underneath, and the check was for an amount that would make even unpropitious Destiny take off his hat and bow politely.

And I tell you that my little Instructor-Baron, with eminent good humor, but with the grand manner, a *Maréchal du royaume,* waved it aside. Turenne could have been no more magnificent.[11] (They do order these matters better in France.) His whole concern—hunger-pinched as he may easily have been at the very moment—his whole concern was to put the embarrassed publisher at his ease, to make this difficulty less difficult.

He assured him that his articles were written *comme ci, comme ça,* for his own amusement, that he could not think of accepting, etc.

And I like to remember that this whole affair, just as if it had been prepared in advance for a popular magazine whose editor insisted upon "happy endings," did end well, and the publisher, who at the moment was involved in the intricacies of a vast correspondence with a Parisian publishing house, found a small position as translator in one of his subdepartments for the little Instructor-Baron who had the great good fortune to suffer the loss of a manuscript—in the right place.

And now the card—engraved, if you please—bears proudly the baron's name, supported by the inscription, "Official Translator and Director of Foreign Correspondence to the Firm of ——— & Co., Publishers."

FICTION WRITING AS A BUSINESS[12]

The exaggerated and exalted ideas of the unenlightened upon this subject are, I have found, beyond all reason and beyond all belief. The superstition that with the publication of the first book comes fame and affluence is as firmly rooted as that other delusion which asks us to suppose that "a picture in the Paris Salon" is the certificate of success, ultimate, final, definite.

---

11 Vicomte Henri de la Tour d'Aubergne Turenne, a seventeenth-century French general.
12 *Boston Evening Transcript,* January 1, 1902, p. 17.

One knows of course that, very naturally, the *Eben Holden* and *David Harum* and *Richard Carvel* fellows make fortunes,[13] and that these are out of the discussion, but also one chooses to assume that the average, honest, middle class author supports himself and even a family by the sale of his novels—lives on his royalties.

Royalties! why in the name of heaven were they called that, those microscopic sums that too, too often are less royal than beggarly? It has a fine sound, royalty. It fills the mouth. It can be said with an air—royalty. But there are plenty of these same royalties that will not pay the typewriter's bill.

Take an average case. No. That will not do, either, for the average published novel, I say it with my right hand raised, is, irretrievably, hopelessly and conclusively, a financial failure.

Take then an unusually lucky instance, literally a novel whose success is extraordinary, a novel which has sold 2500 copies. I repeat that this is an extraordinary success. Not one book out of fifteen will do as well. But let us consider it. The author has worked upon it for—at the very least—three months. It is published. Twenty-five hundred copies are sold. Then the sale stops. And by the word stop, one means cessation in the completest sense of the word. There are people—I know plenty of them—who suppose that when a book is spoken of as having stopped selling, a generality is intended, that merely a falling off of the initial demand has occurred. Error. When a book—a novel—stops selling, it stops with the definiteness of an engine when the fire goes out. It stops with a suddenness that is appalling, and thereafter not a copy, not one single, solitary copy is sold. And do not for an instant suppose that ever after the interest may be revived. A dead book can no more be resuscitated than a dead dog.

But to go back. The 2500 have been sold. The extraordinary, the marvelous has been achieved. What does the author get out of it, royalty of ten per cent. Two hundred and fifty dollars. Two hundred and fifty dollars for three months' hard work. Roughly, less than twenty dollars a week, a little over $2.50 a day. An expert carpenter will easily make twice that, and the carpenter has infinitely the best of it in that he can keep that work up year in and year out, where the novelist must wait for a new idea, and the novel writer must then jockey and manoeuvre for publication. Two novels a year is about as much as the writer can turn off and yet keep to a marketable standard. Even admitting that both the novels sell 2500 copies there is only $500 of profit. In the same time the carpenter

[13] Irving Bacheller, Edward N. Wescott, and Winston Churchill. Each of these novels sold approximately a half-million copies.

has made his $1800, nearly four times as much. One may well ask the question: Is fiction writing a money-making profession?

The astonishing thing about the affair is that a novel may make a veritable stir, almost a sensation, and yet fail to sell very largely.

There is so and so's book. Everywhere you go you hear about it. Your friends have read it. It is in demand at the libraries. You don't pick up a paper that does not contain a review of the story in question. It is in the "Book of the Month" column. It is even, even—the pinnacle of achievement—in that shining roster, the list of best sellers for the week.

Why, of course the author is growing rich! Ah, at last he has arrived! No doubt he will build a country house out of his royalties. Lucky fellow, one envies him.

Catch him unawares and what is he doing? As like as not writing unsigned book reviews at five dollars a week, in order to pay his board bill—and glad of the chance.

It seems incredible. But one must remember this: That for every one person who buys a book, there will be six who will talk about it. And the half-thousand odd reviewers who are writing of the book do not buy it, but receive "editorial" copies from the publishers, upon which no royalty is paid.

I know it for an undisputed fact that a certain novel which has even been called the best American novel of the nineteenth century, and which upon publication was talked about, written about and even preached about, from the Atlantic to the Pacific, took ten years in which to attain the sale of 10,000 copies.[14] Even so famous, so brilliant an author as Harold Frederic did not at the first sell conspicuously. *The Lawton Girl, The Copperhead, Seth's Brother's Wife,* masterpieces though they are, never made money for the writer. Each sold about two thousand copies. Not until *Theron Ware* was published did Mr. Frederic reap his reward.

Even so great a name as that of George Meredith is not a "sesame," and only within the last few years has the author of *Evan Harrington* made more than five or six hundred dollars out of any one of his world famous books.

But of course there is another side. For one thing, the author is put to no expense in the composing of his novel. (It is not always necessary to typewrite the manuscript.) The carpenter must invest much money in tools, must have a shop. Shop rent, tools repaired or replaced cut into his $1800 of profit. Or take it in the fine arts. The painter must have a studio, canvases, models, brushes, a whole equipment; the architect must have his draughting-room, the musician his instrument. But so far as initial expense is concerned, a half-dollar will buy every conceivable necessary

14 Unidentified.

tool the novelist may demand. He needs no office, shop, or studio rent; models are not required. The libraries of the city offer him a quiet working-place if the home is out of the question. Nor, as one has so often urged, is any expensive training necessary before his money-earning capacity is attained. The architect must buy instruction for many years. The painter must study in expensive studios, the musician must learn in costly conservatories, the singer must be taught by high-priced maestros. Furthermore, it is often necessary for the aspirant to travel great distances to reach the cities where his education is to be furthered, almost invariably a trip to, and a residence in Europe is indispensable. It is a great undertaking and an expensive one to prepare for the professions named, and it takes years of time, years during which the aspirant is absolutely nonproductive.

But the would-be novel writer may determine between breakfast and dinner to essay the plunge, buy (for a few cents) ink and paper between dinner and supper, and have the novel underway before bedtime.

How much of an outlay of money does his first marketable novel represent? Practically nothing. On the other hand let us ask the same question of, say, the painter. How much money has he had to spend before he was able to paint his first marketable picture? To reach a total sum he must foot up the expenses of at least five years of instruction and study, the cost of living during that time, the cost of materials, perhaps even the price of a trip to Paris. Easily the sum may reach $5000. Fifty cents' worth of ink and paper do not loom large beside this figure.

Then there are other ways in which the fiction writer may earn money —by fiction. The novelist may look down upon the mere writer of short stories, or may even look down upon himself in the same capacity, but as a rule the writer of short stories is the man who has the money. It is much easier to sell the average short story than the average novel. Infinitely easier. And the short story of the usual length will fetch $100. One thousand people—think of it—one thousand people must buy copies of your novel before it will earn so much for you. It takes three months to complete the novel—the novel that earns the two hundred and fifty. But with ingenuity, the writer should be able to turn out six short stories in the same time, and if he has luck in placing them, there is six hundred dollars earned, more than twice the sum made by the novel. So that the novelist may eke out the alarming brevity of his semi-annual statements by writing and selling "short stuff."

Then—so far as the novel is concerned—there is one compensation, one source of revenue which the writer enjoys and which is, as a rule, closed to all others. Once the carpenter sells his piece of work it is sold for good and all. The painter has but one chance to make money from the sale of his picture. The architect receives payment for his design and there is the end. But the novelist—and one speaks now of the American—may sell the same work over many times. Of course, if the novel is a failure it is a failure and no more is said. But suppose it is a salable, readable, brisk bit of narrative, with a swift action and rapid movement. Properly managed this, under favorable conditions, might be its life history: First it is serialized either in the Sunday press or, less probably, in a weekly or monthly. Then it is made up into book form and sent over the course a second time. The original publisher sells sheets to a Toronto or Montreal house and a Canadian edition reaps a like harvest. It is not at all unlikely that a special cheap cloth edition may be bought and launched by some large retailer either of New York or Chicago. Then comes the paper edition, with small royalties it is true, but based upon an enormous number of copies, for the usual paper edition is an affair of tens of thousands. Next the novel crosses the Atlantic, and a small sale in England helps to swell the net returns, which again are added to—possibly—by the "colonial edition" which the English firm issues. Last of all comes the Tauchnitz edition, and with this (bar the improbable issuing of later special editions) the exploitation ceases. Eight separate times the same commodity has been sold, no one of the sales militating against the success of the other seven, the author getting his fair slice every time. Can any other trade, profession or art (excepting only that of the dramatist, which is, after all, a sister art) show the like? Even (speaking of the dramatist) there may be a ninth reincarnation of the same story and the creatures of the writer's pages stalk forth upon the boards in cloak and buskin.[15]

And there are the indirect ways in which he may earn money. Some of his ilk there are who lecture. Nor are there found wanting those who read from their own works. Some write editorials or special articles in the magazines or newspapers with literary departments. But few of them have "princely" incomes.

RETAIL BOOKSELLER: LITERARY DICTATOR[16]

Of all the various and different kinds and characters of people who are concerned in the writing and making of a novel, including the author, the publisher, the critic, the salesman, the advertisement writer, the drummer—of all this "array of talent," as the billboards put it, which one has the most influence in the success of the book? Who, of all these, can, if he chooses, help or hurt the sales the most?—assuming for the moment

[15] Norris here anticipates the "reincarnations" of *The Pit* (1903), which—with the exception of Canadian and colonial editions—went through this process, culminating in a successful stage version in 1904.
[16] *Boston Evening Transcript,* November 20, 1901, p. 20.

that sales are the index of success, the kind of success that at the instant we are interested in.

Each one of these people has his followers and champions. There are not found wanting those who say the publisher is the all in all. And again it is said that a critic of authority can make a book by a good review or ruin it by an unfavorable one. The salesman, others will tell you—he who is closest allied to the money transaction—can exert the all-powerful influence. Or again, surely in this day of exploitation and publicity, the man who concocts great and skilful and fetching "ads" is the important one.

The author is next included. He can do no more than write the book, and as good books have failed and bad ones have succeeded—always considering failure and success in their most sordid meanings—the mere writing need not figure. But the fact remains that there are cases where publishers have exerted every device to start a book and still have known it to remain upon their hands; that critics have raved to heaven or damned to hell, and the novel has fallen or flown in spite and not because of them; that salesmen have cajoled and schemed and yet have returned with unfilled orders, and that advertisements that have clamored so loudly that even they who ran must have read, and yet the novel in question remained inert, immovable, a failure, a "plug."

All these, then, have been tried and at times have been found wanting. There yet remains one exponent of the business of distributing fiction who has not been considered. He, one claims, can do more than any or all of the gentlemen just mentioned to launch or strand a novel.

Now let it be understood that by no possible manner of means does one consider him infallible. Again and again have his best efforts come to nothing. This, however, is what is claimed: He has more influence on success or failure than any of the others. And who is he?

The retailer. One can almost affirm that he is a determining factor in American fiction, that, in a limited sense, with him is the future. Author, critic, analyst and essayist may hug to themselves a delusive phantom of hope that they are the moulders of public opinion, they and they alone. That may be, sometimes. But consider the toiling and spinning retailer. What does the failure or success of the novel mean to the critic? Nothing more than a minute and indefinite increase or decrease of prestige. The publisher who has many books upon his list may recoup himself on one failure by a compensating success. The salesman's pay goes on just the same whether his order slips are full or blank; likewise the stipend of the writer of "ads." The author has no more to lose—materially—than the price of ink and paper. But to the retail bookseller, a success means money made; failure, money lost. If he can dispose of an order of fifty books, he is ahead by calculable, definite, concrete profits. If he cannot dispose of the fifty his loss is equally calculable, equally definite, equally concrete. Naturally, being a business man, he is a cautious man. He will not order a book which he deems unsalable, but he will lay in a stock of one that promises returns. Through him the book is distributed to the public. If he has a book in stock, the public gets it. If he does not have it, the public goes without. The verdict of the public is the essential to popularity or unpopularity, and the public can only pass verdict upon what it has read. The connection seems clear and the proposition proved that the retail bookseller is an almost paramount influence in American literature.

It is interesting to see what follows from this and to note how the retailer in the end can effectually throttle the sham novelist who has fooled the public once. Were it not for the retailer, the sham novelist would get an indefinite number of chances for his life; but so long as the small book dealer lives and acts, just so long will bad work—and one means by this wholly bad, admittedly bad, hopelessly bad work—fail to trick the reading world twice. Observe now the working of it. Let us take a typical case. A story by an unknown writer is published. By strenuous exploitation the publishers start a vogue. The book begins to sell. The retailer observing the campaign of publicity managed by the publishers stocks up with the volume; surely when the publishers are backing the thing so strong it will be a safe venture, surely the demand will be great. It does prove a safe venture, the demand is great; the retailer disposes of fifty, then of a second order of one hundred, then of two hundred, then of five hundred. The book is now in the hands of the public. It is read and found sadly, sadly wanting. It is not a good story, it is trivial, it is insincere. Far and wide the story is condemned.

Meanwhile the unknown writer, now become famous, is writing a second novel. It is finished, issued, and the salesman who travels for the publishers begins to place his orders. The retailer, remembering the success of this author's past venture, readily places a large order. Two hundred is not in his opinion an overstock. So it goes all over the country. Returns are made to the author and he sees that some fifty thousand have been sold. Encouraging is it not? Yes, fifty thousand have been sold—by the publisher to the retailer, but here is the point—not by the retailer to the public. Of the two hundred our dealer took from the publisher's traveling salesman, one hundred and ninety yet remain upon his counters. The public, fooled once, on the first over-praised, over-exploited book, refuse to be taken in a second time. Who is the loser now? Not the author, who draws royalties on copies sold to the tradesman—the retailer; not the publisher who makes his profit out of the same transaction; but the retailer who is loaded down with an unsalable article.

Meanwhile our author writes his third novel. So far as he can see, his second book is as great a popular success as his first. His semi-annual statements are there to show it—there it is in black and white; figures can't lie. The third novel is finished and launched. At the end of the first six months after publication day the author gets his publisher's statement of sales. Instead of the expected 10,000 copies sold, behold the figure is a bare 1500. At the end of the second six months the statement shows about 250. The book has failed. Why? Because the retailer refuses to order it. He has said to the soliciting salesman, "Why should I, in Heaven's name, take a third book by this man when I have yet one hundred and ninety copies of his second novel yet to sell?"

It is hard for the salesman to controvert that argument. He may argue that the third book is a masterpiece, and—mark this—it may in fact be a veritable, actual masterpiece, a wonderful contribution to the world's literature; it is all of no effect. There stands the block of unsold books, one hundred and ninety strong, and all the eloquence in the world will not argue them off the counter. After this our author's publisher will have none of his books. Even if he writes a fourth and submits it, the publisher incontinently declines it. This author is no longer a "business proposition."

There cannot but be an element of satisfaction in all this and a source of comfort to those who take the welfare of their country's literature seriously to heart. The sham novelist who is in literature (what shall we say?) "for his own pocket every time" sooner or later meets the wave of reaction that he cannot stem nor turn and under which he and his sham are conclusively, definitely and irrevocably buried. Observe how it works out all down the line. He fools himself all of the time, he fools his publisher three times, he fools the retailer twice and he fools the Great American Public just exactly once.

NEWSPAPER CRITICISMS AND AMERICAN FICTION[17]

The limitations of space impose a restricted title, and one hastens to qualify the substantive "criticisms" by the adjective "average." Even "average" is not quite specialized enough; "vast majority" is more to the sense, and the proposition expanded to its fullest thus stands, "How is the vast majority of newspaper criticisms made, and how does it affect American Fiction?" And it may not be inappropriate at the outset to observe that one has adventured both hazards—criticism (of the "vast majority" kind) and also Fiction. One has criticized and has been criticized. Possibly then it may be permitted to speak a little authoritatively; not as the Scribes. Has it not astonished you how many of those things

[17] Syndicated, March 9, 1903.

called by the new author "favorable reviews" may attach themselves—
barnacles upon a lifeless hulk—to a novel that you know, that you know
every one must, must know, is irretrievably bad? "On the whole, Mr.
————'s story is a capital bit of vigorous writing that we joyfully recommend"—"A thrilling story palpitating with life," "One of the very best
novels that has appeared in a long time," and the ever-new, ever-dutiful,
ever-ready encomium, "Not a dull page in the book" (as if by the furthest
stretch of conceivable human genius a book could be written that did not
have a dull page; as if dull pages were not an absolute necessity). All
these you may see strung after the announcement of publication of the
novel. No matter, I repeat, how outrageously bad the novel may be. Now
there is an explanation of this matter, and it is to be found not in the
sincere admiration of little reviewers who lack the ingenuity to invent
new phrases, but in the following fact: it is easier to write favorable than
unfavorable reviews. It must be borne in mind that very few newspapers
(comparatively) employ regularly paid book-reviewers whose business
it is to criticize novels—and nothing else. Most book-reviewing is done as
an odd job by sub-editors, assistants and special writers in the intervals
between their regular work. They come to the task with a brain already
jaded, an interest so low as to be almost negligible, and with—as often
as not—a mind besieged by a thousand other cares, responsibilities and
projects.

The chief has said something like this (placing upon the scribe's table
a column of novels easily four feet high, sent in for review) :

"Say, B———, these things have been stacking up like the devil lately,
and I don't want 'em kicking 'round the office any longer. Get through
with them as quick as you can, and remember that in an hour there's such
and such to be done."

I tell you I have seen it happen like this a hundred times. And the scribe
must "read" and "review" between twenty and thirty books in an hour's
time. One way of doing it is to search in the pages of the book for the
"publisher's notice," a printed slip that has a favorable review—that is
what it amounts to—all ready-made. The scribe merely turns this in with
a word altered here and there. How he reviews the books that have not
this publisher's notice Heaven only knows. He is not to blame, as they
must be done in an hour. Twenty books in sixty minutes—three minutes
to each book. Now, it is impossible to criticize a book adversely after a
minute and a half of reading (we will allow a minute and a half for writing the review). In order to write unfavorably it is necessary to know
what one is writing about. But it is astonishing how much commendatory
palaver already exists that can be applied to any kind or condition of
novel. Is it a novel of adventure (the reviewer may know if it be such by

the ship on the cover design)—it will be appropriate to use these terms: "Vibrant with energy," or "Full of fine fighting," or "The reader is carried with breathless interest from page to page of this exciting romance." Is it a novel of rural life? These may be made use of: "Replete with quaint humor," "A faithful picture of an interesting phase of American life," etc., etc. Is it a story of the West (you can guess that from the chapter headings) it will be proper to say, "A strong and vital portraying of the wild life of the trail and frontier."

And so one might run through the entire list. The books must be reviewed, the easiest way is the quickest, and the quickest way is to write in a mild and meaningless phraseology, innocuous, "favorable." In this fashion is made the greater mass of American criticism. As to effects: It has of course no effect upon the novel's circulation. Only one person is at all apt to take these reviews, this hack-work, seriously.

Only one person, I observed, is at all apt to take these reviews seriously. This way lies the harm. The new writer, the young fellow with his first book, who may not know the ways of reviewers. The author, who collects these notices and pastes them in a scrap-book. He is perilously prone to believe what the hacks say, to believe that there is "no dull page in the story," that his novel is "one of the notable contributions to recent fiction," and cherishing this belief he is fated to a wrench and a heartache when, six months after publication day, the semi-annual account of copies sold is rendered. There is unfortunately no palaver in the writing of this—no mild-mannered phraseology; and the author is made to see suddenly that "this exciting romance" which the reviewers have said the readers "would follow with a breathless interest till the end is reached and then wish for more," has circulated among—possibly—five hundred of the breathless.

Thus, then, the vast majority of criticisms. It is not all, however, and it is only fair to say that there are exceptions—great papers which devote whole supplements to the consideration of literary matters and whose reviewers are deliberate, thoughtful fellows, who do not read more than one book a week, who sign their opinions and who have themselves a name, a reputation, to make or keep. These must have an effect. But even the most conspicuous among them cannot influence very widely. They may help, so one believes, a good book which is already becoming popular. No one of them can "make" a book by a "favorable review," as they could a little while ago in France. No number of them could do it, here in America. There are too many other reviewers. No one man, nor aggregation of men, can monopolize the requisite authority. And then with us the spirit of independent thinking and judgment is no doubt too prevalent.

PART FOUR

REVIEWS

Norris disliked reviewing. As a staff member for the *Wave*, where reviewing was one of his duties, he discussed most books casually and briefly, reserving his occasional longer reviews for books, authors, or problems which captured his interest. During 1901–1902, when he had no regular reviewing obligations, his few reviews are entirely of this second kind. Norris' extended reviews are thus an excellent introduction to his literary interests and concerns. His discussions of Zola's *Rome* and Kipling's *Kim*, for example, reveal that he admired in these seemingly disparate authors their similar exploration of the violent, sensational, and low—that which he called romance in his reviews and naturalism elsewhere. His review of Gibson's drawings contains a clear definition of his idea of "a man's woman," an idea which permeates his characterization of women. And his parodies represent a gallery of those writers who influenced his short stories—Kipling, Davis, Hope, and Bierce.

Norris' reviews, however, reveal not only his literary enthusiasms, but also the concrete applications of his critical beliefs. As often occurs in the transition from criticism to review, he simplified those beliefs in applying them, and narrowed them to two essential criteria—a sincere treatment of "life" and a craftsmanlike form. So Norris praises Howells and Millard for their fictional technique, and Zola, Kipling, and Horton for their presentation of "life." The review which best illustrates his detailed application of both criteria is his analysis of Winston Churchill's *The Crisis*. He discusses Churchill as a writer with an immense following who has chosen to truckle to popular vogues and to write a safe, imitative novel which is also deficient in structure and in selectivity.

Norris' best reviews have that combination of bold insight and vigorous style which characterizes his best fiction. His parodies, for example, indicate his ability to grasp the essence of a writer's theme and style, and then imaginatively recreate that perception into a blatantly comic representation of those tendencies toward the absurd in the writer's work. Moreover, there is little timidity in Norris' reviews. He is willing to strike out against the meretricious, whatever its prestige (*The Crisis* was the nation's best seller when he attacked it), or to praise an infamous Zola or an unknown Horton.

But Norris' reviews also contain weaknesses derived from his total commitment to his critical values. He applauds the naturalism of Zola and Kipling, but fails to recognize the ludicrousness of Zola's sensationalism in *Rome*, the sentimentality of Kipling's treatment of Indian life in *Kim*. His review and parody of Crane indicate his understanding of Crane's impressionism and symbolism, modes which Norris himself had used. He is at a loss, however, when faced with Crane's bitter ironic detachment, and can only attribute that quality to a defective sympathy or an incongruous flippancy. In short, Norris' reviews suggest, contrary to general belief, that the best reviewer is not the critic with a fully coherent and established critical system. For such critics, as in Norris' case, are often blind to defects in works which otherwise affirm some important critical value in their system, and are equally blind to excellencies which have no such role.

Norris is thus weakest when discussing a writer like Crane. Despite some insights into Crane's work, he lacked that sympathetic eclecticism which would allow him to respond to literary experience beyond the limits of his entrenched values and ideas. His reviews are strongest, as with *The Crisis*, when he can frontally assault a work whose flaws or strengths fall readily within his system, and when he can generate a genuine indignation or approval for a writer's neglected or fulfilled responsibilities.

THEORY AND REALITY: AN OLD AUTHOR AND A NEW WRITER CONSIDER THE SAME PROBLEM[1]

There have recently appeared two books, both dealing with the same very delicate sex problem, a problem so delicate in fact that it is almost impossible to consider the books critically. One of these books is by Mr. W. D. Howells and is called *A Parting and a Meeting*.[2] The other is by Mrs. J. R. Jarboe of this city and is called *Robert Atterbury*. Each book has to do with the "ultimate physical relation of man and woman." A dangerous subject truly.

Mr. Howells touches it lightly, delicately, handling it with the greatest subtlety and finesse. Mrs. Jarboe rushes in where Mr. Howells fears to tread, grapples the subject by the throat, sledge-hammers at it, tears the veil from it boldly, uncompromisingly.

Mr. Howells tells a story; Mrs. Jarboe develops a theory. The *Parting and Meeting* is a little tale of how a certain young man of some seventy years ago attempted to prevail upon his sweetheart to join the Shakers with him and to live out the remainder of their lives keeping the relations of brother and sister. In a scene of exquisite delicacy and sympathetic insight, the girl refuses. The man joins the Shakers and the girl marries elsewhere. Sixty years afterward they meet, and though Roger is so old as to be almost in his dotage, he recovers intelligence enough to say, "I'm not so sure but I'd have done about as well to have gone with *you*, Chloe." That is all; this is the whole story, a touch, a suggestion, a hint.

According to Mrs. Jarboe's theory "there is no love which can justify marriage as it is at present understood. There is no law, no blessing of priest or church, which can render it anything but legalized prostitution. It is a crime against nature, against the race, against God." The author proposes as a remedy the Malthusian theory of restraint, a theory beautiful upon paper but which practise and good political economists have long since demonstrated beyond question to be as delusive and impossible as the Ptolemaic system of astronomy. That the increase of the family after marriage should be restrained and limited is a fine and admirable ideal, but the idealists will close their eyes to the fact that men *and women* are after all only human. Even this word "human" is misleading. Is it not

---

[1] *Wave,* XV (May 2, 1896), 8.

[2] Norris' first extensive discussion of Howells' work. Throughout his career Norris had two, not necessarily opposing, views of Howells. On the one hand, he had great respect for Howells' personal character, his critical judgment and integrity, and his fictional craftsmanship. On the other, he deprecated the limited range and depth of Howellsian realism. This dualism became particularly marked after he met Howells in early 1898 and responded warmly to Howells the man. For Norris on Howells, besides the material in this volume, see his fictional portrayal of Howells in "A Lost Story" (republished in Vol. X of *The Complete Edition of Frank Norris* [1928], and *Letters*, pp. 23–24, 33–34.

even truer that so-called humanity still is, and for countless generations will be, three-quarters animal, living and dying, eating and sleeping, mating and reproducing even as the animals; passing the half of each day's life in the performance of purely animal functions? This is lamentable, no doubt, but the grandest theory ever conceived by the mind of the most prodigious thinker is powerless to better the condition of the race, in this respect, as far as immediate results are concerned. There is no prospect for betterment except in the gradual evolution of the type through infinitely vast periods of time.

Mrs. Jarboe, however, does not apply her theory to her hero and heroine—Atterbury and Sara—even after all its elaborate development throughout the first part of the story. In their case the two young people made a virtue of necessity, since one was a consumptive and the other under the shadow of hereditary insanity.

In the case of two healthy, natural young people in real life, or in a good realistic novel, Mrs. Jarboe's fine-spun web of logic would have been rent at the first breath. The greater author of the *Parting and Meeting* knew his real life better. Chloe even refused to consider a union of her life with that of her lover's, conceived upon any such morbid, Utopian principles, and even Roger acknowledges its futility in admitting that, after all, he would have done wiser to have gone back with Chloe.

Mrs. Jarboe presents her subject unskilfully. However admirable her theory—*as* theory—may be, it is not clearly and convincingly expressed in the pages of *Robert Atterbury*. No matter what its purpose or how great a lesson it purposes to teach, the novel should *be* a novel; first and foremost, it should tell a real story, of real people and of real places.

In Mr. Howells's story, even the old chaise horse becomes a character, "making snatches at the foliage and from time to time champing thoughtfully on his bit as if he fancied he might have caught a leaf in his mouth," and Chloe and Roger are flesh and blood characters from first to last. It is what *they* do and what *they* say that interest the reader. In *Robert Atterbury*, however, the people are little more than names and stand for nothing but the various mouthpieces for the author's theory. Chloe and Roger live and act by themselves, while Mrs. Jarboe shifts about the characters like a showman pulling the strings of his puppets. We forget Howells at once in the fortunes of his dramatis personae. We cannot lose sight of the author of *Robert Atterbury* for a single instant.

ZOLA'S *ROME*: MODERN PAPACY AS SEEN BY THE MAN OF
THE IRON PEN[3]

M. Zola has just completed and published the second instalment of his great Trilogy, *Les Trois Villes*. The first was *Lourdes*; the one which is

[3] *Wave*, XV (June 6, 1896), 8.

now in the hands of the reading public the world over—published simultaneously in four different languages—is *Rome*. *Paris* is the next to follow.

The main plot of *Rome* involves the doings of a French priest who visits the Eternal City and obtains an interview with the Pope in order to defend his book, *New Rome,* a work of radical and socialistic tendencies, which is about to be condemned by the Index. But, overwhelmed by the vast and changeless machinery of the Vatican policy, and disheartened by the blind adherence to dogma he is surprised to find in Leo XIII, he, of himself, repudiates his work, altogether disheartened. He is discouraged and can see no hope for the accomplishment of his purposes, when, on the point of leaving Rome, he picks up by chance a school book manual, a humble little work "containing little beyond the first elements of the sciences; still, all the sciences were represented in it, and it gave a fair summary of the present state of human knowledge." It dawns upon the young priest for the first time that here is the germ of the new power that is to revolutionize the world, and overturn and recreate all the great fabric of a purblind and tottering religion. Upon this slender framework M. Zola has constructed a vast panoramic picture of modern ecclesiastical Rome. While, of necessity, lacking in the magnificent action of some of the Rougon-Macquart series, *Rome* is, nevertheless, crammed with tremendous and terrible *pictures,* hurled off, as it were, upon the canvas, by giant hands wielding enormous brushes. As is the rule with this author's works, *Rome* leaves one with an impression of immensity, of vast, illimitable forces, of a breadth of view and an enormity of imagination almost too great to be realized. You lay the book down, breathless; for the moment all other books, even all other *things,* seem small and trivial.

It is almost impossible to criticize such a literary achievement. A few passages only can give one some idea of its character.[4]

. . . .

But *Rome* is not all mere description and ecclesiastical intrigue. A red thread of passion runs through the story. The critics who can see no romance in Naturalism may reflect upon this story of Benedetta and Dario. It involves a thwarted love affair, a stabbing at night in the shadow of a doorway, and culminates in the poisoning of Dario by his rival Prada, and Benedetta's death upon the dead body of her lover, the whole affair taking place in and about an old Italian palace. Certainly all this is romance enough. It is only in the details of some of the scenes and in the manner of their treatment that the naturalism is strong, as, for instance, the scene of the lovers' death. Especially faithful to the Gospel of Nat-

[4] I omit here and below lengthy quotations from the novel.

uralism is the sudden return of the hereditary instincts in Benedetta, the
fierce passion of the race blazing out at the supreme moment.[5]

. . . .

STEPHEN CRANE'S STORIES OF LIFE IN THE SLUMS: *MAGGIE* AND *GEORGE'S MOTHER*[6]

In *Maggie, a Girl of the Streets,* Stephen Crane has written a story
something on the plan of the episode of Nana in *L'Assommoir,* the dialect
and local color being that of the Bowery.[7] Mr. Crane strikes no new note
in his picture of the other half. Most of his characters are old acquaintances in the world of fiction and we know all about—or, at least, certain
novelists have pretended to tell us all about the life of the mean streets
of a great city.[8] In ordinary hands the tale of *Maggie* would be "twice
told." But Mr. Crane is, of course, out of the ordinary. I think that the
charm of his style lies chiefly in his habit and aptitude for making phrases
—short, terse epigrams struck off in the heat of composition, sparks
merely, that cast a momentary gleam of light upon whole phases of life.
There are hundreds of them throughout this tale of *Maggie.* Indeed, it
is the way Mr. Crane tells his story. The picture he makes is not a single
carefully composed painting, serious, finished, scrupulously studied, but
rather scores and scores of tiny flashlight photographs, instantaneous,
caught, as it were, on the run. Of a necessity, then, the movement of his
tale must be rapid, brief, very hurried, hardly more than a glimpse.

One of the best of these "flash-lights" is that of the "truck driver." At
first one is tempted to believe that it is a "long exposure," but on second
thought I conclude that it is merely a great number of snap-shots taken
at the same subject. It is as follows:

Jimmy became a truck driver. There was given to him the charge of a painstaking pair of horses and a large, rattling truck. He invaded the turmoil and
tumble of the down-town streets, and learned to breathe maledictory defiance

[5] One of the few times Norris explicitly mentions hereditary determinism as an element in Zolaesque naturalism.

[6] *Wave,* XV (July 4, 1896), 13.

[7] Norris' first critical estimate of Crane. He later met Crane in Florida during the
Cuban war and found Crane's drinking and behavior not to his taste (Jeannette Norris,
FWC). He discussed Crane disparagingly as the "young Personage" in his article "News
Gathering at Key West." This article, although written for the McClure syndicate, was
not published until 1914—as "On the Cuban Blockade," *New York Post,* April 11, 1914.
Franklin Walker later published it directly from the manuscript in *Letters,* pp. 9–18.
Before 1898 Norris thought that Crane was one of the exciting new writers dealing with
"life" (see p. 27 above). He seldom mentioned Crane in his post-1898 criticism.

[8] Norris alludes particularly to Arthur Morrison's *Tales of Mean Street* (1894), but
also to such other late nineteenth-century slum novels (besides *L'Assommoir*) as George
Gissing's *The Nether World* (1889) and Israel Zangwill's *Children of the Ghetto* (1892).

at the police, who occasionally used to climb up, drag him from his perch, and punch him. In the lower part of the city he daily involved himself in hideous tangles. If he and his team chanced to be in the rear he preserved a demeanor of serenity, crossing his legs and bursting forth into yells when foot passengers took dangerous dives beneath the noses of his champing horses. He smoked his pipe calmly, for he knew that his pay was marching on. If his charge was in the front, and if it became the key-truck of chaos, he entered terrifically into the quarrel that was raging to and fro among the drivers on their high seats, and sometimes roared oaths and violently got himself arrested.

The greatest cases of aggravated idiocy were, to his mind, rampant upon the front platforms of all of the street cars. At first his tongue strove with these beings, but he eventually became superior. In him grew a majestic contempt for those strings of street cars that followed him like intent bugs. He fell into the habit, when starting on a long journey, of fixing his eye on a high and distant object, commanding his horses to start and then going into a trance of observation. Multitudes of drivers might howl in his rear, and passengers might load him with opprobrium, but he would not awaken until some blue policeman turned red and began frenziedly to seize bridles and beat the soft noses of the irresponsible horses.

Good though the story is and told in Mr. Crane's catching style, the impression left with the reader is one of hurry; the downfall of Maggie, the motif of the tale, strikes one as handled in a manner almost too flippant for the seriousness of the subject.

George's Mother seems to me better than *Maggie.* For a short novel it is less pretentious, has fewer characters and more unity, conveying one distinct impression. It is the story of a "little old woman" and her boy George. The boy starts well enough, stays at home in the evening, and even goes—at least on one occasion—to prayer meeting with his mother. But he falls into bad company and becomes perverted. Incidentally the mother dies, of grief and disappointment, so Mr. Crane implies.

There is something about this death of "the little old woman" that rings surprisingly true:

Through the doorway he saw the oilcloth covering of the table catching a glimmer from the warm afternoon sun. The window disclosed a fair, soft sky. ... At intervals the woman out by the stove moved restlessly and coughed.
Over the transom from the hallway came two voices.
"Johnnie!"
"Wot!"
"You come right here t' me! I want yehs t' go t' d' store fer me!"
"Oh, ma; send Sally!"
"No, I will not; you come right here!"
"All right, in a minnet!"
"Johnnie!"

"In a minnet, I tell yeh!"

"Johnnie!"—there was the sound of a heavy tread, and later a boy squealed. Suddenly the clergyman started to his feet. He rushed forward and peered. The little old woman was dead.

It is most remarkable in Crane's novels to observe the truly marvelous fashion in which he feels and seizes the most subtle and hardly expressed moods and emotions. This quality of his was apparent on almost every page of the *Red Badge*. We have it again in *George's Mother*, coming out in such admirable analysis as this where George is beginning to fall in love with Maggie Johnson:

He laid clever plans by which he encountered her in the halls, at the door, on the street. When he succeeded in meeting her he was always overcome by the thought that the whole thing was obvious to her. He could feel the shame of it burn his face and neck. To prove to her that she was mistaken he would turn away from her with a granite stare.

But though these stories make interesting reading, the reader is apt to feel that the author is writing, as it were, from the outside. There is a certain lack of sympathy apparent. Mr. Crane does not seem to *know* his people. You are tempted to wonder if he has ever studied them as closely as he might have done. He does not seem to me to have gotten down *into* their life and to have written from what he saw around him. His people are types, not characters; his scenes and incidents are not particularized. It is as if Mr. Crane had merely used the "machinery" and "business" of slum life to develop certain traits or to portray certain emotions and passions that might happen anywhere. With him it is the broader, vaguer, *human* interest that is the main thing, not the smaller details of a particular phase of life.

A QUESTION OF IDEALS: THE AMERICAN GIRL OF 1896 AS SEEN BY WENZEL AND BY GIBSON[9]

During the last year two men of exceptional talent have been hard at work making pictures of the American girl in all the variety of her moods and tenses, and now in this holiday season the collected results have been put before the public in the shape of two picture books, to wit, *Pictures of People* by C. D. Gibson, and *Vanity Fair* by Albert Wenzel (R. H. Russell & Son, publishers), and it is very interesting to note how these two artists from their separate points of view have regarded and treated the same individual. For despite the mystifying titles it is the American

[9] *Wave*, XV (December 26, 1896), 7.

girl who plays the leading role in *Vanity Fair* and who heads the line in
Pictures of People.[10]

I think that at a very impressionable and formative age—probably a
very early one—Mr. Wenzel fell in love with a very stylish girl who was
short and blonde, with dark eyes and a rather heavy jaw and broad chin.
This girl must have been particularly graceful, given to wearing black
lace over rose-colored silk and must have had a habit of sitting turned
about half way from you while her elbow rested along the back of the
chair and her hand supported her chin—her broad chin. She was a very
pretty girl, by the way, and she went to operas and horse shows and sat
in boxes with highly ornamented hangings and pillars in the background.
At any rate, this is Mr. Wenzel's ideal, and he is very faithful to her and
rarely allows her to escape from a picture. I feel that I know her thoroughly by now and should recognize her at once if I should meet her—at the
opera in a highly decorated box for instance. Mr. Wenzel is fond of her
oftenest in evening dress, with her hair done high and a comb stuck in it
Spanish fashion, and he likes to have her sitting down—rarely do you see
her at full length—in the fore front of a great crowd, from which you
will notice she does not detach herself, but forms a part of it, being made
conspicuous only by virtue of her position. Also, this girl is vivacious, as
you would expect of a short girl, and smiles very easily, as you would
expect of a vivacious one.

But I am rather afraid she is a little superficial. However, she is the
leading figure in *Vanity Fair*. Never, never does she feel any real depths
of passion; never is her sweet high-piled hair disarranged, nor her picture
dress—black lace over colored silk—in disorder. She is always serene and
smiling and happy, and passes her life finding great amusement over
trifles.

But I know another girl who is very beautiful and stylish and all that
who smiles just as readily but who is capable of the graver, sterner note
as well. She is Mr. Gibson's American girl.[11] She has lived an eventful
life. When I first knew her she was (very gently) repudiating foreign
noblemen; then she passed through a period of great distress in her love
affairs; her love would die, or her husband's love, when once it had gone,
was hard to get back again, or she realized her mistake when it was too
late, or her husband persisted in dying and leaving her to weep on a beau-

[10] This review was accompanied by large-scale illustrations of "the American girl" from
the two books. The collection of drawings by Albert Wenzell (not *Wenzel*) is actually
entitled *In Vanity Fair*.

[11] Gibson's popularity had reached its long-maintained height by the mid-1890's, partially owing to his successful collaboration with Richard Harding Davis, whose novels he
illustrated. Many of Norris' heroines have the Gibsonesque combination of statuesque
beauty and firmness of mind. Norris believed that San Francisco women in particular
were Gibson types—tall, handsome, sturdy.

tiful broad divan covered with cushions and letters and things. Of late she has been going about in the costume of a general, or a diplomat, or a minister of the gospel, or a Lord High Chancellor, just as charming and as irresistible as ever in spite of—or perhaps because of—her change of raiment.

Unlike Mr. Wenzel's girl she is very tall and a little slim, and her dignity and imposing carriage are her great characteristics. She is rather grave, doesn't smile often, and then mostly with the eyes. Nor is she so entirely given over to society as the girl of the broad chin and high-piled hair. You see her in states of mind rather than in places, in conditions rather than in circumstances.

As I say, she is tall enough to look down on most men, does so, in fact, very often with her head tilted back and her eyes half closed—not at all the kind of girl you would choose to quarrel with. On the whole, I prefer her to the one of the broad chin. She is more serious, perhaps, and you must keep keyed pretty high to enjoy her society. But somehow you feel that she is a "man's woman" and would stand by a fellow and back him up if things should happen. I do not think Mr. Wenzel's girl would. I would like to put her to the test—if I were the man.

MILLARD'S TALES: PUNGENT EPISODES OF WESTERN LIFE,
SHORT AND POINTED[12]

Mr. F. B. Millard of the *San Francisco Examiner* is out with a collection of stories—some fifteen of them—which the Eskdale Press publishes under the general title of *A Pretty Bandit*.[13] In telling his yarns Mr. Millard has adopted the method employed by the latest successful short-story men. This is not to tell a story, but to strike off an incident or two, clean-cut, sharp, decisive, and brief, suggesting everything that is to follow and everything that precedes. The method is admirable, but it demands an originality and ingenuity on the part of the author that is little short of abnormal. The "motif" of the story must be very strong, very unusual, and tremendously suggestive. More than this, it must be told in sentences that are almost pictures in themselves. The whole tale must resemble, as one might say, the film of a kinetoscope, a single action made up from a multitude of view points. In choosing this method Mr. Millard has volunteered to enlist in the army of the strongest story-writers the world 'round, and some of his stories are quite good enough to bring him well up in the

12 *Wave*, XVI (August 21, 1897), 12.
13 Norris knew Millard personally, and occasionally discussed literary ideas with him, as Millard recalled (not always reliably) in his "San Francisco in Fiction" (*Bookman*, XXXI [August, 1910], 585–597). Millard was the editor responsible for publishing Edwin Markham's "The Man With the Hoe" in the *Examiner* early in 1899, an incident which Norris used in *The Octopus*.

front ranks, notably the "Caliente Trail," "A Notch in a Principality" (our thinking the best story of the book),[14] "The Girl Reporter," and "Horse-In-The-Water." It is a dodge of publishers, as everyone knows, to put the two best stories at the beginning and end of such a collection. But there is little in "A Pretty Bandit" and "The Making of Her" to commend them. Mr. Millard crystallizes a most startling experience in each of these tales, but somehow fails to convince the reader of its "probability"; as, for instance, the hold-up in the first-named story. That a girl should stand up a stage is extraordinary enough for the most sensation-loving reader, but that she should do so upon the impulse of the moment is quite beyond belief—even worse, it is inartistic. In "The Making of Her" (which came very near being the marring of her) Mr. Millard has evidently striven for a contrast of types, the Boston blue-stocking and the Western cowboy. The contrast is sharp enough, but the "events" narrated are not plausible. They all could have happened, it is true, but in story-telling the question is "might" they have happened. One can forgive the impossible, never the improbable. As a whole, however, the tales make capital good reading. Mr. Millard wastes no time—his own nor his readers—in getting down at once to the heart of his work. There is a plainness, a directness in his style that is "the easy reading and hard writing" one has heard so much about. The author has confined himself to California material, which is always good policy, and at the same time impresses his readers with the fact that he is thoroughly posted upon whatever subject is under consideration for the moment, whether it be railroad life, newspaper life, camp life, or ranch life.

PERVERTED TALES[15]

The discovery of California by the editors of the Big Four Magazines of the East has had the lamentable result of crowding from their exalted places, heretofore so secure, a number of the world's most fascinating storytellers. Their places have been filled from the ranks of that little army of youthful volunteers known as Les Jeunes.[16] As a lamentable result old idols have been overthrown, old gods forgotten, and the children in the market place no longer dance to the tune of old pipes. Where once the old favorite received a check, he now receives a printed form with veiled reference to availability, guarded allusions to the plans of the editor—and his

[14] This story, which deals with a wheat farmer in the San Joaquin valley, perhaps had a minor influence on *The Octopus*. Millard attempts to communicate a sense of the vastness of the San Joaquin and its ranches.

[15] *Wave*, XVI (December 18, 1897), 5–7.

[16] Gelett Burgess, Bruce Porter, and Juliet Wilbor Tompkins—all former contributors to the *Lark*—had recently migrated to New York and were beginning to write for the major magazines. Norris himself was soon to be "discovered" by McClure.

*story. With the view to stemming the perverse tide of popular favor—
whose ebb and flow are not reducible to any known law—and, if only for
a moment, sounding again the old notes once so compelling, the editors
of this paper have secured for publication a few of these rejected tales and
here submit them to the public of the West. Their genuineness is as
Caesar's wife, and if additional evidence were wanting the opinions of
experts in type-writing have been secured, which place their authenticity
beyond fear and beyond reproach.*[17]

THE 'RICKSHA THAT HAPPENED[18]

By R——D K——G

Ching-a-ring-a-ring ching-chaw
Ho, dinkum darkey.
                —The unedited diary of Bahlamooca Tah.

Jam yesterday and jam to-morrow
But never jam to-day.*—Native Proverb.*

"*Who's* all right? Rudyard! Who? *Rudyard!*"
                —Barrack-room ballad.

There was a man once—but that's another story. Personally, I do not
believe much of this story; however, you may have it for what it is worth,
to me it was worth five thousand dollars per thousand words.[19]

A friend of mine, who is a *jinricksha* down by Benares, told me this
tale one hot evening outside the Tiddledtypore gate. In the telling of it he
spat reflectively and often into the moat. *Chaprassi simpkin peg,* as Mrs.
Hawkseye says.

Mulligatawney, who is a private soldier and who dines with me at table
d'hôte on Thursdays, and who shares my box at the opera, says the tale
is cheap at a gallon and a half of beer.

"Pwhat nex!" exclaimed Mulligatawney, when he heard it, shifting his
quid to the other side of his mouth (we were at table). "It's *jaddoo,* that's

---

[17] The unusual length of the parodies which follow is explained by the fact that they
appeared in the *Wave's* annual Christmas supplement, in which contributions were considerably longer than those in the regular issues.

[18] Norris here parodies Kipling's basic fictional technique and material rather than a
particular story. However, the title recalls Kipling's "The Phantom 'Rickshaw," and the
character of Stepterfetchit is based on that of "The Boy" in Kipling's "Thrown Away."
Also present are such prominent Kipling characters as Mrs. Hawksbee and Mulvaney,
Ortheris, and Learoyd, the "soldiers three."

[19] A reference to Kipling's reputation as a hard bargainer and as the highest-paid living
writer.

phwat ut is. 'Tis flyin in the face uv natoor to trifle with such brutil and licenshous soldiery as me and Orf-of-this an' Lear-eyed." Here he stole a silver spoon to hide his emotion. *"Choop,* sez oi to im," said Mulligatawney, filling himself another *jinricksha, "choop,* an' he chooped, like *ghairun* gone clane *dal-bat* an' *Kipiri* in hot weather. I waz only a recruity then. But I waz a corpril wanst. I was rejuced aftherwards, but I waz a corpril wanst," and he stared mournfully at the dying embers in the *jinricksha.*

We are a terrible bad lot out here in Indiana, but we can't help that. Here a man's whole duty is to lie *doggo* and not *ekka* more than once a week, and to pray for a war. Also he may keep a *jinricksha* in his stable if he can afford it. As that wonderful woman, Mrs. Hawkseye, says: "It better to *bustee* in a *jampanni* than to have your *jinricksha puckarowed.*" But that's her affair.

Stepterfetchit had just come out from *home.* Now when a man comes out from home, if he is not *jinrickshaed* at the pier landing, he generally does one of three things (*jampanni chorah simpkin bungalow*), either he dies with swiftness, which is bad, or lives with swiftness, which is worse, or marries, which is worst of all. "A single man," says my friend Mulligatawney, "is an ornamint to the service." But as Lear-eyed observes, "when a mon is tewed wi' a lass he's *lokri* in a *bunder,* nothing but *dikh,*" and he flung himself (seven foot four of British soldier), full length upon his *jinricksha.*

Stepterfetchit knew as much of Life (Life with a big L) as a weaning child, until I, who have seen everything worth seeing, and done everything worth doing, and have known everything worth knowing, from Indian magic to the cleaning of codfish, took him in hand. He began by contradicting his colonel, and went on from that to making love to Mrs. Hawkseye (till the lady told him he was a *bungalow,* with no more *pukaree* than a *dacoit*), and wound up by drinking too much *jinricksha* at his club.

Now, when a man takes to the *jinricksha* he is very likely to end at the *shroff.* So I spoke to the Major. You may hit a *marumutta* over the head at the beginning of your acquaintance, but you must not soap the tail of a kitten that belongs to a *Ryotwary,* unless you are prepared to prove it on his front teeth. It takes some men a life time to find this out, but the knowledge is useful. *Sempkin peg, do re mi fa, ching-a-ring-a-ring-ching-chaw,* but that's another story. We arrived—the Major and I—at Stepterfetchit's dak-bungalow on a red hot evening, when the heat blanketed the world like a hot towel round a swelled head. We nearly killed the *jinricksha* in getting there, but a mountain bred can *gawbry* more *jhil* than you would care to believe.

"Hark!" said the Major. We paused on the threshold and the silence of the Indian twilight gathered us in its hollow palms. We both heard a sound that came from Stepterfetchit's window. It was the ticking of an eight-day clock.

People write and talk lightly of blood running cold and of fear and all that sort of thing, but the real sensation is quite too terrible to be trifled with. As the Major and I heard the ticking of that eight-day clock, it is no lie to say that the *bhisti mussick* turned *shikary* in our *khitmatgar*. We were afraid. The Major entered the *bungalow* and I followed and *salaamed* the door behind me.

The *jinricksha* lay dead on the *charpoy* in Stepterfetchit's room. Stepterfetchit must have killed it hours before. "We came too late," groaned the Major. We made no attempt to keep from crying—I respected my self for that. But we gathered up the pieces of the *jinricksha* and sent them to Stepterfetchit's people at Home.

So now you know what I know of the Ricksha that never was.

Stepterfetchit is now a plate-layer somewhere down near Bareilly, on the line of the railroad, where the *Kharki* water tanks [are] that the Rajah of Bathtub built out of stolen government money, when the commissariat bullock train was *puckarowed* by Pathans, in the days of the old *budmash* Mahommud Dinare, and Mulligatawney is away annexing Burmah. When he heard of the affair he said:

"If a *punkah* is goin' to *ayah* niver loose your grip, but I waz a corpril wanst, I was rejuced afterwards," which is manifestly unfair.

Mrs. Hawkseye says that a *"jinricksha* in the hand gathers no moss"—but that's another story.

THE GREEN STONE OF UNREST[20]

By S——N CR——E

A Mere Boy stood on a pile of blue stones. His attitude was regardant. The day was seal brown. There was a vermillion valley containing a church. The church's steeple aspired strenuously in a direction tangent to the earth's center. A pale wind mentioned tremendous facts under its breath with certain effort at concealment to seven not-dwarfed poplars on an un-distant mauve hilltop.

The Mere Boy was a brilliant blue color. The effect of the scene was not un-kaleidoscopic.

After a certain appreciable duration of time the Mere Boy abandoned his regardant demeanor. The strenuously aspiring church steeple no longer

[20] The first sentence of this parody recalls the opening of *Maggie*, but the rest of the piece satirizes *The Red Badge of Courage*.

projected itself upon his consciousness. He found means to remove himself from the pile of blue stones. He set his face valleyward. He proceeded.

The road was raw umber. There were in it wagon ruts. There were in it pebbles, Naples yellow in color. One was green. The Mere Boy allowed the idea of the green pebble to nick itself into the sharp edge of the disc of his Perception.

"Ah," he said, "a green pebble."

The rather pallid wind communicated another Incomprehensible Fact to the paranthine trees. It would appear that the poplars understood.

"Ah," repeated the Mere Boy, "a Green Pebble."

"Sho-o," remarked the wind.

The Mere Boy moved appreciably forward. If there were a thousand men in a procession and nine hundred and ninety-nine should suddenly expire, the one man who was remnant would assume the responsibility of the procession.

The Mere Boy was an abbreviated procession.

The blue Mere Boy transported himself diagonally athwart the larger landscape, printed in four colors, like a poster.

On the uplands were chequered squares made by fields, tilled and otherwise. Cloud-shadows moved from square to square. It was as if the Sky and Earth was playing a tremendous game of chess.

By and by the Mere Boy observed an Army of a Million Men. Certain canon, like voluble but non-committal toads with hunched backs, fulminated vast hiccoughs at unimpassioned intervals. Their own invulnerableness was offensive.

An officer of blue serge waved a sword, like a picture in a school history. The non-committal toads pullulated with brief red pimples and swiftly relapsed to impassivity.

The line of the Army of a Million Men obnubilated itself in whiteness as a line of writing is blotted with a new blotter.

"Go teh blazes b'Jimminey," remarked the Mere Boy. "What yeh's shooting fur. They might be people in that field."

He was terrific in his denunciation of such negligence. He debated the question of his ir-removability.

"If I'm goin' teh be shot," he observed; "If I'm goin' teh be shot, b'Jimminy—"

*   *   *   *   *   *   *   *

A Thing lay in the little hollow.

The little hollow was green.

The Thing was pulpy white. Its eyes were white. It had blackish-yellow lips. It was beautifully spotted with red, like tomato stains on a rolled napkin.

The yellow sun was dropping on the green plain of the earth, like a twenty-dollar gold piece falling on the baize cloth of a gaming table.

The blue serge officer abruptly discovered the punctured Thing in the Hollow. He was struck with the ir-remediableness of the business.

"Gee," he murmured with interest. "Gee, it's a Mere Boy."

The Mere Boy had been struck with seventy-seven rifle bullets. Seventy had struck him in the chest, seven in the head. He bore close resemblance to the top of a pepper castor.

He was dead.

He was obsolete.

As the blue serge officer bent over him he became aware of a something in the Thing's hand.

It was a green pebble.

"Gee," exclaimed the blue serge officer. "A green pebble, gee."

The large Wind evolved a threnody with reference to the seven un-distant poplars.

A HERO OF TOMATO CAN[21]

By B——T H——TE

Mr. Jack Oak-hearse calmly rose from the table and shot the bartender of Tomato Can, because of the objectionable color of his hair. Then Mr. Oak-hearse scratched a match on the sole of his victim's boot, lit a perfumed cigarette and strolled forth into the street of the camp to enjoy the evening air. Mr. Oak-hearse's face was pale and impassive, and stamped with that indefinable hauteur that marks the professional gambler. Tomato Can knew him to be a cool, desperate man. The famous Colonel Blue-bottle was reported to have made the remark to Miss Honorine-Sainte-Claire, when that leader of society opened the Pink Assembly at Toad-in-the-Hole, on the other side of the Divide, that he, Colonel Blue-bottle, would be everlastingly "—————— ————ed if he didn't believe that that ———— ————ed Oak-hearse would open a ————ed jack-pot on a pair of ————ed tens, ————ed if he didn't." To which Miss Ste.–Claire had responded:

"Fancy now."

On this occasion as Mr. Jack Oak-hearse stepped in the cool evening air of the Sierras from out of the bar of the hotel of Tomato Can, he drew from his breast pocket a dainty manicure set and began to trim and polish

---

[21] A parody, of course, of Harte's "The Outcasts of Poker Flat."

his slender, almost feminine finger nails, that had been contaminated with the touch of the greasy cards. Thus occupied he betook himself leisurely down the one street of Tomato Can, languidly dodging an occasional revolver bullet, and stepping daintily over the few unburied corpses that bore mute testimony to the disputations and controversial nature of the citizens of Tomato Can. He arrived at his hotel and entered his apartments, gently waving aside the half-breed Mexican who attempted to disembowel him on the threshold. The apartment was crudely furnished as befitted the rough and ready character of the town of Tomato Can. The Wilton carpet on the floor was stained with spilt Moet and Chandon. The full-length portrait of Mr. Oak-hearse by Carolus Duran was punctured with bullet marks, while the teakwood escritoire, inlaid with buhl and jade, was encumbered with bowie knives, spurs and Mexican saddles.

Mr. Oak-hearse's valet brought him the London and Vienna papers. They had been ironed, and scented with orris root, and the sporting articles blue-penciled.

"Bill," said Mr. Oak-hearse, "Bill, I believe I told you to cut out all the offensive advertisements from my papers; I perceive, with some concern, that you have neglected it. Your punishment shall be that you will not brush my silk hat next Sunday morning."

The valet uttered an inarticulate cry and fell lifeless to the floor.

"It's better to stand pat on two pair than to try for a full hand," mused Mr. Oak-hearse, philosophically, and his long lashes drooped wearily over his cold steel-blue eyes, like velvet sheathing a poignard.

A little later the gambler entered the dining-room of the hotel in evening-dress, and wearing his cordon of the Legion of Honor. As he took his accustomed place at the table, he was suddenly aware of a lustrous pair of eyes that looked into his cold gray ones from the other side of the catsup bottle. Like all heroes, Mr. Jack Oak-hearse was not insensible to feminine beauty. He bowed gallantly. The lady flushed. The waiter handed him the menu.

"I will have a caviar sandwich," affirmed the gambler with icy impassivity. The waiter next handed the menu to the lady, who likewise ordered a caviar sandwich.

"There is no more," returned the waiter. "The last one has just been ordered."

Mr. Oak-hearse started, and his pale face became even paler. A preoccupied air came upon him, and the lines of an iron determination settled upon his face. He rose, bowed to the lady, and calmly passed from the dining-room out into the street of the town and took his way toward a wooded gulch hard by.

When the waiter returned with the caviar sandwich he was informed that Mr. Oak-hearse would not dine that night. A triangular note on scented mauve paper was found at the office begging the lady to accept the sandwich from one who had loved not wisely but too many.

But next morning at the head of the gulch on one of the largest pine trees the searchers found an ace of spades (marked) pinned to the bark with a bowie knife. It bore the following, written in pencil with a firm hand:

Here lies the body
of
JOHN OAK-HEARSE,
who was too much of a gentleman
to play a
Royal-flush
against a
Queen-full

And so, pulseless and cold with a Derringer by his side and a bullet in his brain, though still calm as in life lay he who had been at once the pest and the pride of Tomato Can.

VAN BUBBLES' STORY[22]

By R——D H——G D——S

Young Charding-Davis had been a little unhappy all day long because on that particular morning the valet of his head serving man had made a mistake in the matter of his master's trousers, and it was not until he was breakfasting at Delmonico's some hours later that young Charding-Davis woke to the painful consciousness that he was wearing his serving-man's pants which were made by an unfashionable New York tailor. Young Charding-Davis himself ran over to London in his steam yacht once or twice a week to be fitted, so that the consequences of his serving-man's valet's mistake took away his appetite. The predicament troubled him so that he told the head cook about it, adding anxiously:

"What would you do about these trousers, Wallis?"

"I would keep 'em on, sir," said Wallis, touching his cap respectfully.

"That," said young Charding-Davis, with a sigh of relief, "is a good idea. Thank you, Wallis." Young Charding-Davis was so delighted at the novel suggestion that he tipped Wallis a little more generously than usual.

---

[22] Norris combines a parody of Davis' Van Bibber stories with personal satire of Davis himself, particularly Davis' exploits as a war correspondent. Probably the weakest of Norris' parodies.

"Can you recommend a good investment for this," inquired Wallis, as he counted out the tip.

"Make a bid for the Pacific railroads," suggested young Charding-Davis, "or 'arrive' at the Savoy Hotel."

That night he went to dinner at the house of the Girl He Knew, and in honor of the occasion and because he thought it would please the Girl He Knew, young Charding-Davis put on a Yale sweater and football knickerbockers and the headdress of feathers he had captured from a Soudanese Arab while acting as war correspondent for an English syndicate. Besides this, he wore some of his decorations and toyed gracefully with a golf-stick. During the dinner, while young Charding-Davis was illustrating a new football trick he had just patented, with the aid of ten champagne bottles and the Girl's pet skye terrier, a great and celebrated English diplomat leaned across the table over the center piece of orchids and live humming birds, and said:

"I say, Davis, tell us how you came by some of your decorations and orders. Most interesting and extraordinary, you know."

Young Charding-Davis tossed the skye-terrier into air, and batted it thoughtfully the length of the room with his golf-stick, after the manner of Heavyflinger of the Harvard baseball nine. Then he twirled the golf-stick in his fingers as a Zulu *induna* twirls his assegai—he had learned the trick while shooting elephant on the Zambesi river in South Africa. Then he smiled with becoming modesty as he glanced carelessly at the alarm-clock that hung around his neck, suspended by the blue ribbon of the order of the Pshaw of Persia.

"Really, they are mere trifles," he replied, easily. "I would not have worn them only my serving man insists it is good form. The Cham of Tartary gave me this," he continued, lightly touching a nickel-plated apple-pie that was pinned upon the sweater, "for leaving the country in twenty-four hours, and this chest protector was presented me by the French Legation in Kamschatka for protecting a chest—but we'll let that pass," he said, enveloping himself with a smile of charming ingenuousness. "*This* is the badge of the Band of Hope to which I belong. I got this pie-plate from the Grand Mufti for conspicuous egoism in the absence of the enemy, and this Grand Army badge from a pawnbroker for four dollars. Then I have a few swimming medals for swimming across Whirlpool Rapids and a five-cent piece given me by Mr. Sage. I have several show-cases full of other medals in my rooms. I'm thinking of giving an exhibition and reception, if I could get some pretty girls to receive with me. I've knocked about a bit, you know, and I pick them up here and there. I've crossed Africa two or three times, and I got up the late Greek war in order to make news for the New York papers, and I'm organizing an insurrection in South America for the benefit of a bankrupt rifle manufacturer who wants to dispose of some arms."

While Charding-Davis had been speaking young Van Bubbles, who was just out of the interior of Uganda, had been absent-mindedly drawing patterns in the tomato catsup he had spilled on the table-cloth.

"When I returned from Africa," he said, "this morning I had a curious experience." He fixed Charding-Davis with his glance for a moment, and then let it wander to a corner of the room and afterward drew it back and tied it to his chair leg. Charding-Davis grew a little pale, but he was too well bred to allow his feelings to overcome him. Young Van Bubbles continued:

"I met an old valet of mine on Fifth avenue, who has recently been engaged by the head serving man of one of New York's back-parlor heroes. He was wearing a pair of trousers which seemed to me strangely familiar, and when I spoke to him about the matter, broke down and confessed that he had caused his master's master to exchange trousers with him. You see the point of the story is," concluded Young Van Bubbles, untieing his glance, and allowing it to stray toward Charding-Davis, who drove it away with his golf-stick, "that the back-parlor hero wore his valet's trousers to-day."

There was a silence.

"What an extraordinary story," murmured the diplomat.

"Quite so," said the Girl Charding-Davis Knew.

"Of course," added Van Bubbles, "I took the trousers from him. Here they are," he continued, dropping them on the table. "You see they were no more use to him. I thought, perhaps"—and once more his glance crept stealthily toward young Charding-Davis—"*you* might suggest a way out of the difficulty." He handed the trousers to Charding-Davis, saying: "Keep them, they are a mere trifle, and they may be of some interest to you."

The Girl Charding-Davis Knew saw the point of Van Bubbles' story at once. Charding-Davis tried to catch her eye, but she refused to look at him, and said to her father:

"Why won't he go away; tell him to go away, please."

On the steps outside the house young Charding-Davis reflected what next he should do. He strolled slowly homeward, and, as he came into his rooms, his head serving-man handed him two notes which had arrived in his absence. One was from the Most Beautiful Woman in New York offering him her hand and fortune; the other was written on the back of a ten thousand dollar check, and was from the Editor of the Greatest Paper in the World begging him to accept the vacant throne of the Nyam-Nyam of Khooinooristan in the capacity of Special Correspondent.

"I wonder now," said young Charding-Davis, "which of these offers I shall accept."

AMBROSIA BEER[23]

By A——E B——E.

Sterling Hallmark was one of the most prominent and enthusiastic members of the Total Abstinence Union of San Francisco. His enthusiasm was not only of the passive description. He took a delight in aiding the police in their raids upon the unlicensed beer halls of the Barbary Coast. He helped them break whisky and brandy flasks, and he himself often opened the spigots of the beer kegs and let the foaming liquid run out upon the sanded floor.

On the night of the thirtieth of February, 1868, Sterling Hallmark led the police in a furious attack upon the "Hole in the Wall," a notorious subterranean dive in the vicinity of Jackson street. The battle was short and decisive. The bartender and his assistants were routed and the victorious assailants turned their attention to the demolition of the unsavory resort. Bottles were broken, brandy flasks smashed, the contents of the decanters emptied. In the midst of the confusion Sterling Hallmark advanced with splendid intrepidity towards a large keg, bearing the inscription Ambrosia Beer, extra pale. He set his hand upon the spigot.

But at that moment a terrific crash rent the air. The frail building, in the cellar of which the "Hole in the Wall" was situated, collapsed because it was necessary it should do so at that precise instant for the purposes of this tale. The crazy edifice fell with a loud clatter and clouds of blinding dust.

When Sterling Hallmark recovered consciousness he was not for the moment aware of what had happened. Then he realized that he was uninjured, but that he was unmovably pinioned beneath a mass of debris, and that something was weighing heavily upon his chest. Looking up and around him he perceived in the dim light a ring of metal protruding from a dark object that lay upon his chest. As his senses adjusted themselves to his environment he saw that the dark object was the keg of Ambrosia Beer, and that the ring of metal was the mouth of the spigot. The mouth of the spigot was directly in the line of his lips and not two inches distant from them. The terrible question that now confronted Sterling Hallmark was this, Had he opened that spigot before the collapse of the building, was the keg full or empty? He now found that by great exertion he could move his right arm so that his fingers could touch and clasp the spigot. A horrible fear came upon Sterling Hallmark, drops of cold perspiration bespangled his brow; he tried to cry out, but his voice failed him. His mouth was dry. A horrible thirst tortured him—a thousand fiends seemed

---

[23] A parody of one of Bierce's most famous Civil War stories, "One of the Missing." Norris successfully captures Bierce's typical combination of circumstantial detail, an ingenious denouement, and a cynical conception of fortune.

shouting to him to open the spigot, unseen hands tugged at *his* free hand. He raised this hand to cover his eyes from the sight, but as he withdrew it again it dropped upon his breast two inches nearer the fatal spigot. At length the strain became too great to be borne, Sterling Hallmark became desperate. He laughed aloud in almost insensate glee.

"Ha, Ha!" exclaimed Sterling Hallmark.

He reached up and grasped the spigot and turned it with all his strength.

*   *   *   *   *   *   *   *

An hour later when the rescue party with axes and hatchets found their way into the cellar of the "Hole in the Wall," the foremost of them hauled out Sterling Hallmark.

"Thash a' ri' girlsh," screamed the unfortunate man as his rescuers tried to keep him on his feet. "Thash a' ri', I ne'r him feelsh sho 'appy, as-I-do-t'ni'. Les op'n n'er li'l' bol, girlsh." The patrol wagon was rung for, and the raving inebriate was conveyed to the City Hall. The ride in the open air, however, had the effect of sobering him. He realized that he, Sterling Hallmark, temperance leader, had been *drunk*. He also realized that he could not stand the disgrace that would now inevitably follow him through life. He drew his revolver, and ere the policeman who accompanied him could interfere, had sent a bullet crashing through his brain.

*   *   *   *   *   *   *   *

A few moments after the patrol wagon had departed one of the rescue party discovered the keg labelled Ambrosia Beer, that had been rolled from the breast of Sterling Hallmark. With a few well-directed blows of his ax, he smashed in the head of the keg, and thrust his hand down to the bottom, groping about.

The interior of the keg was full of dust and rusty nailheads.

"Empty for over a year," he exclaimed, in tones of bitter disappointment.

I CALL ON LADY DOTTY[24]

From the Polly Parables

By AN——Y H——PE

Like most women, Lady Dotty is in love with me—a little. Like most men, I am in love with Lady Dotty—a great deal.

Last Thursday afternoon at five o'clock, as I was strolling in St. James'

---

[24] A parody of Hope's subject matter and dialogue form in his *Dolly Dialogues* (1894).

Park (you may have remarked that I always stroll—in St. James' Park—on Thursday afternoons) it occurred to me to call on Lady Dotty. I forthwith presented myself at the house (it is by Van Burgh).

After I had waited some five minutes in the drawing-room Lady Dotty appeared.

"But I am not at home," she said on the threshold. "I am not at home, Mr. Carterer."

"Nor am I," I replied.

"And my husband is—"

"At home?"

"At his club."

"The brute," said I, "to leave you alone."

"There are others," she sighed, with half a glance at me. I had not called in a fortnight.

"I have languished in self-imposed solitude," I murmured with some gallantry.

"Why have you not been to see me in so long."

"My laundress—" I began.

"Your *laundress*, Mr. Carterer?"

"Refused to relent."

"You poor dear. Tea?"

"You are too kind," said I, with a bow.

Lady Dotty's maid, a delicious young creature named Negligee, appeared with the tray and smoking cups and vanished.

Lady Dotty handed me my cup.

"Sit down," she ordered.

There was but one chair in the room. I sat down. Lady Dotty—also sat down.

"Clarence is a beast," she said.

"Most husbands are."

"Sometimes they are not."

"When?"

"When they are other women's husbands."

"Wives," I remarked, "of other men are no less so."

"Why can't other men's wives marry other women's husbands," suggested Lady Dotty.

"The question is worthy of consideration," said I.

Negligee hurriedly entered at this point of our conversation.

"The husband of Madame," she exclaimed.

"Good heavens," said Lady Dotty.

I took my hat.

"Fly, Mr. Carterer," cried Lady Dotty.

"This way," murmured Negligee. "Follow me." She led me out into the dark hall, where the back stairs were.

"It is rather dark, sir. You were best to give me your hand."

"And my heart," I answered.

Our hands clasped.

It was, as Negligee remarked, rather dark.

The charming creature's face was close to mine.

"Were you ever kissed?" said I, boldly.

"I don't know how to kiss," said Negligee.

"We might put our heads together and find out how," I suggested.

As I say, Negligee is a delicious young creature. But a man never knows the usefulness of his watch until he is without it—to say nothing of his scarfpin.

FRANK NORRIS' WEEKLY LETTER[25]

The most abiding impression that one receives from a reading of *The Crisis* is one of regret. Here is a man whose immense public is assured, who is above the necessity of truckling, of bidding for popularity, whose subject is in a sense made to hand, already dramatic, picturesque, interesting; whose theme is enwoven with the career of the most lovable of great men, Lincoln, and yet who has thought it advisable to be cautious, to exercise an undue restraint, to use gray colors. So large a stage, so heroic a theme, so vast an audience, so boundless a popularity and such meager performance, such conservatism, such politeness, such decorum, such cautious holding to old ideas, to trite formulas, to accepted, time-honored, time-worn standards.

The Crisis—the very name implies vigorous action, and the handling of an epic phase of history with a powerful, unrestrained grip, and yet, always the repression of spontaneity, always from page to page, from chapter to chapter, the holding back of impulse. One expects the leap and finds instead only painful, painstaking clambering.

What—a war story and not one scene of battle struck off in the heat of blood! A tale of the death grapple of millions and not one inspiriting encounter. There is, to be sure, the episode in the nineteenth chapter, the capture of Camp Jackson by the Yankees, but how confusedly presented, how diffused the action; cut up into chapters, rendered in piece-meal, instead of en bloc.

It seems to me that this diffuseness, the scattering and partitioning of the drama, is the weakest point in Mr. Churchill's novel. Where is the

25 *Chicago American*, June 22, 1901, p. 8.

grouping? Just what is the writer trying to show? Upon what peg does he hang his story? Up to what pivotal scene does he lead?

Just what is the crisis? Is it in the chapter called "The Crisis" (Chapter V of Book II)? If so, it is strangely out of place in the early part of the novel before the narrative is well begun. By the expression crisis, to just what does Mr. Churchill refer? Is it the crisis in the life of the nation, or in the life of Virginia, or in the life of Abraham Lincoln? It is not clear. Not once in the book is there a single incisive stroke. The story does not seem to be "managed," constructed, arranged, plotted out.

The historical parts are for the most part distinct and unhinged from the fictitious. It is not an historical novel so much as historical events plus a novel.

And such a chance as he had! The story is laid in his native city, familiar to him as the palm of his hand. Yet there is little sense of background, of stage-setting. The place might as well have been New Orleans or Cincinnati. The reader does not see St. Louis. The time of the action is the most dramatic in the history of the country, and yet one misses the drama. It will be argued that in the course of the tale many of the grand scenes of history are included, many of the great figures of the time are introduced. But it is an open question whether this is the right method to be employed to reconstruct a period, to create the atmosphere of a phase.

Much, infinitely much more should have been attempted, or much less. Would not the idea of the civil war times have been more clearly, more forcibly presented by the working out in detail of a single theme, a single line, rather than by the synoptic description of the entire epoch from the time of the Lincoln-Douglas debates to the time of the President's assassination? Suppose Mr. Churchill had elected for his main theme the battle of Gettysburg, the surrender at Appomattox, or the tragedy of Ford's Opera House.[26] Any one of these if worked out in detail would have implied and suggested the whole drama, the entire picture. It would have unified the book, solidified it, made it compact, direct, forceful and infinitely more interesting. No novelist that ever lived or will live could make a picture of the whole of the civil war in the compass of one, nor of one hundred volumes. Yet this is what the author of *The Crisis* sets out to do in 500 pages, and tell the story of Brice and Virginia at the same time.

And to consider now this part of the book—the love story of Virginia Carvel and Stephen Brice. There can be no question of Mr. Churchill's earnestness, no question of his "capacity for taking pains." Yet why in

[26] Charles Norris recalled that one of Frank's plans, after completing the epic of the wheat, was for a trilogy centering on the Battle of Gettysburg. See Charles G. Norris, *Frank Norris: 1870–1902* (New York: Doubleday, Page & Company, 1914), p. 14.

the face of these indubitable powers of his has he elected to sound again, for the hundredth time the old, old note—the story of the Northern man in love with the Southern girl, and the Southern girl responding to this affection in the end, after the usual period of hatred and defiance; the two continually at variance and separated by the violence of their patriotism— the one standing out for the nation and the other for state's sovereignty.

How often have we met these two, how wearisome are their misunder- standings, brought about in the same old way, carried on in the same old fashion, calmly and with dignity by the man, impulsively and hysterically by the girl, and ending in the trite reconciliation and in the girl's discovery of the Northern gentleman's heroism, which he carefully conceals from her and which the other characters in the book are as careful to proclaim. And the girl's father, or uncle, or guardian—it makes no difference so long as he is of the type of the Southern gentleman of the old school. In this case it is Colonel—of course, Colonel—Carvel. It needs not Mr. Christy's illustrations to know that he wears a slouch hat (even in the house in the presence of his daughter, punctiliously courteous though he is) and a goatee and a frock coat. We knew the Colonel long before we knew Mr. Churchill. We have known him ever since the publication— years ago—of the first novel of Southern life.

And Clarence Colfax. We know him, too—type of the young South, hot-headed, generous, worthless and courageous. The instant he comes upon the stage we know how he will end; how he will redeem a misspent life by unheard of courage on the battlefield. How he will be the rival and enemy of the hero and be pardoned and forgiven and saved by the latter's magnanimity. Hopper is an old friend, too, and, oh! the worn out, thread- bare situation where he holds the Colonel's life in his hand and by this means hopes to force the heroine into accepting him as her husband!

So one closes the book with disappointment and a sense of wonder that Mr. Churchill, with all his earnestness, his ability for painstaking work, should have thought fit to truckle to the public with these bids for popu- larity, when his public to the extent of 200,000 readers was assured to him beforehand. Instead of a great, forceful, vivid story of a forceful, vivid time he has given us a "safe book" that may be read without fear and without reproach by the mildest young woman that ever "attended" a seminary. This for the description of Vicksburg:

> First there was a murderous assault and a still more murderous repulse. Three times the besiegers charged, sank their color staffs into the redoubts and three times were driven back. Then the blue army settled into the earth and folded into the ravines. Three days in that narrow space between the lines lay the dead and wounded suffering untold agonies in the moist heat. Then came a truce to bury the dead, to bring back what was left of the living.

"Murderous assault," "murderous repulse," "three times charged, three times driven back," "wounded suffering untold agonies," "what was left of the living," verbiage, empty phrases. Could Mr. Churchill have given us nothing better than this for Vicksburg? Vicksburg!

The best things in the book are the Lincoln portraits, especially the Lincoln of the debates, the Lincoln of the Freeport tavern, telling the story of the Quaker's apprentice and the rats. Then, after the great controversy, taking a child upon his knee and playing his jewsharp. One sees the rugged, human man of the people in these pictures; no heroics, no capitulations, no false colorings—just the plain, honest man he must have been. No doubt that Mr. Churchill has succeeded here. And the split between Colonel Carvel and Judge Whipple—admirably done; one sees and feels the inevitableness of it, understands it all plainly, with no less liking for either of the men.

Then, too, the scene where Brice, at first ashamed to be seen by Virginia in the crowd that are gaping at her as she stands talking to the Prince of Wales, rallies from this sense of false shame, "because of one whom he had known for the short space of one day. . . . Abraham Lincoln would not have blushed between honest clerks and farmers." There is something at once very boyish and very manly to this touch, thoroughly probable and true and persuasive.

But happy touches, be they never so many, do not make a good novel. In the end *The Crisis* is not interesting. It puts sentiment above sincerity. It puts the "small testament" into the hands of the wounded soldier, the fine speeches into the mouths of men and women laboring under great stress, it conceives of the hero as immaculate, of the heroine as without a flaw. It sacrifices truth to a false sense of beauty, and violates probability for the sake of stage effect.

On page 70 there is set forth a rather strenuous dialogue between Virginia and Clarence Colfax. He asks her to marry him and she answers that he must learn self-control.

"You must prove first that you are a man," she says. We are told that just here a doe ran out of the forest not twenty feet away; twenty feet mind you. "But it" (our marriage) "has all been arranged," protests the young man.

"No one shall arrange that for me," replies Virginia promptly, and to avoid him (for he is supposed to step close to her at that) she leaps over the low fence railing, and "the doe fled into the forest whistling fearfully."

Now, just what has this doe got to do with the affair, "whistling fearfully," too? First it comes out of the forest, then it goes in again. Why? What is gained or proved or shown by this bobbing in and bobbing out

of a doe? The doe came out of the forest. The doe goes back into the
forest.

The King of France with forty thousand men
Marched up the hill and then marched down again.

FRANK NORRIS' WEEKLY LETTER[27]

In a period of the most discouraging depression of literary standards
when slovenly work passes current without comment and the plagiarism
of ideas, not even originally worth the pilfering, usurps the place of legitimate fiction, it speaks well for the future of the American novel to come
upon such a novel as Mr. Horton's *Like Another Helen.*[28]

To my mind the importance of this book does not depend upon its
vigor of action, its vividness of presentation, nor the fidelity of what it
sets out to tell; these are minor points—in this book. Vigor of action—
heaven knows—is not wanting in these days of cut and thrust romance,
nor plainness of picture making nor even, sometimes, truthfulness.

But the one thing that is oftenest most lamentably deficient, the single
quality most rarely met with, is just that which impalpably but surely
disengages itself from the story. I mean Sincerity. Write it with a capital,
blow it from trumpets, cry it at the four corners of the country: Sincerity,
Sincerity and again Sincerity; no sham, no pretense, no trading upon another man's success, no pilfering, no quackery, but "my own stuff"
straight from the shoulder. There you have it; I made it, all myself. I
did not take another man's ideas, rearrange them, revamp them, cut a little
here, let out a little there, put on just a different frill at this point, just a
different embroidery at this spot, shake it altogether, slap on a title—that
sounds much like that of the other man's work—flood the market with a
hundred thousand copies and exclaim "Behold!"

The author of *Helen* could have done this—easily; almost anybody
can; grammar and a right hand unparalyzed are all that are necessary. In
Helen George Horton has something to say. Personally and of his own
experience he has seen the Turk and the Greek. He has made up his novel
from scenes he has actually witnessed, from characters he has actually
known, from conditions he has actually studied, and, though his composition is a little disjointed in places, the whole story ramps with life and
rings with the unmistakable timber of truth and sincerity. I know of no
other book—certainly no other novel—that gives a better or truer picture
of the Turk as he is to-day. You feel that it must be true, for there are

[27] *Chicago American,* July 20, 1901, p. 8.
[28] George Horton (1859–1942) was an editor, a diplomat, and an author of poems and
fiction. The novel reviewed by Norris was published in 1901.

unconscious and unstudied irregularities in the picture Mr. Horton makes
—the very crudities and unliterary lapses in the descriptions—by which
one can tell at once that they are true to life, just as the unsymmetrical
unevenness of a piece of inlay work, say, is proof positive that it is hand
work and not the output of a machine.

If *Eben Holden* has sold its thousands, this book should sell its tens
of thousands. If *To Have and To Hold* has reached its two hundred
thousand mark, this book should double it.[29] It is not a great book, its
action is too swift for that, its range by nature of the conditions it portrays
too limited, its movement vibrates rapidly in a small arc, rather than
slowly in a large one. If it were a great book it would not be—could not
be—artistic; proportion forbids. But it is all the more interesting perhaps
for that very reason, more easily read. It is not, thank God, "crammed
with exciting incidents from cover to cover." If it were it would be hopelessly, helplessly, insufferably dull. It leaves something to be desired in
its mechanics. There are chapters—no more than two—which might be
omitted. But does this matter so very much? In some novels it would;
some novels would be better if enough chapters were omitted to cut them
down to the limit of short stories. And for some, most, in fact, it would
be better were they not written at all. But I forgive a man—a writer—
anything so long as he will not lie and does not steal, forgive him slips of
workmanship—in fact, do not think of them. Small virtues these to ask
of a man.

But no one, I take it, likes to be lied to, all the more so when the other
man knows that you know he is lying; and certainly no one enjoys paying
a dollar and half for stolen goods, all the more so when the goods are
found to be upon inspection plated brummagem ware.

But there is no plate, no brummagem about Mr. Horton's *Helen*. I do
not care very much whether or not it be uneven in outline. Knuckle it
and it rings true metal, look close and somewhere you shall find it stamped
with the good word sterling.

MR. KIPLING'S *KIM*[30]

The printing presses of the world go clashing on month after month
turning out the mediocre, the commonplace, the bizarre, the imitation,
and after a time we are content with such and are confused and tricked
by the noise of much advertising and hired clamor, so that we think that
perhaps the enormously popular is of some merit after all. Then, squarely

---

[29] Best sellers by Irving Bacheller and Mary Johnston, the first a "country" novel, the
second a colonial Virginia romance.
[30] *World's Work*, II (October, 1901), 1341–42.

in the midst of all this, true cut as a block of marble, finished and polished as marble, comes such a book as *Kim,* and we stand "attention" with hats off, and the little people shrink back to the tiny niches where they belong and we who have condoned them and excused them are left ashamed, and confused before the Master of the Craft.[31]

The story of *Kim* is simple—merely the initial adventure of the hero's career as an agent in the Indian Secret Service. But upon this insignificant peg is hung as rich and strange a fabric of fiction as ever the mind of romancer conceived.

Nowhere in all his books thus far has Mr. Kipling gone so deep or ranged so widely in the vast under-world of India as in this book. The presentation of the living, moving picture of the Great Road along which the lama and Kim travel, the Serai, the strange shop of that strange man Lurgan Sahib, the native compartments in the railway, the forecourt of the Sahiba's house, the Temple at Tirthankers and last and most powerful of all the breathless enormity of the Himalayas—all pictures so vivid that absolutely the last word upon native India seems to have been said.

The gamin of India—that is Kim, in his elements the same as the London ragamuffin and the New York arab. Thus far we claim him as a brother; it is not far; it is not much, just enough for one to feel the human kinship—and no farther, and no more. It could not be otherwise; for, oh! the wonderful, complex, strange life of him, and his strange friends, and the devious, *louche,* as it were underground ways of him! But he is the New Boy—the New Boy of fiction, brother to Huck Finn and Tom Sawyer and yet as unlike, as removed, as distant, as the Ganges is distant from the Mississippi.

Other boys will come, many will go, but Kim is to stay. By just so much is the reading world the richer, and we can all from now on count one more friend—"the little friend of all the world."

It is the Oriental expression of exactly the same qualities that one finds in the street boy of London, Paris or New York that is the wonder of Kim. He is not only a shrewd, quick-witted, resourceful boy, but his shrewdness, his quick wit, his resource are those of the Oriental. In this is a great achievement of Mr. Kipling. If he had merely made such a boy of his own race it would be a matter of surprise, but to understand—to the very bottom—the hard little, crude little, contradictory little heart of a boy, and to get at it below the perplexing mysterious externals of the Indian life in which it has its being—there is the great thing that Mr. Kipling has done. And the portrait is so vivid that for all its unfamiliarity one knows it to be true.

[31] Norris' praise indicates that his admiration for Kipling, like that for Zola, remained steadfast throughout his career.

And then the troop of minor people—one is compelled to call them minor—for the wonder work of Kim himself dwarfs all else besides—that follow after! Mahbub-Ali, the horse dealer, with the dyed vermilion beard, the Sahiba, garrulous, scheming, shrill and strident, softened and made lovable at the end by the development of the mother affection for Kim; the old lama, the dear, child-like, innocent old lama; Lurgan Sahib —healer of sick pearls—a new portrait in the Kipling gallery—and above all the Babu, the Babu Hurree. Of all the men in the book he is the best, of all the Kipling people up to now he is one of the most successful. Ambitious for the F.R.S., a student of ethnology, able to quote Herbert Spencer; yet frightened at Huneefa's magic. Hear him speak (Huneefa is at work upon her magic over Kim's drugged body). " 'I—I apprehend it is not at all malignant in its operation!' said the Babu watching the throat muscles quiver and jerk as Huneefa spoke. 'It—it is not likely that she has killed the boy? If so, I decline to be witness at the trial. . . . What was the last hypothetical devil mentioned?' "

(Mahbub here says that the devils invoked are not friendly to the Babu's ilk.)

" 'Then you think I had better go?' said Hurree Babu, half rising. 'They are, of course, dematerialized phenomena. Spencer says—'."

And here he is interrupted. An article might be written on just that Babu. He is India in transition, and his humor and his strange courage (he calls himself, and justly, "a fearful man," yet, how he plays the Great Game with the two Russian spies who would slit his throat for a turn of the hand), and his contradictions and consistent inconsistencies are nothing short of superb.

In the matter of picture-making it is to the Himalayas that the mind harks back the first of all when the book is closed. Nothing better, nothing more impressive, more truly great, has come from Mr. Kipling's pen than this gigantic panorama, Kedarnath and Badrinath—these are the two greatest mountains in sight of Kim and the lama as they toil upward. Let experienced mountaineers judge how true is the effect of these lines—and what an impression of vastness they convey!

But for all their marchings, Kedarnath and Badrinath were not impressed; and it was only after days of travel that Kim, uplifted upon some insignificant ten-thousand-foot hummock, could see that a shoulder-knot or horn of the two great lords had—ever so slightly—changed outline.

If one began to quote from the book there would be no end. To quote what is good would practically be the setting down of the whole story. This, however, at random:

Above them, still enormously above them, earth towered away toward snow line, where from east to west across hundreds of miles, ruled as with a ruler, the last of the bold birches stopped. Above them, in scarps and blocks upheaved, the rocks strove to fight their heads above the white smother. Above these again, changeless since the world's beginning, but changing to every mood of sun and cloud, lay out the eternal snow. They could see blots and blurs on its face where storm and wandering Wullie-wa got up to dance. Below them as they stood, the forest slid away in a sheet of blue green for mile upon mile; below the forest was a village in its sprinkle of terraced fields and steep grazing grounds; below the village, they knew, though a thunderstorm worried and growled there for a moment, a pitch of twelve or fifteen hundred feet gave to the moist valley where the streams gather that are the mothers of young Sutluj.

It is such passages as this that only the author of the *Plain Tales* and *Many Inventions* has given us in this generation of writers.

PART FIVE

SALT AND SINCERITY

INTRODUCTION

The six lengthy columns of miscellaneous discussion which Norris wrote for the *Critic* in mid-1902 contain few new ideas. Rather, the pieces are a reprise of his basic themes. He apparently felt no hesitancy in repeating ideas from earlier criticism, since his previous critical writing had been primarily for local magazines and newspapers. Except for several articles in *World's Work*, his *Critic* columns were his first criticism addressed to a national audience.

The title of the series suggests Norris' intent. The "sincerity" refers to his critical method rather than to its use as a topic, and the "salt" implies a lively style laced with occasional acerbity. But sincerity is also inevitably a major theme, as Norris runs the gamut of ideas which he associated with that virtue. Here and there his columns touch on matters of form or of publishing ethics. For the most part, however, they are confined to the familiar demands that the sincere, responsible writer derive his inspiration from "life, not literature," and that he trust in the people's ability to recognize his worth.

Although there are some differences between these columns and Norris' critical writings elsewhere, such differences are primarily of degree. His anti-intellectualism, in his discussions of education, traveling, and academies, is more pronounced and absolute than it was earlier. Some of his ideas are extended to new fields, probably as a result of new experience. For example, his discussion of the lack of responsibility in the drama was no doubt stimulated by his friendship with Hamlin Garland and the Hernes, all militant supporters of a realistic drama of ideas.[1] His analysis of the same deficiency in journalism is directly attributable to his part in defending Dr. William M. Lawlor against San Francisco newspapers.[2]

Norris' technique in his *Critic* pieces was to begin with some item of literary news and then gradually expand it into a discussion of a general idea. Often this method allowed him to combine in one discussion a number of themes, since the ostensible subject was less important than the almost digressive enlargement of it. He began one discussion by reporting Sir Donald Wallace's remark that modern literature was inferior to mid-Victorian. Several thousand words later he had deduced a theory of liter-

---

[1] He met Garland in early 1901 and Katherine and Julie Herne (the widow and daughter of James A. Herne) later that year. The Hernes were interested in a possible dramatization of *The Octopus*. See *Letters*, pp. 80–82. For Garland's and James A. Herne's earlier efforts on behalf of the drama, see my "The Radical Drama in Boston, 1889–1891, "*New England Quarterly*, XXXI (September, 1958), 361–374.

[2] See "Frank Norris Defends Dr. Lawlor," *Argonaut*, LI (August 11, 1902), 87, and Franklin D. Walker, *Frank Norris: A Biography* (Garden City, New York: Doubleday, Doran & Company, 1932), pp. 301–304.

ary progress and decline, had called for a return to a literature of "life" as a necessary prelude to renewed literary progress, and had indicated his faith in the people's ability to recognize and encourage a literature of "life."

Norris' "Salt and Sincerity" columns are therefore primarily valuable as a further guide to his essential beliefs. They are perhaps also significant because of their very repetitiousness, internally and in relation to his criticism published elsewhere. By 1902 Norris was capable of responding with a "set speech" to almost any literary topic, and such facility usually indicates a closed system of ideas which is unlikely to undergo any further major changes.

If the signs of the times may be read aright, and the future forecasted, the volume of short stories is in a fair way of becoming a "rare book." Fewer and fewer of this kind of literature are published every year, and only within the last week one of the foremost of the New York publishers has said that, so far as the material success was concerned, he would prefer to undertake a book of poems rather than a book of stories.[4] Also he explained why. And this is the interesting thing. One has always been puzzled to account for this lapse from a former popularity of a style of fiction certainly legitimate and incontestably entertaining. The publisher in question cites the cheap magazines—the monthlies and weeklies—as the inimical factors. The people go to them for their short stories, not to the cloth-bound volumes for sale at a dollar or a dollar and a half. Why not, if the cheap magazines give "just as good"? Often, too, they give the very same stories which, later, are re-published in book form. As the case stands now, any fairly diligent reader of two or three of the more important monthlies and weeklies may anticipate the contents of the entire volume, and very naturally he cannot be expected to pay a dollar for something he already has.

Or even suppose—as is now generally demanded by the publisher—the author adds to the forthcoming collection certain hitherto unpublished stories. Even this does not tempt the buyer. Turning over the leaves at the bookseller's, he sees two, three, five, half-a-dozen familiar titles. "Come," says he, "I have read three fourths of this book already. I have no use for it."

It is quite possible that this state of affairs will produce important results. It is yet, perhaps, too soon to say, but it is not outside the range of the probable that, in America at least, it will, in time to come, engender a decay in the quality of the short story. It may be urged that the high prices paid by periodicals to the important short-story writers,—the best men,—will still act as a stimulus to production. But this does not follow by any means. Authors are queer cattle. They do not always work for money, but sometimes for a permanent place in the eyes of the world. Books give them this—not fugitive short stories, published here and there, and at irregular intervals. Reputations that have been made by short stories published in periodicals may be counted upon the fingers of one hand. The "life of a novel"—to use a trade term—is to a certain extent indeterminable. The life of a short story, be it never so excellent, is prolonged only

[3] *Critic,* XL (May, 1902), 447–450.
[4] No published source found. Norris may have been reporting a conversation with one of the partners in Doubleday, Page & Company.

till the next issue of the periodical in which it has appeared. If the periodical is a weekly it will last a week, if a monthly, a month,—*and not a day more.* If very good, it will create a demand for another short story by the same author, but that one particular contribution, the original one, is irretrievably and hopelessly dead.

If the author is in literature "for his own pocket every time" he is generally willing to accept the place of a short-story writer. If he is one of the "best men," working for a "permanent place," he will turn his attention and time, his best efforts, to the writing of novels, reverting to the short story only when necessary, for the sake of boiling the Pot, and chasing the Wolf. He will abandon the field to the inferior men, or enter it only to dispose of "copy" which does not represent him at his best. And, as a result, the quality of the short story will decline more and more.

So, "taking one consideration with another," it may be appropriate to inquire if it is not possible that the American short story is liable to decline in quality and standard of excellence.

And now comes again this question addressed to certain authors: "Which book do you consider your best?" and a very industrious and painstaking person is giving the answer to the world.[5]

To what end, it is difficult to see. Who cares which of the *Waverleys* Sir Walter thought his best? or which of the *Rougon-Macquart* M. Zola favors the most? The author's point of view is very different from yours —the reader's. Which one do *you* think the best? That's the point. Do you not see that in the author's opinion the novel he is working on at the moment, or which is in press and about to appear—in fine, the last one written—is for a very long time the best he has done? He would be a very poor kind of novelist if he did not think that.

And even in retrospect his opinion as to "his best book" is not necessarily final. For he will see good points in "unsuccessful" novels that the public and critics have never and will never discover; and also defects in what the world considers his masterpiece that for him spoil the entire story. His best novel is, as was said, the last he has written, or, and this more especially, the one he is *going* to write. For to a certain extent this is true of every author, whether fiction writer or not. *Though he very often does better than he thinks he can, he never does so well as he knows he might.*

His best book is the one that he never quite succeeds in getting hold of firmly enough to commit to paper. It is always just beyond him. Next year he is going to think it out, or the next after that, and instead he compro-

5 Unidentified.

mises on something else, and his chef d'oeuvre is always a little ahead of him. If this, too, were not so, he would be a poor kind of writer. So that it seems to me, the most truthful answer to the question, "What is your best book?" would be:
"The one I shall never write."

Another ideal that such of the "people who imagine a vain thing" have long been pursuing is an English Academy of letters, and now that "the British Academy for the Promotion of Historical, Philosophical, and Philological studies" has been proposed, the old discussion is revived, and especially in England there is talk of a British Academy, something on the same lines as the *Académie française,* which shall tend to promote and reward particularly, the production of good fiction. In a word, it would be a distinction reserved only for the worthy, a charmed circle that would open only to the elite upon the vote of those already admitted. The proposition strikes one as preeminently ridiculous. Literature is of all arts the most democratic; it is of, by, and for the people in a fuller measure than even government itself. And one makes the assertion without forgetting that fine mouth-filling phrase, the "aristocracy of letters." The survival of the fittest is as good in the evolution of our literature as of our bodies, and the best "academy" for the writers of the United States is, after all, and in the last analysis, to be found in the judgment of the people, exercised throughout the lapse of a considerable time. For, give the people time enough, and they will always decide justly.

It was in connection with this talk about an "Academy" that Mr. Hall Caine has made the remark that "no academic study of a thing so variable, emotional, and independent as the imaginative writer's art could be anything but mischievous."[6] One is inclined to take exception to the statement. Why should the academic study of the principles of writing fiction be mischievous? Is it not possible to codify in some way the art of *construction* of novels so that they be studied to advantage? This has, of course, never been done. But one believes that if managed carefully, and with a proper disregard of "set forms" and hampering conventions, it would be possible to start and maintain a school of fiction-writing in the most literal sense of the word "school." Why should it be any more absurd than the painting schools and music schools? Is the art of music, say, any less variable, less emotional, less independent, less imaginative than the fiction-writer's? Heretical as the assertion may appear, one is thoroughly convinced that the art of novel writing (up to a certain point, *bien*

[6] No published source found.

entendue) can be acquired by instruction just as readily and with results just as satisfactory and practical as the arts of painting, sculpture, music, and the like. The art of fiction is, in general, based upon four qualities of mind: observation, imagination, invention, and sympathy. Certainly the first two are "acquired characters." Kindergarten children the world over are acquiring them every day. Invention is immensely stimulated by observation and imagination, while sympathy is so universally a fundamental quality with all sorts and conditions of men and women—especially the latter—that it needs but little cultivation. Why, then, would it be impossible for a few of our older, more seriously-minded novelists to launch a School of Instruction in the Art of Composition,—just as Bouguereau, Lefebvre, Boulanger, and Tony Robert-Fleury founded Julian's in Paris?

At present the stimulus to, and even the manner of, production of very much of American fiction is in the hands of the publishers. No one not intimately associated with any one of the larger, more important "houses" can have any idea of the influence of the publisher upon latter-day fiction. More novels are written—practically—to order than the public has any notion of. The publisher again and again picks out the man (one speaks, of course, of the younger generation), suggests the theme, and exercises, in a sense, all the functions of instructor, during the period of composition. In the matter of this "picking out of the man" it is rather curious to note a very radical change that has come about in the last five years. Time was when the publisher waited for the unknown writer to come to him, with his manuscript. But of late the Unknown has so frequently developed, under exploitation, and by direct solicitation of the publisher, into a "money-making proposition" of such formidable proportions that there is hardly a publishing house that does not now hunt him out with all the resources at its command. Certain fields are worked with the thoroughness, almost, of a political canvass, and if a given State—as, for instance, Indiana—has suddenly evolved into a region of great literary activity,[7] it is open to suspicion that it is not because there is any inherent literary quality in the people of the place greater than in other States, but that certain firms of publishers are "working the ground."

It might not have been altogether out of place if upon the Victor Hugo

---

[7] Indiana was well known in the late nineteenth century for the large number of authors either born or living there. These included James Whitcomb Riley, Booth Tarkington, George Ade, Mary H. Catherwood, Theodore Dreiser, John Hay, William Vaughn Moody, and David Graham Phillips.

monument which has just been unveiled in Paris there had been inscribed this, one of the most important of the great Frenchman's maxims:

"Les livres n'ont jamais faites du mal";[8]

and I think that in the last analysis, this is the most fitting answer to Mr. Carnegie, who, in his address before the Authors' Club, put himself on record as willing to exclude from the libraries he is founding all books not three years old.[9] No doubt bad books have a bad influence, but bad books are certainly better than no books at all. For one must remember that the worst books are not printed—the really tawdry, really pernicious, really evil books. These are throttled in manuscript by the publishers, who must be in a sense public censors. No book, be assured, goes to press but that there is—oh, hidden away like a grain of mustard seed—some bit, some modicum, some tiny kernel of good in it. Perhaps it is not that seed of goodness that the cultured, the fastidious care much about. Perhaps the discriminating would call it a platitude. But one is willing to believe that somewhere, somehow, this atom of real worth makes itself felt—and that's a beginning. It will create after a while a taste for reading. And a taste for reading is a more important factor in a nation's literary life than the birth of a second Shakespeare.

It is the people, after all, who "make a literature." If they read, the few, the "illuminati," will write. But first must come the demand,—come from the people, the Plain People, the condemned *bourgeoisie*. The select circles of the elite, the "studio" hangers-on, the refined, will never, never, clamor they never so loudly, toil they never so painfully, produce the Great Writer. The demand which he is to supply comes from the Plain People—from the masses, and not from the classes. There is more significance as to the ultimate excellence of American letters in the sight of the messenger-boy devouring his *Old Sleuths* and *Deadwood Dicks* and *Boy Detectives,* with an *earnest, serious* absorption, than in the spectacle of a "reading circle" of dilettanti coquetting with Verlaine, and *pretending* that they understand.

By the same token, then, is it not better to welcome and rejoice over this recent "literary deluge" than to decry it? One is not sure but what it is a matter for self-gratulation—not a thing to deplore and vilify. The "people" are reading, that is the point; it is *not* the point that immature, untrained writers are flooding the counters with their productions. The more

---

[8] I have failed to find this quotation in Hugo's work.

[9] Carnegie originally specified one year in his speech before the Authors' Club (*New York Times Saturday Review of Books and Art,* February 15, 1902, p. 11), but the following month, when addressing a group of librarians, he increased the time to three years (*New York Times,* March 20, 1902, p. 8).

the Plain People read, the more they will discriminate. It is inevitable, and by and by they will demand "something better." It is impossible to read a book without formulating an opinion upon it. Even the messenger-boy can tell you that in *his* judgment, No. 3666, *The James Boys Brought to Bay,* is more—or less, as the case may be—exciting than No. 3667, *The Last of the Fly-by-nights.* Well, that is something. Is it not better than that the same boy should be shooting craps around the corner? Take his dime novel from him, put him in the "No Book" condition,—and believe me, he will revert to the craps. And so it is higher up the scale. In the name of American literature, let the Plain People read, anything,—anything, whether it is three days or three years old. Mr. Carnegie will not educate the public taste by shutting his libraries upon recent fiction. The public taste will educate itself by *much* reading, not by *restricted* reading. "Books have never done harm," Victor Hugo said it, and a bad book— that is to say, a poor, cheap, ill-written, "trashy" book—is not after all so harmful as "no book" at all.

Later on, when the people have learned discrimination by much reading, it will not be necessary to bar fiction not three years old from the libraries, for by then the people will demand the "something better," and the writers will have to supply it—or disappear, giving place to those who can, and *then* the literary standards will be raised.

II[10]

A very good friend of mine who is a young man not out of his twenties, and whose work is full of the promise and of an earnest and sober fruition, wrote to me some time since, to enlist my good services to "place" him in New York. "For," says he, "as you very well know, a literary man out of New York is as much out of his element as a meadow-lark in the Mammouth Cave. ——ville, Colorado," he added, "is not exactly a literary centre."

That is very true; "——ville, Colorado," is not a literary centre; but in the implied alternative, does it follow that New York is? At all events I wrote the following heresy to my friend: "Stay in ——ville. For literary work, it is a better place for you than New York. New York is not a literary centre."

And I think the proposition can be proved. It is true that the great publishing houses and magazines are in New York; but by far the larger number of the "best men" do not live in the place. One may see all of them in New York, on different occasions; but they are there only on business. Their trips are flying trips; their interests are not identified with

[10] *Critic,* XL (June, 1902), 550–555.

the city or its people; and they do not exert the slightest influence upon it. It is a mistaken idea this, that New York teems with the important personages in the world of letters. And it is wrong to suppose that the influence of the place itself conduces to the production of the finer, truer, and more enduring types of literary men. Hardly a single one of the writers of the American classics comes from New York. And of the latter-day masters there are not more than two or three at the most who were New Yorkers either by birth or by adoption. Paris is a literary centre, and London, but not New York. Of course a certain number of writers of successful fiction do live in the place; but they do so—and I have heard many of them express themselves upon the subject—they do so under protest, and only count the days till they can get away.

What my young man of ——ville, Colorado, would find in New York would be *not* the Important People, the real masters worth knowing, those who wield an influence; but the imitation, inexpensive, trivial foolery of the literary "clubs" and "circles" and heaven knows what impertinent, impossible "organizations," whose members are occupied during their meetings in log-rolling and in the intervals in back-biting—a motley, melancholy travesty of what they like to think goes on in the European capitals. Not a congenial atmosphere for a half-developed talent surely.

For the best work in the production of good fiction is done in the closet and not on the housetop. The author *as an author* has but two points of view; one in which he sees humanity as if from the "pinnacle of the Temple"—as a whole, a vast, tremendous Conglomerate; the other in which he sees it in his own heart, in an intimacy closer than any words can express. The other view of humanity—the every-day intercourse, the window-outlook,—has no place in his work. The people, the humanity, thus seen is the humanity to which he belongs as a man, not as an author.

And these two outlooks upon the world of men and things, the telescopic and the microscopic let us call them, are quite as possible in ——ville, Colorado, as in New York—are even more so. For from the little isolated village of the Rocky Mountains one gets a perspective upon the outside world impossible to attain in the world itself, or, in other words, in New York. And also the same isolation, remoteness, and seclusion are pre-eminently essential to that quiet meticulous searching of the heart that goes to the making of a master work of fiction. Not much chance for that in the febrile activity and fierce unrest of the great metropolis of the Atlantic seaboard.

It is one of the blessed compensations of the trade of authorship, that, of all others, it is the most independent; and the ingredients for a great novel are scarcely more than these,—ink, paper, a quiet mind, and a gift of persistency.

The death of Mr. Frank R. Stockton brings to mind that as a *constructive* artist he stood probably higher than any other American writer of his generation, and it may even be said that in the list of his native country's writers he will, from a *constructive* point of view, rank second only to Poe. In other words, Stockton more than all others of his contemporaries knew how to put a story together so as to achieve a given effect. In Poe, the effect aimed at was the horrible. In Stockton it was the ludicrous or the puzzling. And in this connection it may be well to note that nearly all writers of fiction fall into either one of two great classifications: they *construct* like Poe, Stockton, or Kipling; or they *explore* like Eliot, Flaubert, or Hardy. In the first class we are interested chiefly in the ingenuity of the author; in the second in the consistency and humanity of his personages. The first deal with events; the second with people. The first build up a situation; the second assume that a certain situation already exists and then proceed to disintegrate it to its elements—some of these elements being episodes, some living human beings. Unquestionably the greater works of fiction belong to the latter class. But the "constructionists" occupy a place of undeniable importance, and in this place the author of "The Lady or the Tiger" and "The Transferred Ghost" must stand preeminent as a master of inventiveness, ingenuity, and construction.

Noted only as the change of residence of an artist of reputation, the return of the sculptor MacMonnies to this his native country impresses one more as an event than as an occurrence.[11] If more of the expatriated American artists and writers had the courage and fine national spirit that animates MacMonnies we would begin to have on this side of the water something like American painting and American fiction. As it is our best novelists have turned their backs upon the home of their birth and have been content to become wholly and irretrievably Anglicized. James and Harland are about as much American in their writings as "Gyp" or Rostand.[12] But if these men had remained in the United States, addressing themselves to the task of picturing and studying their own countrymen, we might have had a series of novels to set side by side with those of Mr. Howells. Frederic of all of them seems to have been sturdiest in clinging to American traditions, but *The Market Place* is more English than native,

---

[11] See "MacMonnies To Work Here. He Intends To Spend the Rest of His Life at Home," *New York Tribune,* January 14, 1902, p. 7. MacMonnies had lived in France for seventeen years. However, he later returned to France, and did not settle permanently in the United States until 1915.

[12] Gyp (pseudonym of the Comtesse de Martel de Janville) and Edmond Rostand were popular French writers of the late nineteenth century. Henry Harland had moved to London in 1890, where he became editor of the *Yellow Book.*

and one is sure would—had not the author died—have marked a transition to a more Anglicized point of view. But while we may note with chagrin the fact that some of our best novelists have turned their backs upon their compatriots it might be pertinent to ask if their compatriots did not first turn their backs upon them. James and Harland were received in England long before they were acknowledged here; and London discovered Stephen Crane before New York did.

In a recent speech of Mrs. Craigie's before the O.P. Club in London she made the following remark apropos of dialogue on the stage: "Dramatic dialogue is a symbol of real conversation and not a verbatim report. It may seem natural, but it cannot be so."[13] It seems to me that there lurks in these words a suggestion of a very sound literary criticism. The novelist is not occupied with life as he sees it, but with life as he *sees it was intended to be*. Civilization has become so complicated that consistency— that is to say, an adequate and harmonious relationship between word and deed—is altogether unusual. Once it prevailed. No doubt if one could go back far enough, one could find some Arcadian community wherein people spoke, lived, and thought consistently, and in a manner true to life. But it is noteworthy that these communities had no fiction. Very naturally, too. They did not need to be revealed to each other through the medium of books. Supposing, however, that a contemporary novelist should have risen in Arcadia. He could have transcribed the life *exactly* as he saw it and his work yet remained both true and accurate. The modern fiction writer can do nothing of the sort. Life itself has become inconsistent, and an accurate representation of it in a story would result in an inconsistent, and therefore improbable story. The thoughtful novelist must make allowances for this falseness to life on the part of life itself. He must readjust the dislocations in the machine; must in a word find Arcadia on Fifth Avenue and discover Beowulf behind the frock coat of a multimillionaire.

All this is pertinent, too, and apropos of the discussion raised by the publication of a novel by Mr. Ernest Williams in which Bernard Shaw figures as one of the characters.[14] The propriety of thus using contemporaneous people as characters in a novel has been questioned and is even now being argued. It seems to me as though there were no room nor occasion for discussion here. Aside from the impertinence and the violation of personal privacy that such a proceeding involves, the results are not, cannot be, satisfactory,—because they cannot be true. Actual living people

[13] Mrs. Pearl Craigie's speech was reported in the *Academy*, XLII (April 5, 1902), 353.
[14] Ernest Williams, *An Exile in Bohemia* (London: Greening Company, 1902), a novel in which Shaw appears as a minor character.

are not true to life. It is the argument of the preceding paragraph over again. It is all very well for the story-teller to take a predominating *trait* for which a certain living being is known, and to develop that. But the result in this case is a character of fiction, not a transcript of the original model. Take a test case. A given character in real life may do, say, or think certain unexplainable, inconsistent things. Yet all the inconsistency in the world will not persuade us that our friend is not lifelike. Put the same person into a book, thinking, doing, and saying identically the same things, and all the argument in the world to prove that the original model did really exist as pictured will not convince a critical reader that the book-person is anything but improbable, unlifelike, and so unreal as to be a mere figment of an untrained imagination.

And now there comes to hand a story of Alphonse Daudet which if true leads to the discovery of what one long since had believed to be an impossibility,—a new form of French depravity. M. Hughes Le Roux, certainly a prominent figure in the world of letters, is its authority. He tells us that at a time when he was an associate of Daudet's household and a student of his style and works, Daudet engaged him to write a novel for an American magazine, and that when the novel was finished Daudet put his name to it, the novel in question being the very well-known *La Belle-Nivernaise*.[15] Now, whether the story be true or not, there is depravity here "of the baser sort" beyond doubt or denial: 1. Either the story is a lie and M. Le Roux is plundering a dead man's chiefest treasures; or, 2. The story is true and Alphonse Daudet instigated and consummated a detestable and petty confidence game to be played upon an American publisher, and through him upon the public at large. I believe that M. Le Roux cites as the justification of the affair the habit of the Renaissance painters—Rubens, for instance—who signed paintings which in part were the work of their students. But even if the cases were analogous, one cannot see that the argument is sound. The practice of deluding the public was just as reprehensible in the sixteenth century as in the twentieth. But it must be remembered that so far as the ultimate result to posterity is concerned, the delusion, in the matter of the paintings, is not wholly evil; for the reason that the students and pupils of the Renaissance painter were often quite as capable as their master and sometimes infinitely more so. Nor did the *personal* element enter into the great religious and allegorical canvases of that period in anything like the same degree as it does in a modern novel. As a matter of fact it is now known that the work of

[15] Reported in the *New York Times,* April 24, 1902, p. 1. Le Roux, who was in the United States on a lecture tour, made the claim in an address before students of the University of Chicago.

these students and pupils was devoted chiefly to the mechanical, or at least to the technical, parts of the work—the drawing of subordinate figures, the completion of backgrounds, perspective, and the like; the student occupying the same relation to the master as the printer, book-binder, proofreader, etc., to the present-day novelist, *not,* as M. Le Roux would persuade us to believe, that of co-laborer.

But on the other hand suppose the story is true. Here we have a prostitution as much more flagrant than the wretched business implied in the literal acceptance of the word, as the mind is superior to the body. A great master, a maker of morals, trusted and confided in by hundreds of thousands, sells what is absolutely the very best, highest, and purest in him for a miserable handful of pennies. If he wanted the money, if he was "in literature for his own pocket every time," why not have allowed the story to be signed Le Roux—or at least Le Roux and Daudet—and then have pocketed the royalties?

A friend and apologist of M. Le Roux has written to a New York paper explaining that many notable French authors have the routine work of their novels done by their pupils, subject to their own revision.[16] One would be glad to know what the apologist means by the "routine" work of a novel. Is it the developing of the characters or the construction of the "plot"? Is it the writing of the descriptions or the elaboration of the moralizing? Is not "revision" itself "routine"? Is there, in heaven's name is there anything of "routine" at all in the writing of novels, except the persistent, patient day to day, hour to hour *penmanship* that makes the whole work one long-continued routine?

Two men of equal talent, or even unequal talent, but dowered with an equally quick sympathy and with similar temperaments, can write a novel, but the resulting work is a unit, so intricately and inextricably woven that it is the work of two minds acting as one. Certainly no genuine literature ever was, will be, or could be produced by one author managing the "routine" and the other the revision.

But in the end it is hard to pardon M. Le Roux even if he has told the truth. A very great man once said that "the truth is not always to be told."[17] Suppose in a moment of weakness or a spirit of bravado Daudet *did* commission the young man to write *La Belle-Nivernaise* and then afterward put his name to the finished work. What small maliciousness, what inexpensive vanity to foster a moment's notoriety at the expense of a dead man's mistakes; betraying his frailty in order to shine in the light of the *ignis fatuus* that burns above his grave. This if his story be true. If

[16] *New York Times,* April 28, 1902, p. 8.
[17] Perhaps George Herbert's "all truths are not to be told," *Jacula Prudentum* (1651).

it is a lie the gentleman in question has proved himself to be merely a new order of ghoul.

The latest word on the subject of the purchase of libraries of fiction at least a year old comes, or did come, I believe, from the late Frank Stockton. Mr. Stockton spoke as a novelist, and he said that he believed if the libraries stopped the purchase of fiction the sale of novels would at once be enormously increased.[18] This would appear to be true at first sight. There is a strong probability even that for the first few years of the experiment, people would buy books they could not obtain in the libraries until a year after their publication. But in the end one is quite sure that the newly awakened desire for the reading of fiction which is now fostered and incited by an easy access to novels would languish and in very many cases die out altogether if new fiction were withheld a twelvemonth. People will read a book which costs them but a few cents where they would ignore it were they obliged to pay the retail price for it at a bookstore. But once let the people, the public, become possessed of a genuine affection for reading and they will prefer to own books instead of borrowing them. Then, too, as this taste for reading spreads through the seventy-odd millions of our population the libraries, to satisfy the demand, will themselves have to buy more books, a fact which will go far to offset the state of things deplored by Mr. Stockton. The great libraries of England now order a new book by the thousands, taking entire editions at a time. Suppose the English libraries should suddenly cut off the supply, does it follow that their subscribers would buy the book in question? It is very doubtful if so much as a fifth part would do so. It is much more probable that the vast majority of the subscribers would promise themselves to buy the book and then forget all about it.

One would be very content, however, to see an embargo at once effective and perpetual imposed upon that element of our national fiction which for want of a better term one may call the super-amiable. With the public just at present, or at the very least, with the publishers, amiability on the part of all the characters of a novel is an infallible commendation. And this amiability is almost invariably symbolized and bodied forth in the person of a young girl. Indeed, one may go so far as to say that the figure of the Amiable Young Girl throws its shadow over the whole scope and range of our latter-day fiction. This fiction is *about* Amiable Young Girls; it is addressed *to* Amiable Young Girls; and—save the mark—is written *by* Amiable Young Girls. Girls are attractive, youth is fine, and amiability is

[18] No published source found.

surely a passport to consideration. But let us not exploit the trinity beyond the bounds of reason and endurance. One had fondly believed that with the passing of the Amandas, Sophronias, and Bellindas of the former generation the ghost had been forever laid. Colorless, mindless "females"! One chose to believe that when the brains were out the girl would die, but now they rise with twenty—flowers—in their crowns to push us from our stools. Is Mr. Charles Dana Gibson and the tremendous vogue he started responsible for this? Was it he who discovered the Amiable Young Girl —or rather resurrected her from *The Children of the Abbey*?[19] At all events she has invaded not only literature but illustration as well. The full pages and high places in the magazines are given over now, not to the sturdy, forthright, rough-hewn fellows of five years ago, but to the "pretty girls," the "smart young women," with wonderful frocks and hats; and not a poster is effective that does not picture the everlasting Amiable in some fresh garb or guise. The noblest study of mankind is—of course— woman. But one may be permitted to protest against this ceaseless exploiting of mere amiability. An amiable woman is, in real life, no doubt a thing to be desired. But in fiction she offers no very interesting problem. The great heroines of literature are anything but amiable. It is the deviation from the normal that makes for interest, and the characterization of a real flesh-and-blood woman, capable of faults, mistakes, even of sins, would not only be a refreshing contrast to the present unending file of well-bred anaemic ladies, but would offer to the novelist an opportunity of exercising all that he has of sincerity, ingenuity, thoughtfulness, and worth. Also it would tend to produce a distinctive American literature.

For be it understood that so long as our novelists limit themselves to a study and portrayal of well-bred people, just so long shall the United States be without a national school of fiction, distinct and separate from those of the Old World. Well-bred people are much the same the world over. Amiability has no nationality. It is the same in England as in France, the same in Russia as in America. Our writers should look for variations from the type rather than conformities to it—variations that are peculiar to us. Politeness, gentility, and the like are beautiful, but they are no more essentially American than brown hair and straight noses. On the surface and at the very bottom, all people are alike. In the "middle ground" come the varieties. It is to this "middle ground" that one looks for strong fiction-characters—unless indeed there should arise a Tolstoy or a Flaubert among us, who dare explore those last and lowest dark places, down at the bottom of things and hearts, where because of elementary forces and basic funda-

---

[19] A very sentimental novel by Mrs. Regina Roche, first published in 1796 and frequently republished thereafter.

mental tendencies, all men and women, as at the surface, come once more
—though in a far different sense—to be alike.

III[20]

There is a certain journal of the Middle West of the United States
which has proclaimed, with a great flourish of trumpets, that Mme. Humbert of Paris would have made a great "fictionist" if she had not elected
to become a great swindler.[21] This is that Mme. Humbert who cheated a
number of bankers, capitalists, and judges out of a great deal of money
with a story of $20,000,000 in a safe which for certain reasons she could
not open. Very naturally, when her hand was forced the safe was empty.
And this person, the Middle-West paper claims, is a great novelist *man-
quée,* "a female Dumas or Hugo." The contention would not be worthy
of notice were it not for the fact that it is an opinion similar to that held
by a great number of people intelligent enough to know better. In a word,
it is the contention that the personal morality of the artist (including
"fictionists") has nothing to do with his work, and that a great rascal may
be a good painter, good musician, good novelist. With painters, musicians
and the like this may or may not be true. With the novelist one contends,
believes, and avers that it is absolutely and unequivocally false, and that
the mind capable of theft, of immorality, of cruelty, of foulness, or falseness of any kind is incapable, under any circumstances, or by any degree
of stimulation of producing one single important, artistic, or useful piece
of fiction. The better the personal morality of the writer, the better his
writings. Tolstoy, for instance: it is wholly and solely due to the man's
vast goodness and philanthropy that his novels carry weight. The attitude
of the novelist toward his fellow men and women is the great thing, not
his inventiveness, his ingenuity, his deftness, or glibness, or verbal dex-
terity. And the mind wholly mean, who would rob a friend of $40,000
(after the manner of the Humbert person), or could even wilfully and
deliberately mar the pleasure of a little child, could never assume toward
the world at large that attitude of sympathy and generosity and toleration
that is the first requisite of the really great novelist. Always you will find
this thing true: that the best, the greatest writers of fiction are those best
loved of troops of friends; and for the reason that, like the Arab philoso-

---

20 *Critic,* XLI (July, 1902), 77–81.
21 Mme. Humbert and her husband, both prominent in Parisian society, swindled
enormous sums from various French banks and companies with an elaborate story of a
temporarily withheld inheritance. See "The Biggest Bunko Game on Record," *New York
Times,* May 5, 1902, p. 1. The midwestern journal mentioned by Norris was probably a
Chicago newspaper.

pher of the poem, they, first of all, have "loved their fellow-men."[22] It is this that has made their novels great. Consider Stevenson, or our own "Dean," or Hugo, or Scott, men of the simplest lives, uncompromising in rectitude, scrupulously, punctiliously, Quixotically honest; their morality —surely in the cases of Stevenson and Hugo—setting a new standard of religion, at the least a new code of ethics. And thus it goes right down the line, from the greater lights to the lesser and to the least. It is only the small men, the "minor" people among the writers of books who indulge in eccentricities that are only immoralities under a different skin; who do not pay their debts; who borrow without idea of returning; who live loose, "irregular," wretched, vicious lives, and call it "Bohemianism," and who believe that "good work" can issue from the turmoil, that the honeycomb will be found in the carcass, and the sweet come forth from the putrid. So that in the end one may choose to disagree with the Middle-West editor and to affirm that it is not the ingenious criminal who is the novelist *manqué*, but the philanthropist, the great educator, the great pulpit orator, the great statesman. It is from such stuff that the important novels are made, not from the deranged lumber and disordered claptrap of the brain of a defective.

In the course of a speech made at a recent dinner given in London Sir Donald Mackenzie Wallace has deplored the fact that our present generation of English writers has produced no worthy successors to the great men of the mid-Victorian period.[23] That there are no names to place beside Scott, Dickens, Thackeray, Browning, or Keats. But he also brought forward extenuating circumstances, chief among which was the fact that the novelists of to-day were working overtime to supply the demands of an ever-increasing public, and that, by implication, their work was therefore deteriorating. One does not believe that this is so. Rapid work may cause the deterioration of a commercial article, but it by no means follows that the authors who are called upon to produce a very large number of books are forced into the composition of unworthy literature. The writer's brain does *not* hold the material for his books. It is not like a storehouse, from which things may be taken till nothing remains. The writer's material is life itself, inexhaustible and renewed from day to day, and his brain is only the instrument that adapts life to fiction. True, this instrument itself may wear out after a while, but it usually lasts as long as the man himself, and is good for more work than the unthinking would believe possible. As

22 Leigh Hunt, "Abou Ben Adhem and the Angel."
23 Wallace was replying for Literature during the after-dinner toasts at the Royal Academy banquet. See *The Times* (London), May 5, 1902, p. 4.

a matter of fact the best novelists have, as a rule, been the most prolific, have been those who had to write rapidly and much to satisfy, if not the demands of the public, then at least other more personal demands, none the less insistent. Scott and Dickens were unusually prolific, yet the rapidity with which they accomplished their work did not hurt the quality of the work itself. Balzac and Dumas produced whole libraries of books and yet kept their standards high. As one has urged before, it is the demand of the People that produces the great writer, not *re*-duces the quality and fineness of his work. If he has the "divine spark," the breath of the millions will fan rather than extinguish it.

One does not choose to believe that the art of fiction nor the standards of excellence have deteriorated since the day of Scott, Dickens, and Thackeray. True, we have no men to equal them as yet, but they are surely coming. Time was, at the end of the seventeenth century, when the dearth of good fiction was even more marked than at present. But one must bear in mind that progress is never along a direct line, but by action and reaction. A period will supervene when a group of geniuses arise, and during the course of their activities the average of excellence is high, great books are produced, and a whole New Literature is launched. Their influence is profound; the first subschool of imitators follow, good enough men, but second-rate. These in turn are followed by the third-raters, and these by the fourth-raters, and no one is found bold enough to strike out for himself until the bottom is reached. Then comes the reaction, and once more the group of giants towers up from out the mass. We are probably living through the era of the Fourth-Raters just now, and one believes that we are rather near to the end even of that. The imitators of the Romantic school have imitated to ten places decimals and have diluted and re-diluted till they can hardly go farther without producing something actually and really new. At any rate, the time is most propitious for a Man of Iron who can be bent to no former shape, nor diluted to no old-time essence. Then will come the day of the New Literature, and the wind of Life itself will blow through the dry bones and fustian and sawdust of the Imitation, and the People will all at once realize how very far afield the Fourth-Raters have drawn them and how very different a good novel is from a bad one.

For say what you will, the People, the Plain People who Read, do appreciate good literature in the end. One must keep one's faith in the People,—the Plain People, the Burgesses, the Grocers,—else of all men the artists are most miserable and their teachings vain. Let us admit and concede that this belief is ever so sorely tried at times. Many thousands of years ago the wisest man of his age declared that "the People imagine a vain thing." Continually they are running away after strange gods; continually they are admiring the fake and neglecting actual worth. But in the end, and at last, they will listen to the true note and discriminate between it and the false. *In the last analysis the People are always right.* Somehow, and after all is said and done, they will prefer Walter Scott to G. P. R. James, Shakespeare to Marlowe, Flaubert to Goncourt. Sometimes the preference is long in forming, and during this formative period they have many reversions, and go galloping, in herds of one hundred or one hundred and fifty thousand (swelling the circulations), after false gods. But note this fact: that the fustian and the tinsel and the sawdust are discovered very soon, and, once the discovery made, the sham idol can claim no single devotee.

In other words, it is a comfort to those who take the literature of the Americans—or even of the Anglo-Saxons—seriously to remember, in the long run and the larger view, that a circulation of two hundred, three hundred or four hundred thousand—judging even by this base-scale of "copies sold"—is not so huge after all. Consider. A "popular" novel is launched and sells its half-million. Within a certain very limited period of time, at most five years, this sale stops definitely and conclusively. The People have found out that it is not such a work of genius after all, and will have no more of it. But how about the circulation of the works of the real Masters, Scott and Dickens, say,—to be more concrete let us speak of *Ivanhoe* and *David Copperfield*,—have not each of these "sold" more than two hundred thousand since publication? Is not two hundred million nearer the mark? And they are still selling. New editions are published every year. Does not this prove that the People are discriminating; that they are—after all—preferring the best literature to the mediocre; that they are not such a mindless herd after all; that in the end, in fine, they are always right? It will not do to decry the American public; to say that it has no taste, no judgment; that it "likes to be fooled." It may be led away for a time by clamorous advertising and the "barking" of fakirs. But there comes a day when it will no longer be fooled. A million dollars' worth of advertising would not to-day sell a hundred thousand copies of *Trilby*. But *Ivanhoe* and *Copperfield*, without advertising, without *réclames* or exploitation, are as marketable this very day as a sack of flour or a bag of wheat.

Mr. Metcalfe, in a recent issue of *Life*, has been lamenting the lack of good plays on the American stage during the past season, and surely no one can aver that the distinguished critic is not right.[24] One cannot forbear a wince or two at the thought of what future art historians will say in their accounts of the American drama at the beginning of the twentieth century.

[24] James S. Metcalfe, *Life*, XXXIX (June 5, 1902), 490.

Frankly and unreservedly the native American drama is just about as bad as it can be, and every intelligent-minded person is quite willing to say so. The causes are not difficult to trace. Two come to the mind at once, which in themselves alone would account for the degeneracy—i.e., the rage for Vaudeville and the exploitation of the Star. The first has developed in the last ten years, an importation from English music halls. Considered at first as a fad by the better class of theatre-goers, a thing to be countenanced with amused toleration like performing bears and the animal circus, it has been at length boosted and foisted upon public attention till, like a veritable cancer, it has eaten almost into the very vitals of the Legitimate Comedy (using the word in its technical sense). Continually nowadays one may see a "specialty"—generally in the form of a dance—lugged in between the scenes of a perfectly sober, perfectly sane Comedy of Manners. The moment any one subordinate feature of a dramatic action is developed at the expense of *vraisemblance* and the Probabilities, and for the sake of amusing the galleries, there is the first bacillus of decay. Vaudeville is all very well by itself, and one will even go so far as to admit that it has its place as much as an Ibsen problem-play. But it should keep to that place. It is ludicrously *out* of place in a comedy—quite as much so as the "Bible Incident" in *Ebsmith* would be in a Hoyt farce.[25] But because the "specialty," because Vaudeville, will "go" with the "gallery" at any time and at any place, the manager and—the pity of it!—the author, too, will introduce it whenever the remotest possibility occurs, and by just so much the tone of the whole drama is lowered. It has got to such a pass by now, however, that one ought to be thankful if this same "tone" is not keyed down to the specialty.

But the exploiting of the Star, it would seem, is, of all others, the great cause of the mediocrity of present-day dramatic literature. One has but to glance at the theatre programmes and bills to see how matters stand. The name of the leading lady or leading man is "scare-headed," so that the swiftest runner cannot fail to see. Even the manager proclaims his patronymic in enormous "caps." But the author!—as often as not *his* name is not discoverable at all. The play is nothing,—thus it would seem the managers would have us believe,—it is the actress, her speeches, her scenes, her gowns, her personality, that are the all-important essentials. It is notorious how plays are cut, and readjusted, and dislocated to suit the Star. Never mind whether or not the scene is artistic, is vivid, is dramatic. Does the Star get the best of it? If not, write it over. The Star must have all the

[25] Arthur Wing Pinero's *The Notorious Mrs. Ebbsmith* (not *Ebsmith*), which played in New York early in 1902, contains a scene in which an "advanced thinker" first throws a Bible into a fire, and then puts her hand in the fire to retrieve it. Charles H. Hoyt (1860–1900) was an American writer of farces.

good lines. If they cannot be built into the Star's part, cut 'em out. The Probabilities, the construction, artistic effect, climax, even good common, forthright, horse sense, rot 'em! who cares for 'em? Give the Star the lime-light—that's the point.

If the audience is willing to pay its money to see Miss Marlowe, Miss Mannering, or Mrs. Carter put through her paces, that's another thing; but let us not expect that good dramas will issue forth from this state of affairs.

Where are the Books for Girls? Adults' books there are and books for boys by the car-loads, but where is the book for the young girls? Something has already been said in this department about literature for the amiable young woman, but this, now, is a very different person. One means the girl of fourteen to eighteen. The boy passing through this most trying formative period finds his literature ready to hand. Boys' books, tales of hunting, adventure, and sport abound. They are good books, too, sane, "healthy," full of fine spirit and life. But the girl, where does she read? Surely the years between fourteen and eighteen are even more trying to a young girl than to a boy. She is not an active animal. When the boy is out of doors, pitching curves or "running the ends," the girl (even yet in the day and age of "athletics for women") is in the house, and, as like as not, reading. And reading what, if you please? The feeblest, thinnest, most colorless lucubrations that it is given to the mind of misguided man to conceive or to perpetuate. It must be this or else the literature of the adult; and surely the novels written for mature minds, for men and women who have some knowledge of the world and powers of discrimination, are not good reading, in any sense of the word, for a sixteen-year-old girl in the formative period of her life.

Besides Alcott, no one has ever written intelligently for girls. Surely there is a field here. Surely a Public, untried and unexplored, is waiting for its author; nor is it a public wanting in enthusiasm, loyalty, or intelligence.

But for all this great parade and prating of emancipated women it nevertheless remains a fact that the great majority of twentieth-century opinion is virtually Oriental in its conception of the young girl. The world to-day is a world for boys, men, and women. Of all humans the young girl, the sixteen-year-old, is the least important—or at least is so deemed. Wanted: a Champion. Wanted: the Discoverer and Poet of the Very Young Girl. Unimportant she may now appear to you, who may yet call her by her first name without fear and without reproach. But remember this, you who believe only in a world of men and boys and women: the Very Young Girl of to-day is the woman of to-morrow, the wife of the day after, and the mother of next week. She only needs to put up her hair and let down her frocks to become a very important person indeed. Meanwhile she has no literature; meanwhile, *faute de mieux,* she is trying to read Ouida[26] and many other books intended for maturer minds; or, worse than all, she is enfeebling her mind by the very thin gruel purveyed by the mild-mannered gentlemen and ladies who write for the Sunday-school libraries. Here is a bad business; here is a field that needs cultivation. All very well to tend and train the saplings, the oaks, and the vines. The flowers—they have not bloomed yet—are to be thought about too.

All the more so that the young girl takes a book to heart infinitely more than a boy. The boy—*his* story once read—votes it "bully," takes down his cap, and there's an end. But the average Very Young Girl does not read her story: she lives it, lingers over it, weeps over it, lies awake nights over it. So long as she lives she will never quite forget the books she read when she was sixteen. It is not too much to say that the "favorite" books of a girl at this age become a part of her life. They influence her character more than any of us, I imagine, would suspect or admit. All the more reason, then, that there should not only be good books for girls, but plenty of good books.

IV[27]

In a recent number of his periodical, the editor of *Harper's Weekly* prints a letter received from a gentleman who deplores the fact that the participants in the Harvard-Yale track teams are given a great place in the daily newspapers while—by implication—his son, an arduous student and winner of a "Townsend prize," is completely and definitely ignored.[28] "I could not but think of my son," writes the gentleman, "a Yale Senior who, as one of the results of nine years' devotion to study, won a Townsend prize." One will ask the reader to consider this last statement. The publicity of the college athletes is not the point here. The point is "nine years' devotion to study" and—"a Townsend prize." Nine years—think of it—the best, the most important of a boy's life given to devoted study! —not of Men, not of Life, not of Realities, but of the books of Other People, mere fatuous, unreasoned, pig-headed absorption of ideas at second-hand. And the result? Not a well-ordered mind, not a well-regulated reasoning machine, not a power of appreciation, not an ability to create. None of these, but—Great Heavens!—a *Townsend Prize!* a rec-

26 Pseudonym of Louise de la Ramée, writer of popular romances.

27 *Critic*, XLI (August, 1902), 178–182.

28 *Harper's Weekly*, XLVI (June 28, 1902), 811. Norris' remarks which follow indicate that he was unaware that the Townsend Prize was awarded to a senior in the law school for the best oration at commencement ceremonies.

tangular piece of the skin of a goat, dried and cured and marked with certain signs and symbols by means of a black pigment; this and a disc of the same metal the Uganda warrior hangs in his ears. A Townsend Prize. And for this a young American living in the twentieth century, sane, intelligent, healthful, has pored over Other People's books, has absorbed Other People's notions, has wearied his brain, has weakened his body, has shut himself from the wide world, has denied himself, has restrained himself, has stultified emotion, has in a word buried his talent in the earth wrapped carefully in a napkin. "And," comments the editor, "the boy who won the Townsend prize for scholarship, if he keeps on, will some day be honored by his fellow-men, when the athletic prize-winner, if he does nothing else, will be a director of a gymnasium. The serious worker comes out ahead every time." But winning Townsend prizes by nine years of study is, we submit, not serious work, but serious misuse of most valuable time and energy. Scholarship! Will we never learn that times change and that sauce for the Renaissance goose is *not* sauce for the New Century gander? It is a fine thing this scholarship, no doubt, but if a man be content with merely this his scholarship is of as much use and benefit to his contemporaries as his deftness in manicuring his finger nails. The United States in this year of grace of nineteen hundred and two does not want and does not need Scholars but Men,—Men made in the mould of the Leonard Woods and the Theodore Roosevelts, Men such as Colonel Waring,[29] Men such as Booker Washington. The most brilliant scholarship attainable by human effort is not, to-day, worth nine years of any young man's life. I think it is Nathaniel Hawthorne who tells the story of a "scholar" who one day, when a young man, found the tooth of a mammoth. He was a student of fossil remains, and in his enthusiasm set out to complete the skeleton. His mind filled with this one idea, to the exclusion of all else, he traveled up and down the world, year after year, picking up here a vertebra, here a femur, here a rib, here a clavicle. Years passed; he came to be an old man; at last he faced death. He had succeeded. The monstrous framework was complete. But he looked back upon the sixty years of his toil and saw that it was a vanity. He had to show for his life-work—the skeleton of a mammoth.[30] And, believe this implicitly: if—as the editor and commentator remarks—if the Townsend prize-winner *keeps on,* this will be the result, a huge thing no doubt, a thing that looms big in the eye, and in the imagination; but an empty thing, lifeless, bloodless, dead, yes and more than dead—extinct; a mere

[29] Colonel George E. Waring (1833–1898) was an American sanitation engineer who directed famous public sanitation programs in New York and Havana.
[30] I do not find this story in Hawthorne's work.

accumulation of dry bones, propped up, lest it fall to the ground, a thing for the wind to blow through and the vulgar to gape at.

But in connection with this subject one may cite so high an authority as Doctor Patton of Princeton, who has recently said that now-a-days men do not go to colleges to become scholars, and that it was time and money wasted to try to make them such.[31] This is a good saying and should be taken to heart by every college faculty between the oceans. Sooner or later there is bound to come a fundamental change in the mode of instruction now in favor in most American colleges. The times demand it; the character of the student body, the character of the undergraduate, is changing. One chooses to believe that the college of the end of the present century will be an institution where only specialized work will be indulged in. There will be courses in Engineering, in Electricity, in Agriculture, in Law, in Chemistry, in Biology, in Mining, etc., and the so-called general "literary" or "classical" will be relegated to the limbo of Things No Longer Useful. Any instructor in collegiate work will tell you to-day that the men in the special courses are almost invariably the hardest, steadiest, most serious workers. The man who studies law at college finishes his work a lawyer, he who studies engineering ends an engineer; the student of biology graduates a biologist, the student of chemistry, a chemist. But the student in the "Literary" course does not—no, not once in a thousand instances—graduate a literary man. He spends the four years of his life over a little Greek, a little Latin, a little mathematics, a little literature, a little history, a little "theme" writing, and comes out—just what it would be difficult to say. But he has in most cases acquired a very pronounced distaste for the authors whose work he has studied in class and lecture room. Great names such as those of Carlyle, Macaulay and De Quincey are associated in his mind only with tedium. He never will go back to these books, never read with enjoyment what once was "work." Even his conscientiousness—supposing him to be animated with such a motive—will trap him and trick him. I do not think that I shall ever forget the spectacle and impression of a student in my own Alma Mater,—a little lass of seventeen (the college was co-educational) with her hair still down her back and her shoes yet innocent of heels, rising in her place in the class room to read before a half-hundred of raw boys and undeveloped girls—not three months out of the high school—a solemn and quite unintelligible "theme" on "The Insincerity of Thomas Babington Macaulay."

Just at the time of the present writing a controversy has been started in

[31] Reverend Francis L. Patton, who resigned as president of Princeton in June, 1902. No published source found for this statement.

London literary circles as to the legitimacy of a reviewer publishing the whole or parts of the same unsigned article in two or more periodicals. Mr. Arthur Symons is the reviewer under fire and his article a critique of the dramas of Mr. Stephen Phillips.[32] It was Mr. Phillips, so we are told, who first started the protest, and he has found followers and champions. And on first consideration there does seem to be ground for complaint here. It has been assumed that the first publisher of the article has a right to expect that for the money he pays to the writer this latter shall give to him all he has to say upon the subject. If he has very much to say—enough for another article—is it not the duty of the scribe to condense and compact so that the matter may be represented as a unit and not as a fragment? Moreover, does it seem fair to Mr. Phillips that three reviews—as was the case—all unfavorable should appear in as many publications, thus giving to the public the impression that a *group* of critics, instead of merely one, was hostile to his work? Lastly, it has been urged that it is not honest to sell a thing twice, that if a horse has been sold by A to B, A cannot sell it again to C.

But none of the objections seems valid. If the space allotted to the article in the paper is not sufficient, that is the fault of the editor, not the writer. The editor pays only for what he prints, the surplusage is still the author's property and can be by him disposed of as such. As for the public considering the single—unfavorable—review as the opinions of three men, and as such unfair to Mr. Phillips, this as well is inadequate and incompetent. Another critic reviewing Mr. Phillips *favorably* is just as much at liberty to split up his work as the adverse reviewer. Last of all, it *is* under certain circumstances perfectly honest to sell the same thing twice. Articles, stories, poems, and the like are continually syndicated in hundreds of newspapers simultaneously, and in this sense are sold over and over again. The analogy between the sale of a horse and the sale of a bit of literature is quite misleading. For the matter of that, the writer does not sell the actual concrete *manuscript* of his work, but merely the right to print it, and unless the word "exclusively" is understood in the agreement he is in no wise bound. The writer is not selling his copy as the owner sells his horse. The analogy would be true if A sold to B the *use* of the horse. When B had got the "use" out of the animal no one will deny the right of A to sell the same "use" to C, D, E, and so on through the whole alphabet. The reviewer of books has a hard enough time of it as it is. It is only fair to give him the same freedom as a livery-stable keeper.

It has often occurred to me as a thing of some importance and certain

[32] See William L. Alden, "London Letter," *New York Times Saturday Review of Books and Art*, June 7, 1902, p. 388.

significance that all great travelers are good writers. And the fact is so well established, the effect flows so invariably from the cause, that there would seem to be here a matter for reflection. One affirms and will maintain that the one is the direct result of the other, that the faculty of adequate expression, of vivid presentation, of forceful and harmonious grouping of words, is engendered and stimulated and perfected by wide journeying.

This is not at all an orthodox view, not at all the theory cherished by our forbears. The writer, according to unvarying belief, is the man of the closet, the bookish man, a student, a sedentary, a consumer of kerosene, a reader rather than a rover. And the idea is plausible. The nomad, he without local habitation, has no leisure, no opportunity, nor even actual concrete place to write. Would it not seem that literature is the quiet art, demanding an unperturbed mind, an unexcited, calm, reposeful temperament? This is a very defensible position, but it is based upon a foundation of sand. It assumes that the brain of the writer is a jar full of a precious fluid—a bottle full of wine to be poured out with care and with a hand so quiet, so restful and unshaken that not a drop be spilled. Very well. But when the jar, when the bottle is emptied—then what? Believe me, the gods give but one vintage to one man. There will be no refilling of the vessel; and even the lees are very flat, be the wine ever so good. The better the grape, the bitterer the dregs; and the outpouring of the "best that is in you" in the end will be soured by that brackish, *fade* sediment that follows upon lavish expenditure, so that the man ends ignobly and because of exhaustion and depletion, with all the product of his early and mature richness making more prominent and pitiful the final poverty and tenuity of his outgiving—ends the butt of critics, the compassion of the incompetent, a shard kicked of every scullion.

And in all the world there is nothing more lamentable than this—the end of a man once strong who has used himself up but who decants lees and not wine. Even when the lees are spent he absorbs them once more and once more gives them forth, each time a little staler, a little thinner, a little feebler, realizing his exhaustion, yet—urged by some whip of fortune—forced to continue the miserable performance till the golden bowl be broken and the pitcher shattered at the fountain.

But suppose the productive power of the writer be considered not as a golden bowl to be emptied and in the end broken, but as a silver cord of finest temper that only needs to be kept in tune. True the cord may be stretched to the breaking point. But its end comes at the very height and in the very consummate fulness of its capacity, and oh the grand world-girdling Note that it sends forth in the breaking! the very soul of it at mightiest tension, the very spirit of it at fiercest strain. What matter the loosening or the snapping when so noble an *Amen* as that vibrates through the nations to sound at once the Height and the End of an entire Life—a whole existence concentrated into a single cry!

Or it may become out of tune. But this is no great matter, because so easily remedied. The golden bowl once emptied there will be no refilling, but by some blessed provision of heaven nothing is easier than to attune the cords of being which are also the cords—the silver singing cords—of expression.

But—and here we come around once more to the *point de départ*—the silver cords once gone *dis*cordant, once jaded and slack, will not, can not be brought again to harmony in the closet, in the study, in the seclusion of the cabinet. Tinker them never so cunningly, never so delicately, they will *not* ring true for you. Thought will avail nothing, nor even rest, nor even relaxation. Of one's self one cannot cause the Master-note to which they will respond to vibrate. The cords have been played on too much. For all your pottering they will yet remain a little loose, and so long as they are loose the deftest fingering, the most skilful touch, will produce only false music.

And the deadly peril is that the cords of Life, and the cords of expression lie so close together, are so intricately mingled, that the man cannot always tell that the cords of expression are singing out of tune. Life and expression are two parts of the same instrument. If the whole life be out of tune how can the man distinguish the false music from the true? There is a danger here, but it is not great. Sooner or later the conviction comes that the productive power is menaced. A little frankness with one's self, a little uncompromising testing of the strings, and the dissonance begins to impress itself.

And—as was said—the remedy is not to be found by the taking of thought, but by an heroic, drastic thrusting out from the grooves and cogs of the life of other men,—of the life of the city and the comfortable stay-at-home hour-to-hour humdrum, and a determined journeying out into the great wide world itself.

The further a-field the better. The Master-note will not be heard within "commuting distance of the city." The whir of civilization smothers it. The click of the telegraph, the hiss of steam, and the clatter of the printing-press drown it out. It is not always and of necessity a loud note. Though Nansen heard it in the thunder of the pack ice of the Farthest North,[33] it came to the ear of Stevenson in the lap of lazy wavelets in the hushed noonday of a South Sea strand.

Travel is the only way. Travel in any direction, by any means, so only it be far—very, very far—is the great attuner of the listless cords of the

[33] Fridtjof Nansen (1861–1930), Norwegian arctic explorer and author of *Farthest North* (1897).

writer's instrument. For again and again and again his power is *not* a bowl to be emptied but an instrument to be played on. To be of use it *must* be sensitive and responsive and true. And to be kept sensitive and responsive and true it must go once in so often to the great Tuner,—to Nature.

We speak of the Mountains, the Rivers, Deserts, and Oceans as though we knew them. We know the Adirondacks from a fortnight in a "summer camp"; the Rivers and the Deserts in kinetoscopic glimpses from the Pullman's windows; the Ocean—God forgive us!—from the beach of a "Resort" or the deck of an Atlantic "greyhound." And I think the gods of the Mountains, Rivers, Deserts and Oceans must laugh in vast contempt of our credulity to suppose that we have found their secrets or heard their music in this timid, furtive peeping and pilfering. For such little minds as these the gods have inexhaustible stores of tinkling cymbals and sounding brasses—Brummagem ware that they sell us for the price of "commutation tickets" and mileage books.

The real knowledge, the real experience that tautens and trims the fibres of being, that tunes the cords, is a very different matter. The trail and the tall ship lead to those places where the Master-note sounds, lead to those un-tracked, un-charted corners of the earth, and dull indeed must be the tympanum that once within earshot cannot hear its majestic diapason. It sounds in the canyons of the higher mountains, in the plunge of streams and swirling of rivers yet without names,—in the wildernesses, the plains, the wide-rimmed deserts. It sings a sonorous rhapsody in the rigging of the clipper ship driven by the trade winds, in the ratlines and halyards of South Sea schooners, and drums "reveille" on the tense, hard sails of the fishing boats off the "Banks." You can hear it in the cry of the lynx, the chant of the wild goose, the call of the moose, and in the "break" of the salmon in the deeper pools below the cataract. It is in the roar of the landslide and in the drone of the cicada; in the war-whoop of the savage and in the stridulating of crickets; in the thunder of the tempest, and in the faintest breath of laziest zephyrs.

And the silver cord of our creative faculty—the thing nearest to perfection in all the make-up of our imperfect human nature—responds to this Master-note with the quickness and sensitiveness of music-mathematics; responds to it, attunes itself to it, vibrates with its vibration, thrills with its quivering, beats with its rhythm, and tautens itself and freshens itself and lives again with its great pure, elemental life, and the Man comes back once more to the world of men with a true-beating heart, and a true-hearing ear, so that he Understands once more, so that his living, sensitive, delicately-humming instrument trembles responsive to the emotions and impulses and loves and joys and sorrows and fears of his fellows, and the Man writes true and clear, and his message rings with harmony

and with melody, with power and with the passion of the prophets inter-
preting God's handwriting to the world of men.

V[34]

There can be no question nor reasonable doubt but that the "language,
institutions, and religion" of fiction writers are at present undergoing the
most radical revolution in the history of literature. And I mean by that
that the men themselves are changing—their characters, their attitudes
toward life; even the mode and manner of their own life. Those who are
not thus changing are decaying. And those others, the Great Un-arrived
who do not recognize the Change, who do not acknowledge the Revolution, will never succeed, but will perish untimely almost before they can
be said to have been born at all.

Time was when the author was an aristocrat, living in seclusion, unspotted from the world. But the Revolution of which there is question
here has meted out to him the fate that Revolutions usually prepared for
Aristocrats and his successor is, must be, *must* be—if he is to voice the
spirit of the times aright, if he is to interpret his fellows justly—the Man
of the People, the Good Citizen.

How the novelists of the preceding generation played the Great Game
is no matter for discussion here. Times were different then. One shut oneself in the study; one wore a velvet coat; one read a great deal and quoted
Latin; one knew the classics; one kept apart from the vulgar profane and
never, never, never read the newspapers. But for the novelist of the next
fifty years of this twentieth century these methods, these habits, this conception of literature as a cult, as a refinement to be kept inviolate from the
shoulderings and elbowings of the Common People is a clog, is a stum-
bling-block, is a pit-fall, a bog, mire, trap—anything you like that is false,
misleading and pernicious.

I have no patience with a theory of literature—and oh, how often one
hears it preached!—that claims the Great Man belongs only to the cultured
few. "You must write," so these theorists explain, "for that small number
of fine minds who because of education, because of delicate, fastidious
taste are competent to judge." I tell you this is wrong. It is precisely the
same purblind prejudice that condemned the introduction of the printing
press because it would cheapen and vulgarize the literature of the day. A
literature that cannot be vulgarized is no literature at all and will perish
just as surely as rivers run to the sea. The things that last are the understandable things—understandable to the common minds, the Plain People,
understandable, one is almost tempted to say, to the very children.

[34] *Critic*, XLI (September, 1902), 267–270.

It is so in every branch of art: in music, painting, sculpture, architecture. The great monuments of these activities, the things that we retain longest and cherish with the most care are plain almost to bareness. The most rudimentary mind can understand them. All the learning, all the culture, all the refinement in the world will not give you a greater thrill on reading your *Iliad* than the boy of fifteen enjoys. Is the "Marseillaise" a thing of subtlety or refinement? Are the Pyramids complex? Are Angelo's Sibyls involved? But the *Iliad,* the "Marseillaise," the Pyramids, the Sibyls will endure and endure and endure while men have eyes to see, ears to hear, and hearts to be moved. These great things, these monuments were *not* written nor composed, nor builded, nor painted for the select, for the cultured. When Homer wrote there were no reading circles. Rouget de Lisle gave no "Recitals."[35] One does not have to "read up" to understand the message of Cheops, nor take a course of art lectures to feel the mystery of the Delphic Sibyl.

And so to come back to the starting place, the Revolution in the character of the writer of fiction. If the modern novelist does not understand the Plain People, if he does not address himself directly to them intelligibly and simply, he will fail. But he will never understand them by shutting himself away from them. He must be—and here one comes to the conclusion of the whole matter—a Man of the World. None more so. Books have no place in his equipment, have no right to be there; will only cumber and confuse him. His predecessor never read the newspapers, but for him the newspaper is more valuable than all the tomes of Ruskin, all the volumes of Carlyle. And more valuable than all are the actual, vital Affairs of Men. The function of the novelist of this present day is to comment upon life as he sees it. He cannot get away from this; this is his excuse for existence, the only claim he has upon attention. How necessary then for him—of all men—to be in the midst of life! He cannot plunge too deeply into it. Politics will help him, and Religious Controversies, Explorations, Science, the newest theory of Socialism, the latest development of Biology. He should find an interest in Continental diplomacy and should have opinions on the chances of a Russo-Japanese war over the Corean question. He should be able to tell why it is of such unusual importance for Queen Wilhelmina of Holland to give birth to an heir,[36] and should know who ought to be nominated for Governor of his native State at the next convention.

No piece of information—mere downright acquisition of fact—need

[35] Claude Rouget de Lisle, a French army officer, was reputed to have composed the "Marseillaise."

[36] It was important because the Queen, who had married in 1901, had no brothers or sisters, and without an heir the succession to the Dutch crown was uncertain.

be considered worthless. Nothing is too trivial to be neglected. I know a novelist of international reputation who told me that the following little bits of knowledge (collected heaven knows where and stored up for years in some pigeon-hole of his memory) had been of use to him, in the composition of a novel he is now at work upon: That great cities tend to grow to the Westward; that race-horses are shod with a long and narrow shoe; and that the usual price charged by an electrician for winding an armature is four dollars. And he seems prouder of the fact that he had these tiny odds and ends at his command, when needed, than he was of the honorary degree just conferred upon him by Harvard University.[37]

I suppose this is an exaggerated case, and it is not to be denied that it is better to have a Harvard degree than to know the shape of a race-horse's shoe, but it surely goes to prove the point that, as far as actual material worth and use were concerned, the fugitive foolish memory-notes were of more present help than the university degree, and that so far as information is concerned the novelist cannot know too much.

In a recent number of *The Bookman* there appears an able article under the title "Attacking the Newspapers."[38] The title is a trifle misleading, since the author's point and text are a defense of modern journalism, or rather let us say an apology. The apology is very well done. The manner of presentation is ingenious, the style amusing, but none the less one cannot let the article pass without protest or at the least comment. The original function of a newspaper was, and still should be, to tell the news— and, if you please, nothing more than that. The "policy" of the paper was (before the days of the yellow press) advocated and exploited in the editorial columns. The whole difficulty lies in the fact that nowadays the average newspaper is violently partisan and deliberately alters news to suit its partisanship. "Not a very criminal procedure," I hear it said; "for by reading the opposition papers the public gets the other side." But one submits that such a course *is* criminal, and that it can be proved to be such. How many people do you suppose read the "opposition" papers? The public that subscribes to the *New York Journal* does not see the *Sun;* and the reader of the *Sun* is almost abashed at being seen with a *Journal.*

---

[37] No "novelist of international reputation" received an honorary degree from Harvard during 1898–1902, the period during which this conversation would presumably have taken place. Yale University, however, awarded honorary degrees to the following novelists during its Bicentennial Celebration, October, 1901: T. B. Aldrich, G. W. Cable, Mark Twain, W. D. Howells, Brander Matthews, and T. N. Page. Howells is the most likely candidate for the "novelist" in this anecdote, though I do not find these "bits of knowledge" in any of his novels of this period.

[38] F. M. Colby, "Attacking the Newspapers," *Bookman,* XV (August, 1902), 534–536.

The American newspaper readers have not time to read "both sides" unless presented to them in one and the same paper.

Observe now how this partisanship works injustice and ruin. Let us suppose a given newspaper is hostile to the Governor of the State. Now every man—even a journalist—has a right to his opinions and his hostilities, and important men in public life must expect to be abused. There are for them compensations; their position is too high, too secure to be shaken by the vituperation of malevolent journals. But these journals have one favorite form of attacking important public men which, though it does not always harm the personage assaulted, may easily ruin the subordinates with which he surrounds himself. This is the habit of discrediting the statesman by defaming his appointees. The Governor, we will say, has appointed John Smith to be the head of a certain institution of the State. But the Governor has incurred the enmity of the *Daily Clarion*—the leading newspaper. Promptly the *Clarion* seizes upon Smith. His career as head of the institution has been a record of misrule (so the *Clarion* reads), has been characterized by extravagance, incompetency, mismanagement, and even misappropriation of the State's money. And here begins the cruel injustice of the business. The editor of that paper will set no bounds upon the lengths to which he will urge his reporters in their vilification of Smith. The editor knows he is a liar, the reporters know they are liars, but the public, ninety-nine times out of a hundred, ignoring motives, unable to see that the real object of attack is the Governor, unable to understand the brute callousness and wretched hypocrisy of the whole proceeding, *believes the calumny,* believes that Smith is an incompetent, a spendthrift, even a thief. And even the better class of readers, even the more intelligent who make allowances for the paper's political prejudices, will listen to the abuse and believe that there "must be some fire where there is so much smoke." Do you suppose for one moment that Smith will ever get a hearing in that paper? Do you suppose its reporters will ever credit him with a single honest achievement, a single sincere effort? If you do, you do not understand modern journalism.

Ah, but the opposition papers! They will defend Smith. They will champion him as vehemently as the *Clarion* attacks. That is all very well, but suppose there are no opposition papers. Politics are very complicated. The press of a given community is not always equally divided between the Republican and Democratic parties. Time and time again it happens that all the leading newspapers of a city, a county, or even a State, Democratic, Republican, Independent, etc., are banded together to oppose some one Large Man. Where then will Smith get his hearing? He cannot fight all the newspapers at once. He is not strong enough to retaliate even upon the meanest. The papers are afraid of nothing he can do. They hold absolute power over his good name and reputation. And for the sake of feeding fat the grudge they bear the Great One they butcher the subordinate without ruth and without reproach. Believe me, it has been shown repeatedly that placed in such a position the modern newspaper will check at no lie however monstrous, at no calumny however vile. If Smith holds a position of trust he will be trumpeted from end to end of the community as a defaulter, gambling away the public moneys entrusted to his care. He will be pictured as a race-track follower, a supporter of fast women, a thief, a blackguard, and a reprobate. If he holds an administrative office, it will be shown how he has given and taken bribes; how he has neglected his duties and ignored his responsibilities till his office has engendered calamity, ruin, and even actual physical suffering. If his work is in the nature of supervision over one of those State institutions where the helpless are cared for,—the infirm, the imbecile, the aged, or sick, or poor,— his cruelty to his wards will be the theme, and he will be written of and pictured as whipping or torturing old men and little children, imprisoning, tormenting, making a hell of what was meant to be a help.[39]

And the man once blackened after this fashion will never again rehabilitate himself in the eyes of the public. The people who read newspapers always believe the worst, and when an entire press, or even the major part of it, unite to defame a man there is no help nor redress possible. He is ruined, ruined professionally and financially, ruined in character, in pocket, and in the hopes of ever getting back the good name that once was his.

And all this is done merely as a political move, merely to discredit the Big Man who put Smith in his place, merely to hurt his chances of renomination, merely to cut down the number of his votes. It is butchery; there is no other word than this with which to characterize the procedure, butchery as cruel, as wanton, and as outrageous as ever bloodied the sands of the Colosseum. It is even worse than this, for the victim has no chance for his life. His hands are tied before the beasts are loosed. He is trussed and downed before the cages are opened, and the benches thunder for his life, not as for a victim to be immolated, but as a criminal to be punished. He is getting only his deserts, his very memory is an execration, and his name whenever mentioned is a by-word and a hissing.

And this in face of the fact that the man may be as innocent of the charges urged as if he had never been born.

Yet Doctor Colby in *The Bookman* article writes: "If we must attack the newspapers let it be as critics not as crusaders, for the people who write

[39] These were the exact charges against Dr. Lawlor, who was in charge of a state home for the feeble-minded. The major San Francisco newspapers—the *Call, Chronicle,* and *Examiner*—were aligned against Governor Henry I. Gage, who had appointed Lawlor.

for them are under no stricter obligations than ourselves." What! the reporter or the editor who by some fillip of fortune is in a position to make public opinion in the minds of a million people under no more obligations than you and I! If every obligation bore down with an all but intolerable weight it is in just his case. His responsibility is greater than that of the Pulpit, greater than that of the Physician, greater than that of the Educator. If you would see the use to which it is put, you have only to try to get at the real truth in the case of the next public character assailed and vilified in the public prints.

Doctor Colby is wrong. It *is* a Crusade and *not* a criticism that will put down the modern yellow newspaper from the bad eminence to which the minds of the hysterical, of the violent, of the ignorant, brutal, and unscrupulous have exalted it.

VI[40]

In the matter of college education touched upon in this department a couple of months ago it seems to me that a further word yet remains to be said. In that paper criticism was offered only upon the so-called "Literary" courses of the modern university. But besides the Literary course, there are other courses of instruction, not technical, which, together with the Literary courses, are sometimes grouped under the general head of *Academic,* in order to distinguish them from the purely scientific or specialized studies, such as law, agriculture, chemistry, and the like.

It is the Academic courses that attract the greatest number of students in the modern college. The Academic course is generally made up of three or four subdivisions, different in name but having a common family resemblance—the Literary course, already mentioned, the Classical course, the Social Science course, or the course in Letters and History, etc., etc., etc.

I have now before me as I write the Register of one of the largest and best universities in the United States, and I shall call your attention to one or two figures in the statement of the summary of students. The total number of undergraduates is given as 1783, divided as follows: Chemistry, 113; Civil Engineering, 50; Mining, 191; Mechanics, 144; Agriculture, 31; Commerce, 21; Natural Sciences, 141; Letters, 266; Social Sciences, 826. This university may be regarded as typical; it is a *modern college* in every sense of the word. It represents about the best the country can offer to the young man in the way of education. Its president is not only a scholar, but a man-of-the-world, a recognized authority in his own work, a man of executive ability, independent, liberal. In a word, an Important Man, a man of Intelligence.[41]

[40] *Critic,* XLI (October, 1902), 363–367.
[41] Norris was using the *University of California Register, 1899–1900* (Berkeley, 1900). The courses which Norris goes on to list are also from this *Register.* Benjamin Ide

And in this college, endowed with enormous capital, presided over by one of the best men in the country, advanced in its views, abreast of the times, wide awake, energetic, with practically limitless possibilities at its command—in this college, I say, 826 students out of 1783 are studying Social Science.

Be pleased to observe the proportion a moment. Eight hundred and twenty-six is very nearly one half of the entire number of the student body of this representative university. If half the number of its undergraduates are enrolled in a given course it is only fair to suppose that the said course must be of considerable value, and alone this Social Science course in question musters a larger number of students than all the *specialized* courses put together.

Let us see now what these eight hundred-odd are studying during the four most important years of their lives. I quote a few studies at random from the Announcement of Courses: *Beowulf,* Histories of English Literature, the Fundamental Propositions of the Euclidean Geometry of Space, Spherical Harmonics, Molecular Physics, Physical Optics, Quantitative Analysis, History of the Renaissance, Mediaeval Life, Constitutional Law, Schiller and Goethe, the *Chanson de Roland,* Voltaire, Zola, and Victor Hugo.

So much for courses these students are *obliged* to take. But in order to make up the amount of work requisite for the degree of A.B., they must elect a certain number of courses from a list of which the following subjects are examples: Philosophy (i.e., Kant, Hegel, the Theory of Knowledge, etc.), Arabic (Brünnow's *Chrestomathy of Arabic Prose Pieces*), Elementary Study of the Cantonese Dialect, Aramaic and Syriac, Ornamental Design, Interior Decoration, and Ceramics.

Be it understood at the outset that, taken *individually,* it is conceded that these studies are admirable. *The Critique of Pure Reason* is an intellectual gymnasium in itself; the ability to read the Gospels in the original is more to be desired than rubies; any form of training that tends to a thorough knowledge of *Beowulf* or the History of the Renaissance is well worth many years of unremitting effort.

It is the appalling mixture that gives us pause. Try to conceive of the state of mind of any young graduate who for four years had *conscientiously* followed such a scheme of work. Just what would be the temper of the intellectual vessel which would retain Ceramics, the *Chrestomathy of Arabic Prose Pieces,* Zola's *La Terre,* and Molecular Physics? Or what is the mental calibre of a brain into which an attempt has been made to force Hegel, Spherical Harmonics, and Syriac dialects?

It is announced in the register of the college under question that the

---

Wheeler, president of the University of California, was a linguistic scholar who also participated actively in politics.

course is designed to furnish a liberal education, and there can be no question as to the wisdom of the design.

Doubt obtrudes itself only as to the possibility of execution. Does it not appear improbable that these subjects—from *Beowulf* to Ceramics—can be adequately studied in the short period of four years? Is it not allowable to doubt that any more than the merest surface acquaintanceship can be obtained in so brief a time? and does a mere surface acquaintanceship with a multitude of widely divergent subjects conduce to a liberal education?

And all this is based upon the assumption that the average college man is a diligent student, taking his work seriously, doing his very best to get the most out of his college, really and honestly trying to fathom Constitutional Law from one to two o'clock, and the formula of narrative construction of Émile Zola from two to three, etc., etc. But, as a matter of fact, the *average* college man is not a diligent student. No one with any knowledge or experience with the species will aver the contrary. One does not submit the fact in the form of adverse criticism; one simply puts the case. The average undergraduate is *not* diligent. He does *not* do his very best to get the most out of his college; he takes only a mild interest in Constitutional Law and the naturalistic theory of fiction to his eye is a bloomless field, remote as the Arabian deserts and about as attractive. If you ask him why he is studying Euclid's geometry he will return you no very definite answer: "Because it's prescribed," is about the most you will get out of him. Push him to a last analysis and it is quite on the cards that he will reply with the ready-made formula that "it trains the mind to exact thinking." But one submits that the day for training the mind to so rigorous a process as "exact thinking" is far past by the time the student is entering college, and the course, it will be remembered, does not propose to conduce to exact thinking, but to a liberal education.

But, it is contended, the Literary, the Classical and Social Science courses do not pretend to do more than show the way to more extensive reading and culture in later life. If this is so it does seem as though much of the labor were in vain. Once the diploma safe, the average college graduate will shut the door upon *Beowulf,* Ornamental Design, Syriac, English Literature, and the like, with a thoroughness and definiteness that forever precludes its reopening. The graduates from this course do not once in a hundred times follow out the lines of the work of their undergraduate days. They enter the Law School, the Medical School, the business world, journalism, etc., and of all the curriculum so carefully and earnestly prepared by the faculty of their alma mater not one feature remains to them either as a material advantage or as a guide in the development of what, for want of a better name, we will call "culture."

This is the fact. It is useless to deny it. There are scores of examples to prove the case in the life and acquaintanceship of nearly every reader of these words. The student of the "general culture" courses in the modern colleges carries away with him after graduation practically nothing—a dim remembrance, perhaps, of a novel theory once enunciated in a classroom, a date or two, a name or two, a confused litter of information, and all the rest blurs and blanks.

And it is better that it should be thus. Of two evils, one holds that it can be proved that there is more hope for a young man who does not take this general culture course very seriously than for the one who does. Imagine the fate of a youth who began life and the struggle of it with a firm belief in Quantitative Analysis or with a clear remembrance of the elements of Cantonese dialect; with convictions as to Euclid and opinions on Spherical Harmonics.

It is very admirable, no doubt, to be able to talk about Physical Optics, Aramaic, and Ceramics, but the occasion very seldom presents itself— away from college—when these topics are appropriate, and when the timely moment *does* come, one's hearers are apt to demand a more intimate and specialized knowledge than the "general culture course has given."

We are eminently a practical people. We want to "get our money's worth." Are we getting it out of the General Culture courses of the American colleges? Let us see. Let us have a few figures.

We will consider only the college in question and the community which supports it.

As was said, out of the 1700 of its undergraduates 800 were enrolled in the General Culture course. At a conservative estimate it costs $600 per year to take a boy through college. This means $2400 for the four-year course for one student. Multiply this by the 800 above mentioned and the figure reaches $1,920,000.

Thus the community from which this particular college draws pays out every four years $1,920,000 to educate its young men in the elements of the Cantonese dialect, the *Chrestomathy of Arabic Prose,* Ornamental Design, Euclid, Philosophy, and a smattering of modern languages; *and the young men hasten to forget the work before the ink is dry on the diplomas.* One may well ask if there is the worth of the money here.

One hears much about "a liberal education." Are we to assume, then, that a knowledge of this astonishing array of subjects affords a liberal education? Certainly, if each of the students gave twenty years of his life to the work. Certainly *not,* if the course is condensed into four years. Take any one of these subjects at random—Mediaeval Life, say. At once the name of Viollet-le-Duc comes to mind.[42] At once it is seen that any one of the studies grouped under the head of Social Science could be *in itself*

[42] Eugène Viollet-le-Duc (1814–1879) devoted his life to the study and restoration of medieval architecture and artifacts.

alone, the work not of twenty years, but of an entire life, *and in itself alone a liberal education.* How much can be got out of it in a course of twenty-odd lectures delivered to young men who are only taking it to fill up the required number of hours per week? A liberal education can be got out of the study of Constitutional Law alone, if the study goes deep enough and is carried on long enough. But what use can a surface knowledge of it be to the young man who after graduation will enter, perhaps, the lumber business?

It is urged again and again by the champions of the culture courses that they do impart to the student a taste for reading and self-improvement in which he indulges in after life. But is it not a fact that the tastes are formed long before college days and that it is this very taste for reading and improvement—developed years previously—that is the cause and not the result of an attendance at college, so that the reading and study in after life would be taken up even if the boy had never so much as seen the university?

And, besides all this, "specialization" is fast becoming the great word of all human activity. Time was when the smith made weapons as well as horseshoes; time was when the scholar knew Greek as well as Hebrew; time was when to be "Literary" was to write as well as to read; time was when Leonardo da Vinci painted pictures and designed siege engines; when Angelo was sculptor, architect, and painter alike.

These were the times when General Culture was attainable; leisurely times, when the student remained a student till the day of his death. But does it not seem, judging of the future by the present and by the immediate past, as though the season and reason for *General* Culture were passing away? There is more than a mere ring of heresy to this, one admits. We have worshipped at the shrine of General Culture so long that to deny its divine right is, apparently, blasphemy. It is difficult to suppose that, ethically speaking, there can be anything finer than General Culture. A "broad education," a "liberal education," a "wide scholarship,"—these are words to conjure with. But the times have changed; the wheels of human existence are moving ever faster. Above all, there are more educated people in the world than ever before. Culture is no longer a monopoly; is no longer so unusual, so admirable,—nor so useful. The useful man, the admirable man, *is he who has studied his one particular subject more than anyone else in the world.* Education, culture, is being divided and subdivided and resubdivided into a thousand specialties. Literature no longer attempts to embrace Literature, but some *phase* of it reduced to its very lowest terms. It is no longer literature, but *dramatic* literature; no longer dramatic literature, but *French* dramatic literature; then *Romantic* French drama; then Hugo; and having gone as far as possible the student halts at Hugo and becomes, or strives to become, an authority on the life and works of the Last Great Frenchman. Time was when men were merely antiquarians; then certain of them became Egyptologists, certain others Assyriologists; certain of these even have already specialized further and are authorities on certain particular dynastics of the Egyptian Empire, or certain particular districts of ancient Assyria.

The range of human knowledge, by discovery, excavation, or forthright original production, has long since become too great for any one student to encompass it—even superficially—and call the result General Culture. Think what a strict interpretation of the term would mean to-day. It would mean a range of reading and research that no living man could attain. If the student were of a character to understand intelligently Pater's *Marius* he would not be of a character to understand, equally intelligently, Zola's *La Terre*.

Observe how things have come about. This specialization of original work, which I have tried to insist upon, has come about in the last hundred years. Where, in the last century, ten men wrote, thought, excavated, built, or painted, there are now ten thousand—and each of the ten thousand in his own "specialized" channel is doing work quite as worthy of study as did the ten before him.

But—and here's the rub—the mind of the student has not expanded to equal this measureless ramification, nor could it so expand. It is physically impossible. The store of human knowledge has become too vast to be even glanced over by any one man, were he dowered with the intellect of Immanuel Kant, the versatility of Macaulay, and the longevity of Von Moltke.

And in the face of this we expect a boy scarce out of his teens to achieve a General Culture in four years of time.

Does it not seem, then, about time to consider this General Culture course in the colleges of these United States,—this General Culture course which is consuming so much invaluable time, and which is costing in the aggregate so many millions of dollars? One does not cry out blindly against the same; one does not presume to say that it is valueless, that it does not have a place. But one does put a question: Is it not time to change our ideas and conceptions of General Culture, and, having changed these, to change the corresponding course of education in the modern American university, so that, at the least, the college man of to-day need not go from a recitation in Abelian functions to a lecture on Moresque art, then spend an hour in the study of the Dynamics of Rotation, and afterwards attend a lecture upon Rabbinic Literature, in order to graduate and become—a Business Man?

BIBLIOGRAPHICAL NOTE

and

CHECKLIST OF NORRIS' LITERARY CRITICISM

Bibliographical Note

Basic biographical information on Norris is contained in Franklin D. Walker's *Frank Norris: A Biography* (Garden City, New York: Doubleday, Doran & Company, 1932) and in his edition of *The Letters of Frank Norris* (San Francisco: Book Club of California, 1956). The best and most recent bibliography is *Frank Norris: A Bibliography* (Los Gatos, California: Talisman Press, 1959) by Kenneth A. Lohf and Eugene P. Sheehy. The most useful critical treatments are still those by Walter F. Taylor in his *The Economic Novel in America* (Chapel Hill, North Carolina: The University of North Carolina Press, 1937) and Ernest Marchand, *Frank Norris: A Study* (Stanford: Stanford University Press, 1942). Also helpful are Lars Åhnebrink, *The Beginnings of Naturalism in American Fiction* (Cambridge, Massachusetts: Harvard University Press, 1950) and the series of articles by Charles C. Walcutt, summarized in his *American Literary Naturalism, A Divided Stream* (Minneapolis: University of Minnesota Press, 1956). The best of the unpublished dissertations on Norris are by Robert D. Lundy, "The Making of *McTeague* and *The Octopus*" (University of California, 1956) and William B. Dillingham, "Themes and Literary Techniques in the Fiction of Frank Norris" (University of Pennsylvania, 1961). Most surveys of American fiction and criticism contain discussions of Norris' critical ideas (see the Lohf and Sheehy bibliography).

Articles which deal primarily with Norris' criticism are: H. Willard Reninger, "Norris Explains *The Octopus:* A Correlation of His Theory and Practice," *American Literature,* XII (May, 1940), 218–227; Malcolm Cowley, " 'Not Men': A Natural History of American Naturalism," *Kenyon Review,* IX (Summer, 1947), 414–435; Joseph J. Kwiat, "Frank Norris: The Novelist as Social Critic and Literary Theorist," *Die Neueren Sprachen,* 2nd Ser., III (1954), 385–392; Charles G. Hoffman, "Norris and the Responsibility of the Novelist," *South Atlantic Quarterly,* LIV (October, 1955), 508–515; and George W. Johnson, "Frank Norris and Romance," *American Literature,* XXXIII (March, 1961), 52–63.

Checklist of Norris' Literary Criticism

The following is a complete checklist of Norris' critical articles and reviews. Items preceded by an asterisk are republished in this volume. Earlier republication is noted at the end of applicable items. I have supplied the signature for each item published before 1901. After that date the lack of signature information indicates that the item was signed by Norris. The dates of Norris' syndicated articles of early 1903 are derived from the bibliography in the 1903 edition of *The Responsibilities of the Novelist,* and have not been verified. (See "A Note on Authorship and the Text" above.) The following abbreviations are used throughout:

BET: Boston Evening Transcript.

FNW: Frank Norris of "The Wave," Introduction by Oscar Lewis (San Francisco: The Westgate Press, 1931).

RN: The Responsibilities of the Novelist (New York: Doubleday, Page & Company, 1903).

1. "Stepterfetchit," *Occident* (a University of California student publication), XX (March 27, 1891), 79 (by "Dick Wincey"); XX (April 3, 1891), 86 (by "Karl Aisle"); XX (April 10, 1891), 104 (by "Mick Auly"); Parodies, Signed "Norrys '94."

*2. "Our Unpopular Novelists: Disappearance of American Fiction from the Book Stores," *Wave,* XIV (October 5, 1895), 7. Signed "Frank Norris."

3. "A Delayed Masterpiece," *Wave,* XV (April 25, 1896), 7. Review of Elizabeth Stuart Phelps, *The Singular Life.* Unsigned in text, but Contents lists as by "F. N."

*4. "Theory and Reality: An Old Author and a New Writer Consider the Same Problem," *Wave,* XV (May 2, 1896), 8. Review of W. D. Howells, *A Parting and a Meeting*; and Mrs. J. R. Jarboe, *Robert Atterbury.* Signed "F. N."

*5. "Zola's *Rome*: Modern Papacy as Seen by the Man of the Iron Pen," *Wave,* XV (June 6, 1896), 8. Review. Unsigned.

*6. "Zola as a Romantic Writer," *Wave,* XV (June 27, 1896), 3. Unsigned.

*7. "Stephen Crane's Stories of Life in the Slums: *Maggie* and *George's Mother,*" *Wave,* XV (July 4, 1896), 13. Review of *Maggie* and *George's Mother.* Unsigned.

8. "Fiction in Review," *Wave,* XV (July 18, 1896), 12. Review of Maria L. Pool, *In a Dike Shanty*; Sarah J. Duncan, *His Honour and a Lady*; Arthur Morrison, *Chronicles of Martin Hewitt*; Elizabeth K. Tompkins, *The Broken Ring.* Signed "F. N." Republished in *FNW.*

9. "A Summer in Arcady," *Wave,* XV (July 25, 1896), 9. Review of the novel by James Lane Allen. Unsigned in text, but Contents lists as by "F. N."

*10. "The 'English Courses' of the University of California," *Wave,* XV (November 28, 1896), 2–3. Unsigned.

*11. "The Modern Short Story," *Wave,* XV (December 26, 1896), 3. Unsigned.

*12. "A Question of Ideals: The American Girl of 1896 as Seen by Wenzel and by Gibson," *Wave,* XV (December 26, 1896), 7. Review of Albert Wenzel, *Vanity Fair;* and C. D. Gibson, *Pictures of People.* Signed "F. N."

*13. "The Decline of the Magazine Short Story," *Wave,* XVI (January 30, 1897), 3. Unsigned.

*14. "An Opening for Novelists: Great Opportunities for Fiction Writers in San Francisco," *Wave,* XVI (May 22, 1897), 7. Signed "Frank Norris."

 15. "The Newest Books," *Wave,* XVI (July 31, 1897), 13. Review of John Fox, Jr., *Hell fer Sartin and Other Stories;* John H. Comstock, *Insect Life;* Thomas Wharton, *Bobo and Other Farces;* Ruth McEnery Stuart, *In Simkinsville.* Signed "F. N."

*16. "Millard's Tales: Pungent Episodes of Western Life, Short and Pointed," *Wave,* XVI (August 21, 1897), 12. Review of Bailey Millard, *A Pretty Bandit.* Signed "N." Republished in *FNW.*

*17. "Fiction Is Selection," *Wave,* XVI (September 11, 1897), 3. Signed "Justin Sturgis."

 18. "The Frivolous Gyp," *Wave,* XVI (September 18, 1897), 12. Review of Martel de Janville ("Gyp"), *En Ballade.* Signed "N."

 19. "Crane in London," *Wave,* XVI (September 18, 1897), 13. Review of Crane's London sketches appearing in the *Saturday Review.* Signed "Justin Sturgis."

 20. "Happiness by Conquest," *Wave,* XVI (December 11, 1897), 2. Editorial based on Horace Fletcher, *Happiness as Found in Forethought and Fear Thought.* Signed "F. N."

 21. "Holiday Literature," *Wave,* XVI (December 11, 1897), 8. Brief comments on illustrated holiday books and calendars. Unsigned in text, but Contents lists as by "F. N."

*22. "Perverted Tales," *Wave,* XVI (December 18, 1897), 5–7. Parodies of Kipling, Crane, Harte, Davis, Bierce, and Hope. Signed "Frank Norris." Republished in *FNW.*

 23. "Reviews in Brief," *Wave,* XVI (December 25, 1897), 12. Brief comments on various works. Signed "N."

*24. "The Unknown Author and the Publisher," *World's Work,* I (April, 1901), 663–665. Signed "A Publisher's Reader."

 25. "Frank Norris' Weekly Letter," *Chicago American Literary and Art Review:* May 25, 1901, p. 8; June 1, 1901, p. 5; *June 8, 1901, p. 5; June 15, 1901, p. 5; *June 22, 1901, p. 8; June 29, 1901, p. 8; July 6, 1901, p. 8; *July 13, 1901, p. 8; *July 20, 1901, p. 8; *August 3, 1901, p. 5; August 10, 1901, p. 5; *August 24, 1901, p. 5; August 31, 1901, p. 8.

*26. "Mr. Kipling's *Kim,*" *World's Work,* II (October, 1901), 1341–42.

Unsigned. Republished in *Frank Norris: Two Poems and Kim Reviewed* (San Francisco: Harvey Taylor, 1930).

*27. "The True Reward of the Novelist," *World's Work*, II (October, 1901), 1337–39. Republished in *RN*.

*28. "A Problem in Fiction: Truth Versus Accuracy," *BET*, November 6, 1901, p. 20. Republished in *RN*.

*29. "Why Women Should Write the Best Novels: And Why They Don't," *BET*, November 13, 1901, p. 20. Republished in *RN*.

*30. "Retail Bookseller: Literary Dictator," *BET*, November 20, 1901, p. 20. Republished in *RN*.

*31. "Novelists of the Future: The Training They Need," *BET*, November 27, 1901, p. 14. Republished in *RN*.

*32. "The Need of a Literary Conscience," *World's Work*, III (December, 1901), 1559–60. Republished in *RN*.

*33. "The Mechanics of Fiction," *BET*, December 4, 1901, p. 22. Republished in *RN*.

*34. "The 'Volunteer Manuscript': Plain Talk to the Ambitious Amateur," *BET*, December 11, 1901, p. 25. Republished in *RN*.

*35. "A Plea for Romantic Fiction," *BET*, December 18, 1901, p. 14. Republished in *RN*.

*36. "Fiction Writing as a Business," *BET*, January 1, 1902, p. 17. Republished in *RN*.

*37. " 'The Literature of the West': A Reply to W. R. Lighton," *BET*, January 8, 1902, p. 7. Republished by Willard Martin, Jr., *American Literature*, VIII (May, 1936), 190–198.

*38. "Simplicity in Art," *BET*, January 15, 1902, p.17. Republished in *RN*.

*39. "New York as a Literary Center," Syndicated, January 19, 1902. Republished in *RN*.

*40. "An American School of Fiction? A Denial," *BET*, January 22, 1902, p. 17. Republished in *RN*.

*41. "The Frontier Gone at Last," *World's Work*, III (February, 1902), 1728–31. Republished in *RN*.

*42. "The National Spirit as It Relates to the 'Great American Novel'," *BET*, February 5, 1902, p. 11. Republished by Willard Martin, Jr., *American Literature*, VIII (May, 1936), 190–198.

*43. "Story-Tellers vs. Novelists," *World's Work*, III (March, 1902), 1894–96. Republished in *RN*.

*44. "The Novel with a 'Purpose'," *World's Work*, IV (May, 1902), 2117–19. Republished in *RN*.

*45. "Salt and Sincerity," *Critic:* XL (May, 1902), 447–450, republished in *RN* (I); XL (June, 1902), 550–555; XLI (July, 1902), 77–81, republished in *RN* (IV); XLI (August, 1902), 178–182, republished in *RN* (II); XLI (September, 1902), 267–270, republished in *RN* (III); XLI (October, 1902), 363–367.

*46. "A Neglected Epic," *World's Work*, V (December, 1902), 2904–2906. Republished in *RN*.

*47. "The Responsibilities of the Novelist," *Critic*, XLI (December, 1902), 537–540. Republished in *RN*.

*48. "The Great American Novelist," Syndicated, January 19, 1903. Republished in *RN*.

 49. "Richard Harding Davis," Syndicated, January 26, 1903.

*50. "The American Public and 'Popular' Fiction," Syndicated, February 2, 1903. Republished in *RN*.

*51. "Child Stories for Adults," Syndicated, February 9, 1903. Republished in *RN*.

*52. "The 'Nature' Revival in Literature," Syndicated, February 16, 1903. Republished in *RN*.

*53. "Novelists To Order—While You Wait," Syndicated, February 23, 1903. Republished in *RN*.

 54. "Chances of Unknown Writers," Syndicated, March 2, 1903.

*55. "Newspaper Criticisms and American Fiction," Syndicated, March 9, 1903. Republished in *RN*.

INDEX